GOOD OLD INDEX:
THE SHERLOCK HOLMES HANDBOOK

Thomas W. Ross

GOOD OLD INDEX:
THE SHERLOCK HOLMES HANDBOOK

*A GUIDE TO THE SHERLOCK HOLMES STORIES BY
SIR ARTHUR CONAN DOYLE: PERSONS, PLACES,
THEMES, SUMMARIES OF ALL THE TALES, WITH
COMMENTARY
ON THE STYLE OF THE AUTHOR*

CAMDEN HOUSE

Published by Camden House, Inc.
Drawer 2025
Columbia, SC 29202 USA

Printed on acid-free paper.
Binding materials are chosen for strength and
durability.

ISBN: 1-57113-049-7

Library of Congress Cataloging-in-Publication Data

Ross, Thomas Wynne, 1923–

Good old index: the Sherlock Holmes handbook: a guide to the
Sherlock Holmes stories by Sir Arthur Conan Doyle, persons, places,
themes, summaries of all the tales, with commentary on the style of
the author / Thomas W. Ross. – 1st ed.
    p.   cm.
    ISBN 1-57113-049-7 (alk. paper)
    1. Doyle, Arthur Conan, Sir, 1859–1930 – Characters – Sherlock
Holmes –Dictionaries. 2. Holmes, Sherlock (Fictitious character) –
–Dictionaries. 3. Detective and mystery stories, English–
–Dictionaries. 4. Private investigators in literature–
–Dictionaries.   I. Title.
PR4623.A3R67   1996
823'.8--dc20   96-749
                                                                  CIP

Acknowledgments

Special thanks are due to my editors, Jim Hardin, Jim Walker, and especially Phil Dematteis, who suggested clarifications and deletions and corrected mistakes. Any errors that remain are of course my own responsibility.

*This book is for Madeline, Tom, Su Jing,
and Emeralda,
who believe in Holmes;
and for Mary, who does not.*

Sidney Paget's illustration for "Silver Blaze"

Contents

Preface

References are to *The Annotated Sherlock Holmes*, 2 volumes, edited by William S. Baring-Gould (London: John Murray, 1968); the American edition is *The Complete Sherlock Holmes*, with a preface by Christopher Morley (New York: Doubleday, 1936). Abbreviations for the titles of the tales are found below, together with a list of additional abbreviations. Boldface type indicates that a word appears as an entry in the index. Quotation marks are used primarily for references to Holmes's cases, recorded and unrecorded. Italics are employed in the customary way to indicate foreign phrases and the names of books, ships, plays, and operas. An asterisk precedes the names of actual personages.

T. W. R.
September 1996

"Hullo! Hullo! Good old index. You can't beat it,"
exclaims Sherlock Holmes in
"The Adventure of the Sussex Vampire."

Introduction

SHERLOCK HOLMES IS the most realistic fictional character in all literature.

More than a century after he first appeared in *Beeton's Christmas Annual* for 1887, readers are still convinced that the great detective not only existed but is alive and well. Hundreds continue to write him at his famous but fictitious address, 221B Baker Street, London. Never mind that Holmes was "born" in the 1850s, people from all over the world – Sri Lanka, Japan, Ukraine, America, and England itself – send him letters every day, asking his advice or expressing their admiration.

Sherlock Holmes *lives,* even though he would by now have reached the Methuselan age of a century and a half. He may have retired to beekeeping in Sussex, but thousands are sure that he maintains a mail drop at the Baker Street address.

The belief in the living Holmes is naive and touching but it is also testimony to the incredible success of Sir Arthur Conan Doyle's portrayal. The author killed him off in 1893 in "The Final Problem" because he was bored with the lanky detective and wanted to spend more time on his historical romances, such as *The White Company* – which, alas, no one reads today.

Readers would not let Holmes die. Conan Doyle acceded to public outcry and resurrected The World's Only Unofficial Consulting Detective in 1903 in "The Adventure of the Empty House."

His creator might have been weary of Holmes, but some of the tales that he wrote after the Resurrection are among his most successful (*see* **best stories, Conan Doyle's own list** [This and all subsequent uses of boldface type for a word or phrase indicates that it appears as an entry in the *Index.*]). Eventually Conan Doyle wrote fifty-six short stories and four short novels, in most of which his detective solves mysteries brought to him at 221B by clients whose social status ranges from **commissionaire**(s) to **royalty, peers, knights.**

How did Conan Doyle do it? First, he created Dr. John (*see* **name**) H. Watson as Holmes's friend and biographer. Through Watson's eyes and from his pen we glean the delicious details about the detective, his exploits, and about the good doctor himself. Watson is an educated man – a physician and, hence, a man of science – but his intellect is not equal to that of his roommate. We know what Watson looked like and how he spoke; how he dressed; what he ate and drank; and that he had a weakness for the turf. (At one point, Holmes has to lock up the doctor's checkbook to prevent him from betting more than he can afford on the gee-gees.)

Detective and doctor are deeply fond of one another (*see* **love**), but Holmes finds it difficult to express any emotion. Watson is a good foil for the brilliant Master of the Science of Deduction. He is no fool, though he was portrayed as such in some films. He sometimes sees the truth when all is dark to Holmes. And he never fails to express his wonderment and admiration when Holmes explains his **chain** of reasoning.

Conan Doyle provides us with a multitude of precise facts about his unforgettable characters and their adventures – visual, auditory (*see* **noise**), and even olfactory (*see* **smell**). He had a fine ear for dialogue, especially in the exchanges between Holmes and Watson (*see* **pawky humour,** for instance). And he devised some highly inventive plots – murder by serpent and by spectral hound; ingenious jewel thefts; romantic tales of true love triumphant, including Watson's own wooing and marriage (*see* **Morstan**).

Each tale is different from the rest, but it is obvious that Sir Arthur also worked by **formula,** and we delight in the familiar preliminaries and the inevitable outcomes as we read and reread the stories.

His **style** is good, but typical, mid-Victorian: formal and graceful. It is also sometimes polysyllabic, repetitive, and florid. It is sometimes absurd . . . as, indeed, is Sherlock Holmes. The Persian slipper for the tobacco and the jackknife for the unanswered correspondence are extravagant details – quirky, exotic, unforgettable – but absurd. Holmes is maddeningly self-assured and implausibly successful (but *see* **ass; cases, mistakes**). He can be irritable and irritating, even to Watson.

He is close-mouthed, especially when in the midst of his cerebrations. We eventually learn a little about his family (*see* **Holmes, Mycroft; *Vernet, Émile Jean Horace**) and we discover that he attended a **university** but took no degree and made only a couple of friends while at Oxbridge or Camford. He is impatient with minds less agile than his own and can be patronizing to the lowly born. Conversely, he is not unduly impressed by the upper-class clients who seek his help (e.g., **Bohemia, King of; St. Simon,** Lord Robert).

Thus, Holmes embodies the best and sometimes the worst of Victorian England. He is a rational man – an intellectual who draws on the vast knowledge he has amassed for himself and on deductive reasoning. He also employs modern technology (e.g., the **microscope**). He is always a gentleman. Even when roughing it upon the forbidding moor in *The Hound of the Baskervilles* he provides himself with civilized food, including a flask of spirits, and his linen is as impeccable as it would have been in his Baker Street sitting room. He is unfailingly courteous to women, though he despises and mistrusts the fair sex.

We love the tales, then, not just because of Holmes and Watson but because Conan Doyle brings Victoria's England to life. London is foggy and gaslit. Its **architecture** is depressing, but it is the center of the civilized world. The Empire is secure, and only in the last stories is there a hint of the changes that will occur after 1914. For the upper classes, life is quite comfortable. One takes for granted the persistent presence of the poor. Without a twinge of conscience, a gentleman can enjoy good music, sport, men's clubs, the theater, abundant food and drink, good tobacco, and stately women – who know their place as disenfranchised second-class personages. Class and racial **prejudice** are natural to the Victorian gentleman, who looks askance at anything non-British (*see* **foreigners**). There is plenty of suffering and **violence,** but one can be sure that justice will triumph. Though Holmes coolly commits **burglary** and in other ways circumvents the **law,** he and his fellow Victorians are confident of their legal institutions.

The police are another matter. Inspectors Lestrade and Gregson are well-meaning and energetic but without **imagination.** Sherlock Holmes manages to correct their mistakes and gleefully lets them have the credit.

Science and technology are making their increasingly rapid strides. Electricity is gradually replacing gaslight; the London Underground is expanding; and we witness the advent of motorcars, telephones, and electric bells.

Victorians revere the monarchy as it is embodied in the Queen, but they have some doubts about the **Prince of Wales**. Great Britain is a mighty world power kept in place by the Royal Navy. Education is elitist, but Sherlock Holmes himself welcomes the advent of universal schooling (*see* **board schools**).

Conan Doyle seems to have mistrusted everything that was not English. He liked **Americans,** however. Many of them appear in the stories. They are amusing naïfs, though uncultured and with too much newly acquired money. Holmes also likes them, and he predicts that one day there will be a quartering of the Union Jack and the Stars and Stripes. Perhaps he was born in America: he knows a great deal about the country, and he can speak Yankee **dialect** (*also see* **slang**). He may sound absurdly exaggerated to Americans, but his lingo is good enough to persuade a clever German spy that the tall man with the Uncle Sam goatee – Holmes in disguise – is what he pretends to be, an Irish-American traitor named Altamont.

Conan Doyle also has a begrudging admiration for the **French.** All other foreigners are unfathomable and potentially dangerous grotesques.

Thus, the author places his ideal gentleman in a Victorian England that he portrays as he saw it, ignoring the unpleasant and the seamy (*see* **sanitary arrangements,** for instance), as did most of his fellow writers. Holmes himself is a published author (*see* **Holmes Bibliography**): learned monographs, no fiction (but *see* **write them yourself**). He is a master of minutiae, which he catalogues in an immense set of commonplace books that he refers to as his good old index. His knowledge is broad and often deep: *see* **actor; architecture; ashes; atavism; bees; blood; boots (and bootlaces); boxers; burglary; butter; candle; celts; chalk; charters; cigars; codes; Cornish; dialect; disguises; dust; fingertips; foreign languages; frequency of letters; glue; golf; hands; medieval pottery; miracle plays; music; newspapers; number** (for ciphers, perfumes, tyres); **palimpsest; pinna, points, postmarks, scales, scissors,**

shoes, single-stick, sleeves, stairs; thumb; typefaces; warships; watches; watermarks; wheels.

Occasionally his vast knowledge and his **analytic mind** fail him. He has been beaten by clever malefactors, and he errs more often than even the admiring Watson is aware (*see* **cases, mistakes**). Watson intrigues us when he refers to adventures other than those chronicled in the sixty-four narratives. Some of these "titles" are evidence of Sir Arthur's sense of humor, particularly "the politician, the lighthouse, and the trained cormorant," "the red leech," ("repulsive" affair!), "the aluminium crutch," and "the giant rat of Sumatra, a tale for which the world is not yet prepared."

There remain absurdities and extravagances of style. Conan Doyle could, without a blush, call a sawed-off shotgun a "truncated fowling-piece" and make Holmes admit that "we are suffering from a plethora of surmise." He also employed formulas, not only of plot but of phrasing, as well (*see* **repetitions**).

Sir Arthur admitted in his autobiography, *Memories and Adventures* (1924), that he had never been "nervous about details." His sometimes hasty writing leaves the reader with tantalizing problems. Most notorious are Watson's **wound** and **name.** For more, *see* **problems.** There are also differences, some substantial, between American and English **editions** of the tales.

But such difficulties do not deter the millions of Holmesians, who return to the stories again and again. Holmes may be blunt, arrogant, and humorless (but *see* **laugh**); he may not be the **best and wisest** man (as Watson said of him) that we have ever known, but we feel that we do know him and love him in spite of his **vices.**

The Granada Television series (shown in the United States on the PBS *Mystery* series and on the Arts & Entertainment cable network in the early 1990s), starring the late, incomparable Jeremy Brett, makes the detective familiar, through another medium, to yet another generation of Sherlockians. Brett is a twitchy, neurotic Holmes – quite right! The scriptwriters have wisely retained most of the Conan Doyle dialogue and the delightful minutiae.

Good Old Index: The Sherlock Holmes Handbook is intended to intensify the reader's – and the television viewer's – enjoyment of Sir Arthur Conan Doyle's remarkable stories and their captivating protagonist. It is meant for the first- or second-time reader.

But it is also for the specialist – the Sherlockian, the Holmesian, the Baker Street Irregular. These are Holmes fans, both organized and unorganized, throughout the world, who take the Canon seriously – they refer to the stories thus, as if they were Holy Writ. Most of these aficionados, of course, only pretend to assume a serious critical and scholarly posture, declaring that Holmes, Watson, Moriarty, and everybody else actually existed and that Sir Arthur was merely Watson's literary agent. Even such specialists as these Irregulars and members of the so-called Scion Societies of the Baker Street Irregulars will, I hope, find useful and surprising entries in my compendium.

These Holmesians have compiled a body of articles and books that probably exceeds, in bulk if not in quality, all the critical writing about, say, the poet Edmund Spenser. If the reader is curious about this often delightful Sherlock Holmes "criticism," he may turn to the American periodical *The Baker Street Journal* and to the selective bibliography "The Writings About the Writings" at the end of Baring-Gould's second volume, listing more than five hundred items published by the faithful acolytes of the Literary Agent. Since lists of these "scholarly" treatises are readily available elsewhere, it is not necessary to include them here. Furthermore, it would be inappropriate to burden this light-hearted study with scholarly impedimenta such as bibliographies and footnotes. The necessary references are included in the text.

I do not take Sherlock Holmes or Sir Arthur Conan Doyle *too* seriously. Holmes was assuredly a titanically successful literary creation, but there are confusions and contradictions in his persona. His creator was a minor Victorian, comparable perhaps to Galsworthy. He could write beautifully and compellingly, but he was sometimes careless and repetitious. And he betrayed a rather vulgar affection for words such as *plethora,* as did the late sportscaster Howard Cosell.

Both creator and creation are sometimes preposterous. But they are never dull. And they are lovable – delightful – fun! That's what *Good Old Index* is all about – the fun available from the Sherlock Holmes stories. I trust that as a handbook to the tales it will enhance the reader's pleasure.

Abbreviations, Dramatis Personae, and Thumbnail Synopses of the Tales

(Abbreviations for the tales are those in common use. Major characters' names are listed – not including Holmes, who, of course, is always present, and Watson, who almost always is.)

ABBE
: The Adventure of the Abbey Grange
Brackenstalls, Croker.
Wine dregs reveal that swinish peer was justifiably killed.

BERY
: The Adventure of the Beryl Coronet
Holders, Burnwell.
Prince of Wales offers coronet as surety for loan; banker's son wrongfully accused of tearing beryls off.

BLAC
: The Adventure of Black Peter
Carey, Neligan, Cairns.
Sea captain harpooned for stolen securities.

BLAN
: The Adventure of the Blanched Soldier
Dodd, Emsworths.
Boer-War veteran hidden because of his (misdiagnosed) leprosy.

BLUE
: The Adventure of the Blue Carbuncle
Baker, Ryder.
Christmas goose has gem in crop.

BOSC
: The Boscombe Valley Mystery
McCarthys, Turners.
Australian past catches up with squire.

BRUC
: The Adventure of the Bruce-Partington Plans
Mycroft Holmes, Cadogan West, Walters, Oberstein.
Plans for submarine retrieved.

CARD
: The Cardboard Box
Cushings, Browner.
Severed ears sent to wrong lady; adultery, double murder.

CHAS
: The Adventure of Charles Augustus Milverton
Milverton, Brackwell.
Blackmailer shot dead by lady victim.

COPP
: The Adventure of the Copper Beeches
Hunter, Rucastles.
Governess cuts her hair to impersonate employer's daughter.

CREE
: The Adventure of the Creeping Man
Bennett, Presburys.
Professor takes monkey-gland injections for sterility.

HOUN   The Hound of the Baskervilles
Baskervilles, Mortimer, Lyons, Barrymores, Stapletons, Frankland.
Spectral beast trained by putative heir to fortune; almost kills rightful heir.

IDEN   A Case of Identity
Sutherland, Windigate.
Maiden-lady seduced by step-father in disguise.

ILLU   The Adventure of the Illustrious Client
Gruner, de Mervilles, Winter.
German baron has seduced English heiress; Prince of Wales interested.

LADY   The Disappearance of Lady Frances Carfax
Carfax, Shlessingers, Green.
After Continental travels, English lady almost loses life at hands of phony clergyman.

LAST   His Last Bow
Von Bork.
Holmes poses as Irish-American traitor to trap German spy.

LION   The Adventure of the Lion's Mane
McPherson, Murdoch, Stackhurst, Bellamys.
Venomous sea creature kills, maims; but justice is done.

MAZA   The Mazarin Stone
Cantlemere, Sylvius, Merton.
Crown jewel returned to peer by trickery.

MISS   The Adventure of the Missing Three-Quarter
Overton, Staunton, Mount-James, Armstrong.
Cambridge rugby star marries secretly, is eventually found.

MUSG   The Musgrave Ritual
Musgrave, Brunton, Howells.
Butler solves puzzle of ancient family ritual which leads to buried treasure (crown jewels); suffocates.

NAVA   The Naval Treaty
Phelps, Harrisons, Holdhurst.
Treaty returned by trickery.

NOBL   The Adventure of the Noble Bachelor
St. Simon, Doran, Millar, Moulton.
Pompous and penurious nobleman's marriage annulled; American girl reunited with long-lost husband.

NORW   The Adventure of the Norwood Builder
McFarlanes, Oldacre.
Suburban contractor fakes his own death (hides behind wall) as vengeance for disappointment in love.

SIGN	The Sign of the Four (Baring-Gould); The Sign of Four (Doubleday) Morstan, Sholtos, Small, Tonga. Agra treasure lost in Thames, but Watson meets future wife.
SILV	Silver Blaze Ross, Straker, Simpson, Brown. Holmes identifies fast-running horse by washing its face.
SIXN	The Adventure of the Six Napoleons Hudson, Beppo, Brown, Sandeford, Venuccis. Missing jewel found in the last of six smashed busts of the emperor.
SOLI	The Adventure of the Solitary Cyclist Smith, Carruthers, Woodley, Williamson, Morton. Rural music-teacher followed on bicycle; marriage by force is thwarted, partly by pistol shots.
SPEC	The Adventure of the Speckled Band Stoner, Roylott. Serpent summoned by whistle to frighten stepdaughter and to prevent her marriage; thwarted when serpent bites its owner.
STOC	The Stockbroker's Clerk Pycroft, Pinner(s). Clerk lured away from broker's office by disguise (imperfect because of gold-filled tooth); violent end.
STUD	A Study in Scarlet (The first published tale.) Drebber, Stangerson, Hope; Part 2, Ferriers. American avenges crimes perpetrated by murderous Mormons.
SUSS	The Adventure of the Sussex Vampire Fergusons. Jealous crippled boy guilty of neck-biting.
THOR	The Problem of Thor Bridge Gibsons, Dunbar. American bully and millionaire falls in love with governess; wife's suicide by pistol makes nick on bridge.
3GAB	The Adventure of the Three Gables Stockdale, Dixie, Klein. Black thug tries to frighten Holmes from discovering book-manuscript which will reveal crimes.
3GAR	The Adventure of the Three Garridebs Garrideb, Evans. American stages hoax to find pal's counterfeiting machine.

3STU	The Adventure of the Three Students
	Soames, Bannister, Gilchrist, Ras, McLaren.
	Muddy athletic shoes betray student who stole proofs of Greek examination.
TWIS	The Man with the Twisted Lip
	Whitneys, St. Clairs.
	Respectable English suburbanite poses as disfigured beggar who hides in opium den.
VALL	The Valley of Fear
	Douglases, Barker; Part 2, McGinty, Baldwin, Shafters. American living in England fakes his own death to avoid being hounded by secret-society thugs; eventually drowned by Moriarty's henchmen.
VEIL	The Adventure of the Veiled Lodger
	Ronders, Leonardo.
	Female circus-performer, disfigured by lion claws, gets vengeance.
WIST	The Adventure of Wisteria Lodge
	Eccles, Garcia, Burnet, Henderson.
	South American patriot (now British suburbanite) invites respectable Englishman to country house to establish alibi; fails.
YELL	The Yellow Face
	Munros.
	American-born English wife hides mulatto daughter from husband.

Additional abbreviations: q.v. = which see; qq.v. = which see (plural); s.v. = under the entry for; cf. = compare; OED = *Oxford English Dictionary*.

GOOD OLD INDEX

*Note: The index entries are referenced to the stories in which they occur using the standard four-letter abbreviations for the Holmes stories, which can be found on the preceding pages under Abbreviations, Dramatis Personae, and Thumbnail Synopses of the Tales. In some of the more extensive entries (such as the one for **flora**) no abbreviations are given, although many of the more significant subentries found in them are also listed as separate entries in their own right. In those entries, story abbreviations are given. The index entries are not meant to be exhaustive, and were chosen arbitrarily.*

Abbas Parva: small Berkshire village where Ronder died and his wife was lion-clawed; Holmes is surprised that Watson does not remember the events, although the two were together at the time VEIL.

"Abbey School": (= PRIO) BLAN.

Abdullah Khan: one of the Four SIGN.

"Abergavenny murder": no hint of the details, though Holmes says it is coming up for trial PRIO; *see* **"Ferrers documents."**

"Abernetty family": we are told that it was a dreadful business but no more SIXN; *see* **butter.**

abominable: *see* **"Merridew, of abominable memory"; "Ricoletti of the club foot and his abominable wife"; smile.**

"Abrahams, old, in mortal terror of his life": we do not know why the old man was so terrified LADY.

absurdities – some occasioned by differences in English and American usages: passed out

BERY, DEVI; *see* **barrels** (of pistol); **boots** (reversed); **child** (in chimney); **kid** (tethered); **knocked up; mind** (Watson's, utterly submerged; **outhouse; propose; relations; shiver** (of assent, passes through drooping tail); **threw up.**

absurdly simple: (Holmes remarks) DANC, SIGN, TWIS; quite simple RETI; (very) commonplace NAVA, STUD; absurdly commonplace LADY; very (remarkably) superficial CARD, CROO, RESI; *see* **Elementary.**

accent: *see* **dialect.**

Achmet: merchant carrying Agra treasure; Small abets the merchant's murder by throwing his firelock between his (Achmet's) legs SIGN.

acid: used as weapon BLUE, ILLU; splash on forehead REDH; prussic, sent to Holmes VEIL; strong, Holmes's hand stained with STUD; *see* **chemistry; vitriol; weapons.**

Acton, Old: neighbor of the Cunninghams; the burglary of his

house gives the Cunninghams
the idea for their own fake burglary REIG; for the peculiar as-
sortment of items stolen from Acton, *see* **collections, singular.**

actor: (Holmes) MAZA, SIGN; *see*
professions; stage.

Adair, Hon. Ronald: shot because
he knew that Moran was a cheat
EMPT.

Adams: culprit in the **"Manor
House case,"** q.v. GREE.

"Addleton tragedy": Holmes has
solved the case GOLD.

Adler, Irene: (first name probably
pronounced "ee-RAY-nay" or
"ee-RAY-nuh") BLUE, IDEN,
LAST, SCAN; in Holmes's good
old index, her biography appears
between those of a rabbi and an
authority on fish SCAN; to Holmes, *the* woman; *see* **daintiest
thing under a bonnet on this
planet;** *cf.* **Bellamy.**

admiration: popular applause (no-
toriety) hateful (abhorrent) to
Holmes LADY, SECO; averse to
publicity, public applause DEVI,
NORW; Holmes says, I cannot
agree with those who rank modesty among the virtues GREE;
egotism a strong factor in Holmes's character, says Watson
COPP; admits that he has great
powers, which he shares with
Mycroft BRUC; always warmed
by admiration, the characteristic
of the real artist VALL; accessible
to flattery REDC; smile shows he
is pleased by Hayter's REIG and
Lestrade's SIXN compliments;
admits he is hurt – just a little –
when Mortimer says that Bertil-

lon is the foremost criminal expert in Europe, which Mortimer
then emends to But as a practical
man of affairs it is acknowledged
that you stand alone; that
soothes   Holmes's   feelings
HOUN; he can be self-dep-
recating: *see* **ass; beetle; fool; lunatic; mole;** *also see* **automaton.**

A D P: = Alfred Dunhill Pipe
SILV.

affair: Holmes arranged one for
Hobbs REDC.

affaire de cœur: oscillation on the
pavement always means (Holm-
es opines) IDEN.

Afghanistan: Watson's service
there and in India has inured
him to heat CARD, RESI; and has
taught him to pack quickly for
travel BOSC; Watson tries, to no
avail, to entertain Phelps with
stories of Afghanistan and India
NAVA; Holmes's first remark to
Watson: You have been in Afghanistan, I perceive STUD; ab-
ductors take Wood there (and to
India, Nepal) CROO.

Africa: Sterndale has lived in West
and Central; collects *radix* powder in Ubanghi country DEVI; *see*
South Africa.

Agar, Dr. Moore: advises complete
rest for Holmes DEVI.

Agatha: housemaid; Holmes engaged to CHAS.

age doth not wither . . . : Holmes
paraphrases Shakespeare, *Antony
and Cleopatra* EMPT.

aged seaman: Holmes's disguise
SIGN.

agency, detective: Holmes's LADY, SUSS.

agents: foreign (spies): *see* La-Rothière, Louis; Lucas (Eduardo); Meyer, Adolph; Oberstein, Hugo; Holmes's, disguised as muffled passers-by, loungers, guardsmen, a scissors-grinder EMPT, SCAN; *see* Mercer; Warner; both Holmes and Milverton call themselves agents – disingenuously CHAS.

agony column: (roughly = "personals" in American newspapers) BRUC, ENGR, 3GAR, VALL; columns snipped by Holmes are filed in a great book REDC, evidently different from **good old index**, q.v.

Ainstree, Dr.: authority on tropical diseases; Watson wants to summon him DYIN.

Airedale terrier: McPherson's, dead, stiff, eyes projecting LION.

air-gun: EMPT, MAZA; *see* Straubenzee; Von Herder.

airy nothing: Holmes quotes Shakespeare, *The Tempest* FINA.

Albert chain (for pocket watch): heavy STUD; brassy REDH; gold IDEN; *see* **watch-chain.**

*Alcuin: real name Albinus Flaccus (735-804), English scholar, educator, and religious reformer; his *Vox populi, vox Dei* quoted by Holmes ABBE.

"Aldridge": perhaps one of the official police; *see* **"bogus laundry affair."**

Alexis: betrayed by Coram; in Siberia GOLD.

Algar: Holmes's colleague in Liverpool CARD.

aliases: the following assume one or more: **Antonio; Armitage** (James); **Baldwin, Ted; Baskerville; Becher, Dr.; Beddington; Bohemia, King of; Clay, John; Evans** ("Killer"); **Holmes, Sherlock; Lopez; Lucas** (Eduardo); **Murillo, Don Juan; Oberstein, Hugo; Oldacre, Jonas; Peters, Henry** ("Holy"); **Prescott, Rodger; Ross** (Duncan); **Ryder** (James); **St. Clair** (Neville); **Sergius; Straker** (John); **Sutton; Watson, John H.; Windibank, James,** qq.v.; aliases assumed: **Altamont; Angel, Hosmer; Anthony; Barton, Dr. Hill; Basil, Captain; Beddoes; Blessington; Boone, Hugh; Coram, Professor; Cornelius, Mr.; Darbyshire; Douglas** (John [Jack]); **Escott; Ferguson** (Mr.); **Fournaye** (Henri); **Garrideb** (John); **Hargrove; Harris; Henderson; Holmes, Sherlock; Lucas** (Mr.); **McMurdo, Jack; Morecroft; Morris** (William); **Pierrot; Pinner, Harry, Arthur; Porlock, Fred; Price; Pycroft, Hall; Robinson, John; Shlessinger, Dr. and Mrs.; Sigerson; Spaulding, Vincent; Trevor** (old); **Vandeleur; Von Kramm, Count; Waldron; Winter** (James), qq.v. Two Lucases: Eduardo Lucas takes the alias Fournaye, while Lopez assumes the name Lucas. Beddington/Blessington: Beddington poses as Pycroft, while Sutton poses as Blessington. Baskerville's aliases include Stapleton, Vandeleur, and Sherlock Holmes.

Holmes himself poses as Altamont, Basil, Escott, Harris, Sigerson; *see* **disguises.**

Alice: Doran's dour maid NOBL.

"Alicia": a cutter that was lost in a patch of mist; an unfinished case whose records are at Cox and Co. THOR; *cf. Anderson (Sophy); "Phillimore, James."*

alkaloid, vegetable: poison; Stamford says Holmes might give a pinch to a friend, just to see the effects STUD.

Allardyce's: butcher's, where Holmes tries to impale a pig carcass with a harpoon BLAC.

Allen, Mrs.: relieves Mrs. Douglas of household cares; buxom, cheerful, somewhat deaf VALL.

all is well that ends well: (Holmes) SIGN; probably not quoting Shakespeare play title, since the phrase is proverbial.

alliteration: Conan Doyle's stylistic habit – examples: walk where we would, we could not walk ourselves clear of the danger that was dogging our footsteps; rattle and roar, beating a blast FINA; gurgling, gargling STOC; creak and crackle EMPT; a new sound mingled with it, a deep, muttered rumble, musical and yet menacing, rising and falling like the constant murmur of the sea HOUN.

Alpha Inn: (probably to be identified with the Museum Tavern, Great Russell Street) BLUE.

Alpine-stock: (spelled thus in Doubleday edition; *alpenstock* in Baring - Gould edition) Holmes leaves behind at Reichenbach FINA.

Altamont: Irish-American traitor; actually, Holmes's alias (also Conan Doyle's father's middle name) LAST.

"aluminium crutch": crutches were usually made of wood, so this one is unusual, but we know nothing else about its significance MUSG; Straker carries an aluminium pencil case SILV.

"Amateur Mendicant Society": members had a luxurious club in the lower vault of a furniture warehouse FIVE; an adventure evidently unrelated to TWIS, where St. Clair is a professional mendicant who works alone.

Amati violins: Holmes knows all about them, of course STUD; *see* **Cremona; Stradivarius.**

Amazon (River): twenty years ago, Pinto adored Gibson on its banks THOR.

Amberley, Josiah, and wife: repulsive murderer and adulteress; Holmes prevents him from committing suicide by poison pill RETI; for the co-respondent in this triangle, *see* **Ernest.**

America: it is always a joy to meet an American, Holmes says; he foresees a quartering of the Union Jack and the Stars and Stripes NOBL; settings STUD, VALL; weapons (Smith and Wesson, Winchester, sawn [sawed]-off shotgun) VALL; American men of affairs characteristically have round, fresh, clean-shaven faces; criminal escapes from penitentiary through political influence 3GAR; Coventry says, These Americans are readier with their pistols than we are THOR; was Holmes born in America? – *see* **Atlanta; Buffalo; California; Chicago; Cleveland; Florida; Kansas; Lone Star; New York; North America; P-E-N.**

Americans: *see* **Adler, Irene** (born New in Jersey); **Altamont; Baldwin, Ted; *Beecher, Henry Ward; Castalotte, Tito; Cormac, Tiger; Cubitt** (Elsie); **Dixie, Steve; Doran** (Aloysius and Hatty); **Drebber, Enoch J.; Evans** ("Killer"); **Ferrier** (John and Lucy); **Garrideb** (Alexander Hamilton); **Gibson** (Neil); **Hebron** (John); **Hope** (Jefferson); **Hopkins** (Ezekiah); **Leverton; Marvin, Captain Teddy; McGinty, John (Black Jack); Morris** (Brother); **Moulton** (Francis Hay); **Munro** (Effie); ***Poe, Edgar Allan; Scanlan, Mike; Slaney, Abe; Smith** (*Joseph); **Stangerson, Joseph; Starr, Dr. Lysander; *Thoreau, Henry David; Winter** (James); ***Young, Brigham;** Conan Doyle gave what he thought were typical American Christian names to the men: Aloysius, Ezekiah, Ted, Teddy, Jefferson, Alexander Hamilton, Abe; and the women: Elsie, Hatty, Lucy, Effie; for immigrants to America, *see* **Douglas** (John ([Jack]); **Edwards, Birdie; Lucca** (Gennaro and Emilia); **Gorgiano, Giuseppe; McMurdo, Jack; Openshaw** (Elias); **Shafter;** *also see* **Apaches; native Americans;**

also see entries for South and Central Americans: **Anthony; Durando, Signora Victor; Garcia; Lopez; Murillo, Don Juan; Pinto** (Maria); **Stapleton** (Beryl).

Ames: butler; quivering from shock; quaint, gnarled, dried-up; capable VALL.

analytic: reasoning backward, says Holmes, as compared with synthetic STUD; Watson concedes that some cases baffled Holmes's analytical skill FIVE; Holmes recognizes that a woman's impression may be more valuable than a conclusion of an analytical reasoner TWIS; respects Miss Presbury's intuition CREE; Holmes says, I value a woman's instinct in such matters LION.

Anderson: Emsworth's fellow soldier in South Africa BLAN; village constable; big, gingermoustached; slow, solid Sussex breed – a breed which covers much good sense under a heavy, silent exterior LION; "Anderson murders in North Carolina": Holmes uses this case as a precedent, but we are not told how he came to know about it HOUN; "*Sophy Anderson*": British bark that was lost; Holmes evidently solved the case FIVE.

Anerley Arms: hotel where McFarlane stays NORW.

Angel, Hosmer: Windibank's alias IDEN.

Angels, Avenging: Mormon secret police, also known as the Danite Band STUD.

Anglo-Indian: *see* **clubs.**

animals: *see* **fauna;** for man-eating animals, *see* **crocodile; jackal.**

aniseed: *see* **syringe.**

ankle(s): Holmes feigns a sprained PRIO; bare, Roylott's protrude SPEC; Watson seized by his CHAS; *see* **bulldog; telegram, -graph, -phone** (Holmes's hotel room ankle-deep in congratulatory telegrams).

Anna: Coram's near-sighted wife; long, obstinate chin; brown with dust; a Nihilist GOLD.

Anstruther: takes Watson's practice BOSC.

antennæ of an insect: Gruner's moustache ILLU; Mortimer's fingers HOUN.

Anthony: doddering Stapleton servant; actually Antonio, a Costa Rican; Holmes says that Anthony is not a common name in England HOUN; *see* **dialect.**

Antonio: *see* **Anthony.**

Apaches: thought to be guilty of murdering Moulton; actually only kidnapped NOBL; the Apaches who assault Le Brun (ILLU) are French street thugs; *see* **native Americans.**

ape: -like face STUD; monkey-faced (Small) SIGN; Mrs. McFarlane calls Oldacre a malignant and cunning ape NORW; *see* **Baboon; Beppo; serum.**

applause: *see* **admiration.**

Appledore, Sir Charles: father of the Duchess of Holdernesse PRIO.

apocrypha of the agony column VALL; *see* **style.**

aqua tofana: an arsenic poison said to have been devised by seventeenth-century Sicilian secret societies STUD.

aquiline: Holmes TWIS; Brackenstall ABBE; Coram GOLD; Von Bork LAST; Norton SCAN; Burnet WIST; *see* **face; hatchet; nose.**

Arab: street (ragged lad), summons four-wheeler in response to whistle SIGN; the Baker Street Irregulars are sometimes called street Arabs CROO, SIGN; caterer's men disappear like genii in *Arabian Nights* NOBL.

Archie: Clay's partner, alias Duncan Ross and William Morris REDH; perhaps to be identified with Stamford, who has the same first name SOLI.

architects: Holmes and Watson pose as SPEC.

architecture: *see* **Elizabethan; Tudor; Jacobean; Palladio; Queen Anne; Georgian; Victorian; awful;** *bijou;* **clump; dingy; feeble; flat-chested; flat-faced; griffins; heraldic; high; lions; nightmare; old (staring) brick.** Stoke Moran is built of gray lichen-blotched stone; two curving wings like the claws of a crab; interior walls are brown worm-eaten oak SPEC; Charlington Hall has a gateway of lichen-studded stone SOLI; Abbey Grange has a couple of wings, several bedrooms, kitchen, butler's pantry, gun-room, billiard-room, dining room ABBE; Baskerville Hall has oak-panelling, baulks of age-blackened oak, crenellations, mullioned windows, twin towers, high chimneys, great-hall with gallery, twin staircases, many bedrooms, minstrel's gallery, billiard-room, candles and torches (no gas) HOUN; Birlstone is weather-stained and lichen-blotched; it has many gables and small diamond-paned windows; double moats, one forty feet broad; drawbridge VALL; Tuxbury Old Hall is large and rambling – a regiment might be hid away in it BLAN; Ferguson's house has towering Tudor chimneys and a lichen-spotted, high-pitched roof; half-paneled walls; fireplace dated 1670 SUSS; the Cunninghams' fine old Queen Anne house has 1709 (**Malplaquet**, q.v.) on the lintel REIG; Thor Place is widespread, half-timbered, half Tudor, half Georgian THOR; Wisteria Lodge is an old tumble-down building in a crazy state of disrepair WIST; St. Luke's College has some really curious pieces of mediæval domestic architecture 3STU.

Arctic expedition: Holmes, alias Captain Basil, advertises a phony one to lure unemployed seamen to his rooms BLAC.

Armitage: James, Trevor's real name GLOR; Percy, Stoner engaged to SPEC.

arm(s): Klein holds Holmes's 3GAB; long, Moriarty's; thrown around Holmes; Holmes's, Watson grips him by EMPT; Holmes's – long, thin, nervous – shoots out from the sheets in the Turkish bath

ILLU; Holmes's wiry, round Watson 3GAR.

Armstrong, Dr. Leslie: foul-tempered medico; brooding eyes; at the conclusion, he calls Holmes a good fellow MISS.

"Armsworth Castle": no details about this adventure except that Holmes used the "Fire!" ruse SCAN; see **"Darlington Substitution Scandal."**

Army: British STUD; Indian, Watson's service in THOR; for regiments, see **Berkshires; Coldstream Guards; Fifth Northumberland Fusiliers; Middlesex Corps;** commissions depend upon education: Barclay has an education and was already marked for the sword-belt, says Wood CROO; cf. **Navy; queen.**

arsenal: Gibson, a violent American, has one in his house THOR.

art: in the blood is liable to take the strangest forms (Holmes, re his and Mycroft's gifts) GREE; for art's sake (upper-case *Art... Art's* in Baring-Gould edition), Holmes solves case without fee (*L'art pour l'art* is sometimes attributed to *Victor Cousin, [1792-1867]) COPP, REDC, RETI; Some touch of the artist wells up within me, and calls insistently for a well-staged performance (Holmes) VALL; Holmes loves his art (detection) NAVA; Holmes's voice exhibits the joy and pride that an artist takes in his own creation (actually, the wax bust of Holmes is Meunier's creation) EMPT; an oasis of art in the howling desert of south London, Sholto describes his house thus SIGN; Holmes invites Watson to spend time with him in a Bond Street picture gallery HOUN; *see* **game.**

artificial kneecaps: false address leads to manufacturer of REDH.

ashes: Holmes scrapes off lamp (only half, leaving the rest for the official police) DEVI; *see* **cabbage; cigars; Holmes Bibliography; number.**

asphalt: paving that leads to stablegates SILV.

ass: write me down as one, says Holmes BRUC; *see* **beetle; fool; lunatic; mole; slow-witted.**

astronomy: Holmes's knowledge of nil, according to Watson STUD; *see* ***Copernicus, Nikolaus; ecliptic; equation.**

atavism and hereditary aptitudes: Holmes discourses on GREE.

Athene: bust of CHAS.

"Atkinson brothers of Trincomalee": victims or criminals? We know nothing except for the locale SCAN.

Atlanta: Holmes has some knowledge of YELL.

attenta: Final *a* means it is addressed to a woman (Holmes reveals his ignorance of Italian; the -*a* is the inflection for informal imperative singular – no sex or gender involved); also, the Italian alphabet does not use *K*, so Holmes's counting of flashes is in error REDC.

Aurora: steam launch SIGN.

Australia(n): past – shameful or criminal ABBE, BOSC, EMPT, GLOR; future – Wilder, guilty of a felony, is permitted to escape and seek his fortune there PRIO; Maynooth is governor of one of the Australian colonies EMPT.

automaton; calculating machine: Watson calls Holmes SIGN; Holmes is a reasoning machine – but for an instant he betrays a human love for admiration and applause SIXN; *see* **admiration; inhuman; red Indian; scientific.**

Aveling: mathematics master PRIO.

avidity: Holmes displays when asking for six thousand pounds from Holdernesse; he pats the cheque affectionately PRIO; hastens to cash cheque for five hundred pounds LAST.

awful gray London castle: de Merville's house on Berkeley Square ILLU.

baboon: One of Roylott's pets; *see* **cheetah** SPEC; baboon-like faces: Drebber STUD, Beppo SIXN.

back, long, thin: Holmes's DANC; *cf.* **fingers.**

backgammon and draughts (checkers) FIVE; *see* **games.**

Backwater, Lord: guest at St. Simon wedding NOBL; his horse entered in the Wessex Cup SILV.

badger: one of Sherman's pets; *see* **slow-worm; stoat** SIGN.

Bagatelle: *see* **club.**

Bain, Sandy: jockey SHOS.

Baker, Henry: amiable drunk, loses goose and hat BLUE.

Baker Street Irregulars: boys who do the dogsbody work for Holmes, receiving one shilling a day; *see* **Cartwright; Simpson; Wiggins;** one of them, surprisingly, owns a **handkerchief,** q.v.

Baker Street, 221B: first-floor (= American second-floor) flat DYIN; Holmes describes it as a suite: two bedrooms, sitting-room, two broad windows STUD; spare bedroom NAVA; bow-window BERY, MAZA; front door with fanlight BERY; a second exit through the bedroom leads behind curtain MAZA; at least two lumber-rooms SIXN; Moriarty's aides set fire to FINA; there are many references to the Baker Street neighborhood – Oxford, Welbeck, Wigmore, Bentinck, and Vere Streets, and Park Lane; *see* **bearskin hearthrug in 221B; butter-dish; correspondence; gasogene; mantel; number; V.R.**

Baldwin, Ted: murderous Scowrer; registers at the Eagle Commercial Hotel under the alias of Hargrove; curved nose; American dialect (gettin') VALL.

ball: gigantic, of **newspapers,** q.v. BOSC; small, black dough or clay with sawdust in it 3STU; thin white slit of, beneath Pinner's eyelids STOC.

Ballarat: in Australia; Watson has been there SIGN; young McCarthy hears last two syllables, a rat BOSC; *see* **dying mumbles, half-understood.**

balls: met by two in the face (Menzies, Scottish engineer) VALL.

Balmoral: Duke and Duchess of NOBL; Lord, Moran wins four hundred and twenty pounds from him and **Milner, Godfrey,** q.v. EMPT; Duke of – his horse entered in race SILV; are these all the same peer?

*Balzac, Honoré de (1799-1850): French novelist; Angel quotes in one of his letters IDEN.

bang: (spelled *bhang* in Baring-Gould edition) drug made from hemp SIGN; *see* **drugs.**

Banks: City and Suburban, Holmes prevents robbery of REDH; Worthingdon, robbed of seven thousand pounds RESI; Capital and Counties, Cadogan West's BRUC, St. Clair's TWIS; Holmes uses the Oxford Street Branch PRIO; Dawson and Neligan BLAC; Holder and Stevenson BERY; Moriarty uses six different banks for household expenses VALL; Lady Frances refuses to leave her jewels with her banker, Silvester's LADY; Oldacre's bankbook reveals a low balance NORW; Watson's account is depleted CARD, RESI; *see* **Cox & Co.; racing.**

Bannister: college dip or servant; plump, twitching face, nervous fingers; former butler to Sir Jabez; dandled young Gilchrist on his knee 3STU.

Barclay, Colonel, and wife, Nancy (Devoy): the very model of a middle-aged couple; he is afraid of the dark; when angry, she has blazing eyes CROO.

Bardle, Inspector: member of Sussex constabulary; steady, solid, bovine man with thoughtful eyes; burly, phlegmatic LION.

Barelli, Augusto: father of Signora Lucca REDC.

baritsu: Japanese system of wrestling; Holmes uses it to save his life at the Reichenbach Falls EMPT.

Barker: Holmes's hated rival on the Surrey shore RETI; James Cecil: prize-fighter face, masterful black eyes VALL. One suspects that these two Barkers are the same man. Having learned Holmes's methods at the Master's feet, Cecil becomes a private investigator.

barmaid, Bristol: young McCarthy thinks he is married to one BOSC.

Barnes: innkeeper of the Green Dragon; spaniel delivered to him SHOS.

barney: Dodd's slang term for an argument BLAN.

Barnicott, Dr.: bust owner SIXN.

barometric pressure: Holmes asks, How is the glass? Twenty-nine, I see . . . and draws conclusions therefrom BOSC.

Barraud of London: watchmaker; *see* **watch.**

barrels: of pistol (error for chambers); Holmes fires five HOUN; lady fires barrel after barrel CHAS; two barrels DANC; Watson rightly calls them chambers SIGN; of creosote SIGN; of beer? booze? McGinty sits on one, hurls Baldwin across one VALL.

Barrett: constable, discovers Lucas's body SECO.

Barrymore, John and Eliza: Baskerville servants, in service for four generations; he is pale and, fortunately, rather deaf; her eyes are red, with swollen lids HOUN; *see* **beards; Selden.**

Barton, Dr. Hill: Watson's pseudonym; Holmes provides him with a card, duly printed ILLU.

Bart's: St. Bartholomew's Hospital; Stamford had been a dresser there under Watson; Holmes and Watson first meet in the chemistry laboratory STUD.

baryta, bisulphate of: Holmes identifies; baryta = barium oxide IDEN.

Basil, Captain: Holmes's pseudonym BLAC.

Baskerville: Sir Charles, head was half Gaelic, half Ivernian; frightened to death by the hound; Sir Henry, baronet; large hazel eyes, head of a Celt, which carries inside it the Celtic enthusiasm and power of attachment (Mortimer says); Rodger, father of "Stapleton"; Hugo, the forebear who hunted down the yeoman's daughter and was killed by the hound, giving rise to the legend; John; William; estate worth seven hundred and forty thousand pounds HOUN; *see* **Desmond; money; sucker.**

Bass Rock: Croker's new ship ABBE.

Bates, Marlow: neurotic manager of Gibson estate THOR.

bathroom: *see* **key.**

battery: Holmes wonders how one feels when it pours electricity into a non-conductor DYIN.

Baxter: Edith, maid SILV; *Richard (1615–1691), Holmes's error for *John Bradford (1510–1555) BOSC.

Baynes, Inspector: country detective; stout, puffy, red; extraordinarily bright eyes; later, small eyes, mentioned several times WIST.

beards: chinchilla (Ferguson) ENGR; full black (Barrymore); bushy black, false (Stapleton) HOUN; short, dark, false (Carruthers); black, either false or later shaved off (Pinner) STOC; white, later gray (Williamson) SOLI; white, stained yellow (Coram) GOLD; great brindled (Carey) BLAC; golden at fringes, white near lips; brindled (Sterndale) DEVI; long, dwindling, vivid red; streams down on table (Holdernesse) PRIO; flaming red (Bellamy) LION; drooping, mid-Victorian whiskers of a glossy blackness (Cantlemere) MAZA; pointed, grizzled brown (Baker) BLUE; short, black (Brackenstall) ABBE; light (Walter) BRUC; straggling gray (Emsworth) BLAN; goat's (N Garrideb) 3GAR; lionlike (hair and beard, Gregory) SILV; long, light (V Walter) NAVA; tangled (Turner) BOSC; little, pointed, thready, ill-nourished (Kemp) GREE; bristling black (Slaney) DANC; bristling, diamond twin-

kles through fringe of (McGinty) VALL: six black, two white, two red, two bristling. Moustaches: Watson has one; others include Anderson's (ginger), Croker's (golden), Gruner's (antennæ of an insect), Moran's (grizzled), Norberton's (heavy), Windibank's (false), Woodley's (red).

Holmes and Watson in the Musgrave Ritual.
Paget illustration

bearskin hearthrug in 221B HOUN, PRIO.

Beaune: wine, Watson drinks at lunch; makes him short-tempered SIGN.

Becher, Dr.: Ferguson's real name (or alias?) ENGR.

Beddington: Pinner's brother; famous forger and cracksman; poses as Pycroft STOC.

Beddoes: alias Evans; invites Trevor to his estate for shooting;

writes to Trevor in code; disappears, after having avenged himself on Hudson (Holmes hypothesizes) GLOR.

*Beecher, Henry Ward (1813–1887): American abolitionist; Watson has a framed portrait; he is distressed by Beecher's reception in England, as a spokesman for the North during the Civil War, by the more turbulent of our people CARD, RESI.

beef, Berkshire: stationmaster says that a little of this would do Stark no harm ENGR.

beer: drunk in pubs, by Holmes and others BLUE, SOLI; but also at 221B – *see* **cold beer.**

bees: *see* **fauna; Sussex;** Admiralty buzzing like overturned bee-hive BRUC; beeswing = wine dregs ABBE; beeswax: *see* **make-up.**

beetle: blind, Browner CARD, Holmes PRIO, and Pycroft STOC call themselves; like one on a card, Carey is pinned to the wall BLAC; Prendergast says the ship is beetle-ridden GLOR; *see* **ass; mole.**

bell: electric MAZA, PRIO; mechanical, quivers, rings or does not ring NAVA, WIST; Holmes stops Lady Hilda from ringing, then rings himself SECO; distant tinkle, as lodger rings for lunch REDC; clang of NORW, violent peal of STUD, at 221B; Holmes asks Watson to touch to summon Mrs. Hudson BLUE; Armstrong rings furiously MISS; violent ring at Birlstone VALL; Sir Henry rings to ask Barrymore

about the woman's sobs HOUN; *see* **bell-rope.**

belladonna STUD; *see* **drugs; make-up.**

Bellamy: Tom, owns all the boats and bathing-cots; daughter Maude, son William; Holmes describes Maude as a most complete and remarkable woman: Who could have imagined that so rare a flower would grow from such a root and in such an atmosphere? LION; *cf.* **Adler.**

Bellinger, Lord: austere, high-nosed, eagle-eyed, dominant; quick, fierce gleam in his deep-set eyes; twice Premier SECO; *see* **nose.**

bell-rope (-pull) ABBE, CROO; dummy SPEC.

Belminster, Duke of: father of Lady Hilda SECO.

benefactor of the race: Watson calls Holmes REDH; *see* **best.**

benevolence, -ent: *see* **peering.**

Bennett, Trevor: called Jack; medical degree CREE.

Bentley's: private hotel, Overton and the Cambridge 'varsity stay at MISS.

Benz: one hundred-horsepower motor-car LAST; *see* **vehicles.**

Beppo: murderous Italian thief; worker in a bric-a-brac factory; swift and active as an ape; snaps at Watson's hand SIXN.

bereavement: Watson's; Holmes consoles him EMPT; *see* **Morstan.**

Berkeley (Barclay?) Square: *see* **awful; Sinclair.**

Berkshires: Watson's regiment STUD; *see also* **Fifth;** *cf.* **beef.**

Bernstone, Mrs.: housekeeper SIGN.

***Bertillon, Alphonse (1853–1914):** French criminologist HOUN, NAVA; in Mortimer's estimation, the foremost criminal expert in Europe, at which judgment Holmes takes some umbrage HOUN.

best and wisest: Watson, speaking of Holmes, perhaps echoing the final passage of Plato's *Phaedo,* where the subject is Socrates; *see* **benefactor of the race; heart;** *cf.* **Milverton, Charles Augustus; Moran, Colonel Sebastian.**

best stories, Conan Doyle's own list, in order: SPEC, REDH, DANC, FINA, SCAN, EMPT, FIVE, SECO, DEVI, PRIO; evidently he considered the short stories only; most readers would include the novels HOUN, VALL; *see* **worst stories.**

Bevington's: pawnbroker's, where Lady Frances's jewelry is pawned LADY; *cf.* **Jews.**

Bible, Holmes quotes: wages of sin CROO; nothing new HOUN; schemer falls 3GAB; possess our souls in patience VALL; *see* **David, Uriah, Bathsheba.**

bicycle PRIO, SOLI, VALL; Holmes rides one MISS; MacDonald says it would be a grand help to the police if these things were numbered and registered VALL; *see* number; **Rudge-Whitworth; tyre.**

Biddle: crook RESI; *see* **Sutton.**

Big Ben: name of the great bell in the Clock Tower of the Houses of Parliament, often mistakenly applied to the clock itself; clock reads twenty-five to eight as Holmes and Watson fly by in a hansom on the way to a funeral scheduled for eight o'clock; bell strikes eight as they tear down the Brixton Road LADY.

bijou villa: Holmes's description of Briony Lodge, Adler's house SCAN.

Bill: Breckinridge's boy BLUE.

billiards: Watson plays DANC; *see* **chalk.**

Billy: Name of (apparently) two different pages at 221B, one in 1880s VALL, the other after 1894 MAZA, THOR; unnamed servant at 221B referred to as the boy GREE, the boy in buttons IDEN, the page SHOS, our page-boy NAVA, NOBL, YELL.

billycock: like a derby or bowler but with a lower crown; from it Holmes deduces that Baker drinks, his wife has ceased to love him, and he has no gas in his house BLUE.

binomial theorem: mathematical theorem devised by Sir Isaac Newton for raising any two terms connected by a plus or minus sign to any power; Moriarty's treatise on it had a European vogue FINA; *see* **Dynamics of an Asteroid, The.**

bird: strange, lank, with dull gray plumage and black top-knot (Holmes resembles) DANC; hawk-like nose, pipe like bill of some strange bird (Holmes again) STUD; clear-cut, hawklike (Holmes yet again) SIGN; vulture's beak (Colonel Emsworth's nose) BLAN; eagle's beak (Sylvius's nose) MAZA; nose like a beak (Mortimer's) HOUN; horrible bird of prey (Amberley looks like) RETI; vulture-faced (Harraway) VALL; *see* **eye(s); fauna; nose.**

"Bishopgate jewel case": Jones admits that Holmes has set the official police on the right track SIGN.

bitter curse: Holmes utters and hurls a telegram into the grate; such strong language is rare; it is perhaps justified by the message, from the London police, that the gang has been captured but that its leader, Moriarty, has escaped FINA; Watson utters and shakes his fist at the lonely abode of the Stapletons; perhaps justified, because Watson thinks Stapleton has murdered Watson's charge, Sir Henry HOUN; for other things described as bitter, *see* **snarl; sneer; tears.**

bitterly cold ABBE, CHAS.

black business: Holmes calls the case COPP; *cf.* **shadows.**

black fellows: Indians; Sholto says they can be disregarded; Small calls mutineers black devils, black fiends SIGN; *see* **Indians.**

blackguard: Lyons's artist-husband was one HOUN; so was Oldacre NORW.

Blackheath: Watson's public school SUSS; Staunton played rugby for MISS; Yes, I went there, says Holmes, but he appears to mean that he visited the town to dig up dirt on Oldacre NORW.

black-letter editions: Holmes collects; at least, he buys one early book, *De Jure,* q.v. REDH.

blackmail BOSC, CHAS, GLOR, HOUN, REIG, SCAN; Holmes has (or pretends to have) a blackmail case that will prevent him from being in Devon HOUN; citizens pay public blackmail to McGinty; Scowrers are a ring of blackmailers VALL; *cf.* **murderers; thieves.**

black reaction: Sir Henry falls into, after excitement HOUN; for Holmes's melancholy, *see* **fits.**

Black Swan Hotel: Holmes and Watson lunch there COPP.

black villainy brewing: Barrymore thinks HOUN.

Blackwater, Earl of: son at the school PRIO; *see* **Backwater,** evidently a different peer.

blazing hot CARD.

bleak: and windy WIST; and boisterous EMPT.

bleat, Watson – unmitigated bleat!: Holmes cries, referring to **agony column,** q.v. REDC; *cf.* **twaddle.**

Blessington: Sutton's alias RESI.

blind: *see* beetle; mole; Von Herder.

blizzard, keen VALL.

*Blondin, Charles (1824–1897): real name Jean François Gravelet, acrobat and funambulist SIGN.

blood: fresh, Holmes digs into finger with long bodkin to obtain; Holmes deduces that writing was done by man's forefinger dipped in; gushes from Hope's nose; little ribbon, little pool (Stangerson's) STUD; Holmes simulates with red paint SCAN; on window sill BRUC, TWIS, VALL; on rope SIGN; steps are red with; ghastly crimson halo of REDC; ghastly pool of HOUN; Hatherley's coat-sleeve drenched with ENGR; rivers of, pail of WIST; Barclay CROO and Venucci SIXN lie in pools of their own; sucking of SUSS; extravasated (Holmes's term), in wounds LION; fresh, James McCarthy's right hand and sleeve stained with BOSC; bicycle horribly smeared and slobbered with PRIO; with brains, all over the room, including seat of oaken chair ABBE; slight smears and discolourations, but undoubtedly fresh NORW; side of Elsie's face red with DANC; runs down Garrideb's face 3GAR; spurts from front of Woodley's waistcoat SOLI; blood-letting, adventure cost Watson a 3GAR; blood-bespattered room; notebook stained with BLAC; stains are slight BRUC, NORW; drops of blood on snow BERY; Brunton's will be on Musgrave's head MUSG; Browner asks that the

blood might rot in Sarah Cushing's veins CARD; strange, outlandish in Murdoch LION; and brown sherry GLOR; *see* art; criminal; test; Tudor.

bloodhound: Holmes SIGN, Hope STUD, McMurdo VALL compared to; Blessington's cheeks, loose pouches, like those of a bloodhound RESI; *see* dogs; hound.

"Bloomsbury Lodger": original title of REDC.

blotting-paper CREE, MISS, TWIS.

Blount: student who, along with Sudbury, finds dead dog LION.

"blue carbuncle" (= BLUE) COPP; Holmes says that the gem has been the cause of two murders, a vitriol-throwing, a suicide, and several robberies.

blue, electric: *see* dress.

bluff: Sterndale accuses Holmes of; Holmes says that the bluff is on Sterndale's side DEVI; Holmes admits that he bluffed Gibson THOR.

blunder: Holmes admits he has made – a more common occurrence than anyone would think, he says SILV; Shlessinger says to Holmes, You've blundered badly; you've made a silly blunder LADY.

blurt, Holmes's tendency to: tells Mortimer his marriage was bad (because it disarranged Holmes's deductions) HOUN; almost tells McFarlane that he is gratified by McFarlane's imminent arrest NORW.

A NEW SHERLOCK HOLMES STORY by A. CONAN DOYLE

blush: My blushes, Watson, Holmes murmurs in a deprecating voice; the occasion is Watson's exhibition of pawky humour VALL; *see* **flush**, which is somewhat more common.

Blymer estate: gambled away by Sylvius MAZA.

Board schools: hundreds of bright little seeds in each, out of which will spring a wiser, better England, Holmes predicts NAVA.

*Boccaccio, Giovanni (1313–1375): Italian author; copy of his *Decameron* in Drebber's pocket is evidence of Drebber's dissolute character STUD.

body: Holmes's gives a wriggle of suppressed excitement NORW (*see* **fingers**); dead, atop Underground train BRUC; Norberton's sister's: dreadful witchlike features, all nose and chin, projecting at one end, the dim, glazed eyes staring from a discoloured and crumbling face SHOS; bodies thrown from Bar of Gold into Thames TWIS; *see* **cadaver.**

"bogus laundry affair": Aldridge helped in this case, but we are not told which was bogus, the laundry or the affair CARD.

Bohemia, King of: strongly marked German accent, foppish dress; Holmes knows his full name: Wilhelm Gottsreich Sigismond von Ormstein, Grand Duke of Cassel-Felstein; alias Count Von Kramm; he is six-feet-six SCAN; case mentioned COPP, IDEN; *see* **dress.**

Bohemian: soul, habits, Holmes's ENGR, MUSG, SCAN; dealer (Dorak) CREE; bachelors 3GAR; *see* **Murger, Henri.**

bolted: Holmes tells Watson to send this single word from the nearest telephone exchange if Amberley breaks away or returns RETI.

bones: discovered HOUN, SHOS; at bottom of Thames (Tonga's) SIGN; crushed, Cadogan West's (head) BRUC; charred, platter heaped with pieces of (lamb or kid) WIST; charred, of dog or rabbit, which police are meant to identify as human NORW; from one bone, a whole animal described FIVE; surgeon's deposition refers to injuries to parietal and occipital (Watson marks spot on his own head) BOSC; fossil, cleared away to make places for Holmes and Watson to sit 3GAR; *see* **condyle; mummy; skeleton.**

boob: = fool; Evans's American slang term for Garrideb.

book: Gruner's, in which he collects women; brown leather, locked, coat-of-arms on cover ILLU; *Book of Life, see* **Holmes Bibliography;** books: *see* **blackletter; *Murger, Henri; yellow-back.**

bookseller: Holmes's disguise; he carries *Origins of Tree Worship, British Birds, Catullus, The Holy War*; disguise consists of a pile of white hair, seedy frock-coat, hunched posture to take a foot off his stature EMPT.

bookworm: Coram calls himself a poor GOLD.

Boone, Hugh: St. Clair's alias TWIS.

boot(s): elastic-sided BERY, IDEN; square toes BOSC, RESI, SIGN, SILV, STUD; peculiarly long, sharp toes DANC; missing: Sir Henry has two and a half pairs but donates a pair (through Barrymore) to Selden; clink of Holmes's upon stone HOUN; patent-leather STUD; reversed EMPT; mismatched and half-buttoned IDEN; buttoned awry WIST; shooting, thick-soled; maid shows to Holmes BOSC; resoled: evidence that Holdhurst is not rich NAVA; bloody mark of boot-sole; muddy boots VALL; two nail-marks from British workman's boots; from Watson's, Holmes deduces that he can afford a hansom CROO; Watson's from Latimer's of Oxford Street LADY; Holmes identifies boot as American by pointing at toes VALL; Holmes kicks off boots and stockings (tells Watson to hold them) to make a naked footprint SIGN; Watson and Sir Henry take theirs off to stalk Barrymore HOUN; Watson ties his in a certain way LADY; Warren tells Holmes and Watson to leave theirs on the landing REDC; Brunton leaves his behind but wears slippers MUSG; nickname for page CARD, STUD (*cf.* **buttons**); for bootlaces, *see* **sleeves;** *also see* **shoes.**

***Borgias:** powerful Italian Renaissance family; black pearl of the SIXN.

bosom: Morstan's, *see* **pearl;** Lady Hilda's, *see* **key;** Munro's, *see*

locket; murderess's, *see* **revolver;** Anna's, *see* **packet.**

*Boswell, James (1740–1795): Friend and biographer of Dr. Samuel Johnson; Holmes calls Watson his Boswell SCAN.

*Bouguereau, Adolphe William (1825–1905): French painter; work by, in Sholto's collection SIGN.

boulder: big, Holmes and Stackhurst use to kill *Cyanea* LION; used as weapon against Hope STUD.

bowling-alley: (outdoors; bowling-on-the-green) wedding setting SOLI.

box: small black and white ivory; sharp spring like a viper's tooth, envenomed DYIN; deal (wooden), sliding lid, of bricks (child's blocks) TWIS; small wooden, sliding lid (contains mementos of case); squat, brass-bound, wooden (contains royal treasure) MUSG; match (contains remarkable worm) THOR; despatch (contains incriminating letter) SECO; small tin cash (contains record of newspaper advertisements) BRUC; tin (contains securities) BLAC; strong (contains Acton's claim against Cunningham estate) REIG; big black (contains Blessington's assets; he mistrusts banks) RESI; little (contains Ming saucer, evidently property of the Prince of Wales) ILLU; small chip (contains poison pills) STUD; small cardboard (contains pearls); Benares iron-work (contains Agra treasure) SIGN; small brass (contains Klan papers)

FIVE; tin, on Stapleton's shoulder (contains butterflies) HOUN; something like a box on Wood's shoulder (contains mongoose) CROO; coffin (for Holmes, Culverton Smith threatens) DYIN; bulky boxes (contain counterfeit half-crowns) ENGR; crates (contain 30,000 napoleons) REDH; *see* **snuff-box;** *also see* **Cox & Co.**

Boxer cartridges: (not in OED) Holmes fires at wall in 221B for target practice; *see* **V.R.**

boxers: *see* **Dixie, Steve; McMurdo** (Mr.); **Merton, Sam; Norberton, Sir Robert; Trevor** (old); **Williams;** Holmes himself is a boxer; he could have aimed high as a professional SIGN; he indulges in the good old British sport of boxing SOLI; Colonel Wardlaw's horse is named Pugilist SILV; *see* **Barker** (James Cecil: his face); *also see* **baritsu.**

box-room: Holmes's mind LION, STUD; *see* **mind.**

Brackwell, Lady Eva: author of compromising letters (very sprightly, says Milverton), engaged to Dovercourt CHAS.

Brackenstall: Sir Eustace: title, money, false London ways; Lady Mary, née Fraser ABBE.

Bradley: Watson's and Holmes's tobacconist, of Oxford Street; Holmes orders a pound of shag from; identifies Watson by discarded cigarette with Bradley printed on butt HOUN.

Bradshaw: railroad time-table; its vocabulary is terse but limited (Holmes) COPP, VALL.

Bradstreet, Inspector BLUE, ENGR, TWIS; accompanied by a plain-clothes man ENGR; *see* **He! he! You are a funny one!**

brain(s): Moriarty pays for – the American business principle VALL; you are proud of your brains (Smith to Holmes) DYIN; great, Mycroft's, everything is pigeon-holed in; Holmes has the power of throwing his brain out of action BRUC; Watson does not distract Holmes's intent brain WIST; strange how the brain controls the brain (Holmes) DYIN; I am a brain. The rest is a mere appendix (Holmes) MAZA; abnormally active MISS; brain without a heart GREE; razor brain, blunted and rusted with inaction; accuses himself of softening of the brain (Holmes) VALL; from his hat size, Holmes deduces that Baker has a large brain: cubic capacity = intellect BLUE; mutineer mercifully blows out wounded sergeant's brains GLOR; Wood says it was in his heart to knock Barclay's brains out CROO; Holmes remarks, Ah, me! it's a wicked world, and when a clever man turns his brains to crime it is the worst of all SPEC; *see* **God; mind; *Wild, Jonathan.**

Brambletye Hotel: Holmes and Watson stay there, as does Neligan BLAC.

brandy: usually for resuscitative purposes BLUE, EMPT, FIVE, GLOR, HOUN, LION, NAVA, PRIO, SECO, SIGN, SPEC, 3STU;

and water (with breakfast) ENGR; and soda WIST; and bandages ENGR; and ammonia GREE; Wood gulps a whole bottleful to save his life LION.

brazen tripod: Holmes hurls into the garden GREE.

bread-crumbs: Holmes arranges to illustrate pattern of cow tracks PRIO.

break: Gibson threatens Holmes, I have broken stronger men than you . . . . I can make or break, and it is usually break THOR; Moriarty threatens that Holmes will be trodden under foot FINA; *cf.* **Crush.**

breakfast: Holmes foregoes, Watson eats NORW; Holmes persuades Watson to forego 3STU; hurried, Holmes and Watson snatch GOLD; Holmes precedes Watson at, and then eats nothing until 10 P.M. FIVE; Holmes demands, before he will explain injury to his hand; Holmes and Watson usually have **toast**, q.v.; but on this occasion Mrs. Hudson, unbidden, brings in tea, coffee, and three covered dishes: curried chicken, eggs, the treaty NAVA; before breakfast, Murdoch insists upon algebraic demonstration LION.

breast: Holmes's head sunk upon DANC, TWIS; Jack coos and nestles his head upon his father's SUSS; Conan Doyle does not use *breast* for the female anatomy; indeed, such references are rare – *see* **bosom;** *cf.* **cheek.**

breath: two Ladies (Hilda Trelawney Hope NAVA and Frances

Jeremy Brett as Holmes (courtesy PBS)

Carfax LADY) draw; Holmes gasps for DYIN; finest girl that ever had the breath of life between her lips – Wood re Nancy Barclay CROO; Holmes and Watson breathless BLAC.

Breckinridge: irascible poulterer and gambler BLUE.

brewer: Mrs. St. Clair is daughter of TWIS; *see* **Melville.**

Brewer, Sam: moneylender SHOS.

bridge: Holmes strikes with his cane THOR.

bright, crisp, snowy BERY.

*Brinvilliers, Marchioness: actually Marie d'Aubray, Marquise de Brinvilliers (circa 1630–1676): French poisoner; alluded to in *Daily Telegraph* article about Drebber murder STUD.

"British barrow": singular contents; Holmes solves the case GOLD.

British government: *see* **Holmes, Mycroft; Prime Minister; Whitehall;** *cf.* **Empire, British;** government officials lose things (submarine plans BRUC, letter SECO, treaty NAVA), but Holmes, of course, finds them.

British Medical Journal: Watson reads STOC; for Watson's other reading, *see* ***Murger, Henri; novel; pathology; *Russell, William Clark; surgery; Trevelyan, Percy.**

British Museum: Holmes reads up on voodooism in WIST; Baker works in, or pretends to BLUE; **Montague Street,** q.v., is just behind it; **Great Orme Street,** q.v., is on the northeast side.

Broadmoor: hospital for the criminally insane; Holmes thinks that Amberley will go there rather than to the scaffold RETI.

brokers: debt collectors, Mrs. Tangey runs away from NAVA; pawnbroker: *see* **Jew.**

"Brooks": one of fifty men who wants Holmes's life BRUC.

Brook Street Mystery: journalists' term for RESI.

Brown: Josiah, bust owner SIXN; Silas, irascible stable owner; Holmes calls him bully, coward, sneak, old horse-faker SILV; Sam, Jones's police colleague SIGN.

Browner, Jim: married Mary Cushing; handy with a blunt knife; devil's light in his eyes; Fairbairn sees death in them CARD.

brows: Holmes's are frequently drawn, as in HOUN; *see* **eyebrows.**

Bruce-Partington: submarine; Mycroft says, 1) I thought everyone had heard of it; 2) It has been the most jealously guarded of all government secrets; Watson to Holmes, re the latter's solution of the case: A masterpiece. You have never risen to a greater height BRUC; for its patented secret mechanism, *see* **double.**

Bruce Pinkerton: prize, Trevelyan wins RESI.

Brunton, Richard: butler; well-grown, handsome man, with a splendid forehead; speaks several languages and plays every musical instrument; suffocates MUSG.

brute!, the: Watson exclaims twice, Holmes exclaims once, a little later HOUN; Ryder calls a goose a brute BLUE.

*Buddha, Gautama: originally Prince Siddhartha (563?–483? B.C.), Indian religious leader; hasp of Agra treasure chest in shape of a sitting Buddha SIGN; Holmes sits on floor like some strange Buddha as he consults good old index VEIL; Buddhism of Ceylon, Holmes discourses on SIGN.

Buffalo, New York: Holmes spends time there in preparation for his role as an American spy LAST.

bull: enraged, Cairns BLAC and Prendergast GLOR bellow like; mad, Dixie enters like one 3GAB; Holmes wonders if Heidegger has been gored by PRIO; John Bull will be on his hind legs and fair ramping, says Altamont LAST.

bulldog: Lestrade HOUN; chin (Boone) TWIS; eyes (Gregson) WIST; face (Cairns) BLAC; brave as a (Jones) REDH; bull-pup: Watson tells Holmes, at their first meeting, that he keeps one, but it never turns up STUD; bull-terrier, Trevor's, freezes onto Holmes's ankle GLOR.

bullet: elephant, Emsworth's shoulder wounded by BLAN; revolver, soft, expanding, discharged from air-gun; Mrs. Hudson picks it up from carpet EMPT; one remains in body after penetrating heart; the second passes through front of brain; the third makes a hole in the window-sash: Holmes finds because he was looking for it DANC; *see* **ventilator; vesta;** for other bullets, *see* **Boxer cartridges; Jezail; Martini bullet.**

Bull Inn: Holmes and Watson stay at WIST.

bull's-eye: lantern SIGN; *see* **dark lantern.**

bumper: a glassful: Holmes proposes that he, Watson, and Athelney Jones drink one each (of port) to the success of their journey on the Thames SIGN.

Burberry: brand of raincoat LION.

burglary: mostly by Holmes, sometimes abetted by Watson BRUC, CHAS, GREE, ILLU, LADY, MAZA, NAVA, RETI, SCAN, 3GAB; amateur domiciliary visit (Holmes's euphemism for) BRUC; unselfish and chivalrous (Watson) CHAS; tools include two drills, jemmy (jimmy in American edition), skeleton keys, dark lantern, chisel, diamond-tipped glass-cutter BRUC, CHAS; in BRUC, Watson brings tools to Holmes; Holmes uses pocket-jemmy on coffin SHOS; opens tin box with chisel BRUC; Shlessinger (Peters) calls Holmes a common burglar LADY; Holmes says burglary could have been his alternative profession, And I have little doubt that I should have come to the front RETI (*see* **criminal**); apparent, of country-houses ABBE, REIG; Blessington's talk of burglary was the merest blind RESI; Stapleton probably perpetrated at Folkestone Court HOUN; burglaries for busts SIXN; King of Bohemia has twice had Adler's house burgled, without success SCAN; *see* **circle.**

Burnet, Miss: *see* **Durando, Signora Victor.**

burning: *see* **letters.**

Burnwell, Sir George: dangerous, dissolute BERY.

bus: Mount-James takes, even though faced with a grave emergency, because he is miserly MISS.

bushes: Holmes and Watson hide in BLAC, CREE; *cf.* **shrubbery.**

business: man lured away from REDH, STOC.

bust: Napoleon's SIXN; for ladies', *see* **bosom.**

busybody: Holmes addressed thus by Williamson SOLI; by Roylott SPEC; by Sylvius MAZA; *see* **jack-in-office.**

butler: Gruner's, would have adorned a bench of bishops ILLU; Doran's, ejects Millar, with help of footman NOBL; Trevor gives Hudson job as GLOR; butlers, footmen, maidservants: overfed, underworked (says Holmes) WIST.

butlers: *see* **Ames; Bannister; Barrymore** (John)**; Brunton, Richard; Gruner, Baron Adelbert; Jacobs; John; khitmutgar; Ralph; Staples; Stephens;** *see* **violence** (for Roylott's native butler).

butt: misshapen, of air-gun, Moran cuddles to his cheek, with a sigh of satisfaction; of revolver, Watson uses on Moran EMPT; *see also* **Bradley; cigarette** (-ends).

butter: parsley sinks in, to a depth measured by Holmes, thus compromising the criminal SIXN; *see* **"Abernetty family."**

butter-dish: criminal relics in, at 221B MUSG.

butterflies: Stapleton catches (one variety named for him) HOUN; Nathan Garrideb collects 3GAR; *see* **Cyclopides.**

buttons: metal, left after Oldacre sets fire to his own trousers in the woodpile NORW; nickname for page; *see* **Billy.**

buxom: Allen, Mrs.; Merrilow, Mrs., qq.v.

cab: fog so thick that one is useless BRUC; Holder walks, since cabs go slowly through the snow BERY; nicknamed a growler STUD; *see* **vehicles.**

cabbage and potato: difference between – Holmes's analogy for differences in tobacco-ash, evident to an expert such as he SIGN.

Cabinet: awaits Holmes's final report with utmost anxiety BRUC; *see* **Holdernesse, Duke of.**

cabinet photograph: size larger than a carte de visite (OED) SCAN; *see* **photo.**

cabmen: Holmes has the two who transported Sylvius MAZA.

cadaver: Holmes beats STUD; cadaverous face (Garrideb's) 3GAR; *see* **body;** for more beating by Holmes, *see* **bridge; pavement.**

Cadogan West: Arthur, murdered government employee; engaged to Westbury, who says he was the most single-minded, chivalrous, patriotic man upon earth; his mother, a dazed old lady BRUC.

Café Royal: Holmes attacked outside of ILLU.

calabash: never mentioned; *see* **pipe, smoking, and tobacco.**

Cairns, Patrick: sea-captain; fierce bulldog face, tangled hair and beard BLAC.

calculation: Holmes throws himself into an intricate and elaborate one, to break the code DANC; *see* **height; rate; trigonometry.**

calf: dog as large as COPP; *see* **pony.**

California: Holmes has some knowledge of ILLU, STUD.

Calhoun, Captain James: Holmes sets the pips on him FIVE.

C. A. M.: Milverton's initials on card he sends to Holmes CHAS.

"Camberwell poisoning case" FIVE.

Cambridge: Holmes calls it an inhospitable town; one travels *down* to it from London MISS; Willoughby Smith GOLD, Overton, Staunton MISS, Phelps NAVA attended the university; *see* **rugby.**

Camden House: opposite 221B; Holmes and Watson await Moran there EMPT.

camel: Wood's back is like CROO.

Camford: = Cambridge + Oxford CREE; Holmes calls it a charming town, ergo = Oxford (*see* **Cambridge**) CREE.

*Campbell, Sir Colin, Lord Clyde (1792–1863): British army officer; appears simply as Sir Colin in SIGN.

Canada: Sir Henry has spent time there; Meyers, Toronto, is printed inside his boot HOUN; *see* **C. P. R.**

canary: Teddy tries to catch, from which Holmes deduces that he is carnivorous CROO; *see* **Wilson.**

candle: unguttered DANC; burned only half-inch VALL; burned out, guttered DEVI (from all of which Holmes deduces lapsed time, open window); moved at window as signal HOUN, REDC; Holmes throws on floor REDC; stump, red wax, on mantel STUD; wavers in Walters's trembling hand WIST; steady light from, in hut BLAC; tallow-stains on Baker's hat BLUE; bedroom candle held by Lady Brackenstall ABBE and Holmes HOUN.

Cantlemere, Lord: suspicious patrician MAZA.

canula: (variation of *cannula;* tube for draining body cavities) Bennett looks for CREE.

cap: greasy leather, Boone's TWIS; blue cricket cap with white chevron, Saltire's, found in a gypsy van PRIO; cloth caps are used for traveling or country wear; *see* **dress.**

capitalists: McGinty rails against mine owners as; his Marxism is a mask for hooliganism; McMurdo speaks of class war and capitalist millions, McGinty of capitalist outrage VALL.

Carbonari REDC, STUD; *see* **secret societies.**

card, visiting: Holmes throws his at Rance STUD; Holmes scribbles a few words on the back of his, for Lestrade CARD; Holmes sends his in to Armstrong, who is not pleased MISS; Holmes gives his to Carruthers SOLI; Holmes sends his to shipping-line manager, ensuring instant attention ABBE; Holmes's commands Johnson's respect BRUC; Holmes takes Amberley's (rather soiled) from the table RETI; Hatherley presents his to Holmes, via maid ENGR; Milverton sends his to Holmes, who throws it on floor; on it he describes himself as an agent; in fact, he is a professional blackmailer CHAS; Holmes's eyebrows rise when presented with Lady Hilda's SECO; Green sends his to Holmes and Watson on a salver LADY; Morstan sends hers to Holmes on brass salver; Holmes instructs Watson to tie one round his (Holmes's) neck, for reasons never disclosed (perhaps misprint for *cord*) SIGN;

cards, playing: Holmes has in his pocket REDH; Sir Henry and Mortimer play HOUN; Tregennises play DEVI; colour card, Holmes has none, says Gruner ILLU; Holmes to Dunbar: All the cards are against us THOR; Holmes: I see the fall of the cards BRUC; Holmes: We are getting some cards in our hand; we have added one card to our hand SHOS; the case is like a three-card trick 3STU; cards, gambling at, *see* **Adair, Hon. Ronald; McLaren, Miles; Moran, Colonel Sebastian; Prendergast** (Major); *and see* **games.**

"Carère, Mlle": step-daughter of Montpensier, thought dead but found (by Holmes ?) alive and well in New York HOUN.

Carey, Peter: has wife and daughter, whom he flogs; attacks Cairns, spitting and cursing BLAC.

Carfax, Lady Frances: stray chicken in a world of foxes LADY.

Carina: singer RETI.

Carlo: mastiff COPP; spaniel SUSS.

*Carlyle, Thomas (1795–1881): British author; Holmes claims not to know of him STUD, yet he quotes Carlyle's definition of genius SIGN.

Carlton: *see* club.

carrion crow amongst eagles: Holmes suggests that Norberton may be SHOS.

Carruthers: Bob, and musical daughter; he curses: by the living Jingo, by the Lord, by George! SOLI.

"Carruthers, Colonel": Holmes and Watson locked him up WIST.

Carter: Scowrer treasurer, yellow parchment skin VALL.

Cartwright: boy, employed by express office, recruited for moor duty; evidently not a Baker Street Irregular, but he does Irregular work; *see also* **urchin** HOUN; crook, hanged RESI.

cases, criminal escapes: ABBE, BERY, BLUE, BOSC, CHAS, CROO, DEVI, ENGR, FIVE, IDEN, GOLD, GREE, HOUN, NAVA, PRIO, SCAN, SUSS, 3GAB, 3STU,

TWIS, VALL, WIST – Holmes permits culprit to escape or he or she escapes despite Holmes's efforts; some die or disappear.

cases, mistakes by Holmes in: Holmes errs in at least a half-dozen cases FIVE, LADY, LION, SECO, VALL, YELL; admits he has mismanaged HOUN; has blundered SILV; admits to a miscalculation CREE; had come to an entirely erroneous conclusion, based on insufficient data SPEC; beaten four times – three times by men and once by a woman (Adler); some cases have baffled his analytical skill FIVE; many startling successes and a few unavoidable failures SOLI; *see* **chaotic; hopeless; supposititious.**

cases, no crime involved BLAN, COPP, CREE, IDEN, LION, MISS, NOBL, SHOS, SUSS, 3STU, TWIS, VEIL.

cases, number of Holmes's: Watson says Holmes has had seventy SPEC, five hundred HOUN, many hundreds SECO, over one thousand FINA; of Holmes's fifty-two last cases, police got credit in forty-nine NAVA; handles ten to twelve simultaneously IDEN; but Watson says that Holmes would never permit cases to overlap HOUN.

cases, referrals: from official police ABBE, BLAC, BOSC, CARD, GOLD, RETI, SHOS, SILV, SIXN, STUD, VALL; from former classmates GLOR, MUSG; Watson says he has brought Holmes only two, ENGR and "Colonel Warburton's madness" (he forgets about NAVA, which involves

Watson's old schoolmate Phelps); word of mouth accounts for the rest – recommendations from all walks of life from landladies REDC to European royalty SCAN.

cases, unpublished: cases handled by Holmes that are mentioned in various stories but not described in detail; *see* "Abergavenny murder"; "Abernetty family"; "Abrahams, old, in mortal terror of his life"; "Addleton tragedy"; "Aldridge"; "*Alicia*"; "aluminium crutch"; "Amateur Mendicant Society"; "Armsworth Castle"; "Atkinson brothers of Trincomalee"; "Bishopgate jewel case"; "bogus laundry affair"; "British barrow"; "Brooks"; "Carère, Mlle"; "Camberwell poisoning case"; "Carruthers (Colonel)"; "Conk-Singleton forgery case"; "Coptic Patriarchs, two"; "Crosby the banker, terrible death of"; "Darlington Substitution Scandal"; "Dowson, Baron"; "Dundas separation case"; "Etheredge, Mrs."; "Farintosh, Mrs."; "Ferrers documents"; "Folkestone Court"; Forrester, Mrs. Cecil; "French government case"; "*Friesland*"; "Hammerford will case"; "Harden, John Vincent"; "Hobbs, Fairdale"; "Huret, the Boulevard assassin"; "Long Island cave mystery"; "Lynch, Victor"; "Manor House case"; "Margate, woman at"; "Marseilles, intricate matter from"; "Matthews"; "*Mathilda Briggs*"; "Maupertuis, Baron"; "Meridew, of abominable memory"; "Montpensier, Mme"; "Morgan, the poisoner"; "Netherland-Sumatra Company"; "Nonpareil Club"; "Paradol Chamber"; "Patersons, Grice, in the Island of Uffa"; "Persano, Isadora, well-known journalist and duellist"; "Phillimore, James"; "politician, lighthouse, trained cormorant"; "Pope, his Holiness the"; "Prendergast, Major"; "rat, giant, of Sumatra, a story for which the world is not yet prepared"; "red leech, repulsive case of"; "Ricoletti of the club foot and his abominable wife"; "St. Pancras case"; "Second Stain"; "Stevens, Bert"; "Tankerville Club"; "Tarleton murders"; "Tired Captain"; "Tosca, Cardinal"; "Trepoff murder in Odessa"; "Turkey, Sultan of"; "Upwood, Colonel"; "Vamberry, wine-merchant"; "Vatican cameos"; "Vigor, Hammersmith wonder"; "Warburton, Colonel, madness of"; "Woodhouse"; "Woodman's Lee, tragedy of."

Castalotte, Tito: partner in Castalotte and Zamba, fruit importers; great firm REDC.

cat: frightens Watson CHAS; let loose in aviary NORW; purring, Holmes calls Gruner ILLU; Holmes asks Stoner if there is one in Roylott's safe SPEC; large, black – Martha strokes LAST; Holmes makes a feline pounce VALL; Holmes has a catlike love of personal cleanliness HOUN.

*Catullus, Gaius Valerius (circa 87–54 B.C.): Roman poet; Holmes, in disguise, offers Watson a book by EMPT.

Caunter: Saltire's older schoolmate PRIO.

C. C. H.: initials on Mortimer's stick, standing for Charing Cross Hospital, though Watson interprets them as Something Something Hunt HOUN.

celts (stone axes), arrowheads, shards: Holmes discourses upon DEVI; *cf.* **flint.**

Central America: *see* **South America.**

cesspool: London, into which all the loungers and idlers of the Empire are drained STUD; world would become, if the least fit took monkey-gland serum or similar treatments to prolong their worthless lives, Holmes says CREE.

chain: none stronger than its weakest link (Watson's bright remark) VALL; Watson supplies missing links EMPT; all missing links there ABBE; missing links in a very simple chain; strange chain DANC; long chain, every link rings true (Watson, re Holmes's deductions) REDH; Holmes reconstructs a very remarkable chain of events NAVA; curried mutton, first link in Holmes's chain of reasoning SILV; chain between great brain and dead man; first link in Moriarty's is Moran VALL; British government – Woolwich Arsenal – technical papers – Brother Mycroft, the chain is complete

BRUC; Holmes: When two chains of thought intersect, you find the truth LADY; Holmes: trunks from Italy may be the missing link 3GAB; Holmes: a link; Watson, the next link? 3GAR; Holmes: Every link is now in its place and the chain is complete THOR; singular chain of events, chain of reasoning SIXN; Holmes has forged and tested every link of his chain GOLD; from a single fact the ideal reasoner deduces the entire (mysterious and inexplicable) chain FIVE; lamp and ash – successive links in a fairly obvious chain DEVI; Surely my whole

Paget's portrayal of Holmes's nemesis, Professor Moriarty

chain of reasoning cannot have been false. It is impossible! Chain of logical sequences without break or flaw STUD.

chair: Watson picks up to use as weapon CHAS; Lady Brackenstall tied to ABBE.

Chaldean: Holmes thinks **Cornish,** q.v., has Chaldean roots; surely he (or the author) must have known of Indo-European, whose roots are those of almost all European tongues, including Cornish and the others of the Celtic branch.

chalk: marks, on waistcoat pocket, from which Holmes and Mycroft deduce that a man is a billiard-marker GREE; Mount-James could chalk his billiard cue with his knuckles (he suffers from gout) MISS.

chamois leather bag, heavy: King of Bohemia carries under his cloak; it contains three hundred pounds in gold, seven hundred in notes, for Holmes's current expenses SCAN.

champagne: McGinty and his Scowrers drink (highly unlikely!) VALL.

chance: universe ruled by? (asks Holmes); unthinkable (he answers himself) CARD; see **religion;** chance meetings or sightings BRUC, CROO, VALL.

Chandos, Sir Charles: Ames's former employer VALL.

chaotic case: Holmes, re WIST.

charlatanism: Watson accuses Holmes of SIGN; *cf.* **witchcraft.**

Charles Street: side entrance to Phelps's office; *King* Charles Street runs from Whitehall alongside the Foreign Office NAVA.

Charpentier, Mrs. (or Madame); daughter Alice, son Arthur: Drebber's landlady and family STUD.

charters, early English: Holmes does research on with striking results (we never learn what they are) 3STU; *see* **Holmes Bibliography.**

chauffeur: thick-set; Watson's disguise LAST.

*Chaucer, Geoffrey (1340?–1400): English poet; *see* ***Spenser, Edmund.**

Check, (cheque): Holmes pats his fee affectionately PRIO; -book, Watson's, *see* **racing.**

cheek(s): (Holmes's) hectic flush upon either, hectic spots, rouge over the cheek-bones DYIN, slight flush sprang into his thin CROO, feverish flush; tinged with colour GOLD, touch of colour upon his sallow BERY, little fleck of feverish colour upon either SIGN; flushed with the exhilaration of the master workman who sees his work lie ready before him PRIO; warmer hue VALL; flushed: Peterson's BLUE, Trevelyan's RESI; tinge touch of colour on Gibson's sallow, touch of colour on Dunbar's wan THOR; bloodhound (Blessington) RESI; pressed to breast (Lucy and Hope) STUD; haggard (Johnson's); stained (Walters') BRUC; ivory (De Merville's)

ILLU; dreadful livid (McPherson's) LION.

cheetah: one of Roylott's pets; *see* **baboon** SPEC.

chemistry: Holmes's researches include acetones COPP; coal-tar derivatives in France EMPT; organic, unspecified GLOR; he knows about carbolic acid and rectified spirits as preservatives CARD; dissolves a hydrocarbon SIGN; uses hydrochloric acid for experiment, identifies bisulphate of baryta IDEN; weird, malodorous scientific procedure, experiments DANC, DYIN, SIGN; uses Bunsen burner, retort, two-litre measure, test-tube, pipette, and litmus-paper NAVA; props test-tube in rack and begins to lecture DANC; knows that Roylott used a poison (snake venom) undetectable by any chemical test SPEC; his fees have made him financially independent, and he can concentrate his attention upon his chemical researches – after Moriarty is disposed of FINA; Sholto's chamber is outfitted as a chemistry laboratory, like Holmes's SIGN; *see* **acid; baryta; nitrite; test.**

Chequers: inns where Holmes and Watson stay in Camford CREE and Sussex SUSS.

chess: literal, metaphorical BLAN, FIVE, HOUN, ILLU, MAZA, PRIO, RETI, SIGN; Holmes says that excellence in playing is a mark of a scheming mind RETI; *see* **games.**

chevy: Watson chevied (taunted) Phelps and hit him over the shins with a wicket when they were in school together NAVA.

chianti: Sholto offers SIGN.

Chicago: Holmes has knowledge of crooks of DANC; he travels there in preparation for his role as an Irish-American spy LAST.

chicken: curried, and ham and eggs NAVA; plucked, Blessington's neck stretched like RESI; for more fowl figures of speech, *see* **Carfax, Lestrade, Susan.**

child: in the chimney, wind sobbed and cried like a FIVE; scream of tortured COPP; could not be drowned in moat (it is so shallow) VALL; Watson at first thinks baboon is a hideous and distorted child SPEC; Mason has the firm, austere expression which is only seen upon those who have to control horses or boys SHOS; Conan Doyle does not usually portray children sympathetically: the noble Lucy Ferrier (STUD) is the exception; monsters like Edward (COPP) and Jack (SUSS), or brats like Jack (SIGN), are the rule; **Wiggins** and the other Irregular lads are portrayed in a kindly way but Holmes treats them sternly and condescendingly; *see* **dogs; kid.**

chimpanzee: Wood crawls with a stick like a CROO.

chin: Holmes's, on breast REIG, on chest SILV; smooth, linen perfect, though he has been camping on the moor HOUN; leans it on his hands to study mud SILV; scratches it in some perplexity SPEC; jaw on fists TWIS; Smith's, heavy double DYIN; Rucastle's great, heavy; rolls down in fold after fold upon his throat COPP; Anna's, long, obstinate, GOLD; chins on hands, Holmes, Watson, and Morstan SIGN.

Chinese crockery: in Gruner's study; actually Ming porcelain ILLU; *see* **box.**

chivalrous: Watson's term for a burglary CHAS; Scowrers' term for murder VALL.

chloroform LADY, LAST, MAZA, 3GAB.

*Chopin, Frédérick François (1810–1849): Polish pianist and composer; Holmes sings melody, Tra-la-la-lira-lira-lay; opus not identified STUD.

chokey: Small's slang for prison SIGN.

Chowdar, Lal: one of Sholto's servants SIGN; *see* **Rao.**

*Christ, Jesus (4–8? B.C.–?A.D. 29): by the Cross of, McMurdo swears VALL.

*Christie's: auctioneers and art dealers; actual firm ILLU, 3GAR.

*Chubb: lock SCAN; key GOLD; *see* **key.**

chuckle: Clayton the cabman chuckles at Holmes HOUN; Holmes chuckles – *see* **laughter.**

Church Row, Hampstead: Holmes and Watson take a hansom as far as, on way to burgle Milverton's house CHAS.

Church Street, Kensington: Holmes, in disguise, says his bookshop is there; location of a real bookshop EMPT.

Church Street, Stepney: site of works where busts of Napoleon were made SIXN.

cigarette(s): by Ionides of Alexandria; Holmes chain-smokes, upsets box, to divert attention GOLD (*cf.* upset oranges REIG, watering-pot DEVI, hat BLAN); Holmes has caseful of BOSC; cloud from Holmes's SCAN; Holmes soothes himself with; carries silver case (used as a paperweight) FINA; Holmes smokes one, sedates McFarlane with another NORW; Holmes pushes one towards Musgrave MUSG; Holmes lights one, lays it down; Mortimer rolls his own HOUN; Garcia smokes endless WIST; Watson and Sir Henry smoke, while waiting to trap Barrymore; Watson throws one away outside Holmes's moor hut HOUN; end, short, smoked by clean-shaven man (Holmes deduces) REDC; -ends, Holmes's carpet littered with NORW; *see* **Bradley.**

cigars: Holmes keeps his in coal-scuttle MAZA, MUSG; varieties include lunkah SIGN, Trichinopoly SIGN, STUD, bird's-eye SIGN, Indian BOSC, SPEC; ash from cigar showed how long Sir Charles Baskerville stood at gate; cigar drops from Stapleton's hand, later he smokes (the same?) one with Sir Henry HOUN; Old Trevor (Armitage) invites Holmes into the billiard-room for a quiet GLOR; Havana, imported from Dutch East India RESI; pungent reek CHAS; Holmes smokes one EMPT, offers one to

Lestrade NOBL and to Small SIGN; gives one to Gregson STUD; offers one to Von Bork (it is declined) LAST; gives Croker one to bite on CARD; Lestrade puffs thoughtfully at one SIXN; one for Holmes, one for Hopkins GOLD; Watson smokes one on the train SILV; Jones smokes one SIGN; restaurant proprietor's is less poisonous than one would expect (Holmes opines) BRUC; half-smoked, sodden (Holmes's) LAST; Holmes settles Croker's nerves with one ABBE (*cf.* **cigarettes; coffee**); Holmes and Watson discuss case over a couple CARD; cheroots SIGN; two glowing ends of Von Bork's and Von Herling's might have been the smouldering eyes of some malignant fiend LAST; Milverton's projects at an insolent angle CHAS; Havana, Dutch: victim and murderers smoke RESI; McGinty's is eternal, half-chewed, half-smoked; he bites it VALL; for ash, see **number; Holmes Bibliography**.

cipher: Porlock tells Holmes to burn it VALL; *see* **codes.**

circle: of glass, Holmes removes to commit burglary CHAS; Red, Italian secret society REDC.

circumstantial evidence: tricky, says Holmes BOSC; occasionally very convincing, says Holmes NOBL; *see* ***Thoreau, Henry David.**

Civil War, American: Watson is distressed when he recalls it – a useless waste of life CARD, RESI; *see* ***Beecher, Henry Ward.**

clang: door of Baskerville Hall clangs HOUN.

*Clarendon, Lord (Edward Hyde, Earl of [1608–1674]): English chancellor whose history of the English Civil War was recommended in the Baskerville manuscript HOUN.

claret: French wine; Windibank worked for a firm that imported IDEN; Holmes and Watson share a bottle, and the afternoon softens into a mellow glow CARD; and biscuits DYIN; *see* **milk.**

Claridge's: hotel THOR; Holmes will meet Martha there LAST.

classical references: *see* **Athene; *Catullus, Gaius Valerius; *Euclid; Hercules; Hippocratic smile; *Horace; Jupiter, descending; Parthian shot; *Petrarch; *Plato; Scylla and Charybdis; *Thucydides;** *also see* **best and wisest; foreign languages.**

claws: Lestrade and Gregson have them into one another STUD; Sahara King has real ones VEIL; crab, *see* Stoke Moran, s.v. **architecture.**

Clay, John: young man, but not a youth; a supercilious criminal REDH; *see* **Eton; royal duke; Spaulding, Vincent;** for the significance of clay on toe-caps, *see* **earth.**

Clayton, John: Stapleton's cabman HOUN.

clergyman: Holmes's disguise SCAN (*also see* **priest**); phony COPP, LADY; Wilson poses as chaplain GLOR.

Cleveland, Ohio: Holmes has knowledge of STUD.

clever: I thought you had done something clever; Harrison (Joseph) NAVA and Wilson REDH utter this same annoying remark after Holmes has explained a deduction; *cf.* Cunningham's sneer at Holmes: I thought you Londoners were never at fault. You don't seem to be so very quick, after all REIG; and Garrideb's I've read of your tricks, Mr. Holmes 3GAR.

clinkers: Dunn, mine manager, dies kicking and clawing among a heap of VALL.

clock: three chimes from, tell Phelps it is a quarter to ten; later Holmes hears the church-clock in Woking strike the quarters NAVA; church chimes strike half-past two BLAC; great church clock strikes eleven, seeming to sound the dirge of Holmes's, Watson's, Lestrade's, and Mycroft's hopes BRUC; Watson hears a far-away clock chime the quarter hours HOUN.

clogs of curious peasants: interfere with Holmes's observations HOUN; *see* **peasants.**

close, rainy day RESI.

cloud: Holmes effuses in the early morning, See how that one little cloud floats like a pink feather from some giant flamingo SIGN; *cf.* **ostrich;** for other clouds, *see* **cigarettes; newspapers.**

club: weapon (q.v.): Wood's cane, hard carved wood with bone handle, mistakenly identified as murder weapon CROO; Leonardo's, set with five claw-like nails VEIL; men's: Anglo-Indian (Moran's) EMPT, Diogenes (Mycroft's) BRUC, GREE, Carlton (Damery's) ILLU, Bagatelle (Adair's, Moran's) EMPT; Watson belongs to one (unnamed), and Holmes knows that he has spent the day there because of the immaculate condition of his hat and boots HOUN; *see* **"Nonpareil Club"; "Tankerville Club."**

clump of a house, square and prosaic: Pondicherry Lodge SIGN.

coach: = private tutor; Army: Moriarty FINA; Murdoch, Stackhurst LION.

coachman: hard-faced, gnarled HOUN.

coat: Holmes orders Watson to help him on with his DYIN; coats-of-arms: on Gruner's book ILLU; on envelope that Milverton holds CHAS.

Cobb, John: McCarthys' groom BOSC.

cobra: poisonous as, Gruner ILLU; Teddy catches CROO.

cocaine SCAN, SIGN, TWIS, YELL; syringe MISS; habits . . . perhaps less excusable (Watson says) CREE; seven-per-cent solution SIGN; *see* **morocco; morphine; opium; vices.**

cock: white, for voodoo WIST; pheasant 3GAR.

cock-a-doodle: Lestrade's little victory cry NORW.

Cockney: Holmes admires this class; Pycroft is one STOC.

Cocksure, Mr.: Breckinridge calls Holmes BLUE.

cocoa Holmes tells Watson that there is some waiting in the next room; Watson probably drinks it before he and Holmes go out to examine bicycle- and cow-tracks PRIO.

cocoanut matting in hallways: confusing, but no footprints GOLD.

codes: secret DANC, GLOR, LAST, REDC, VALL, WIST. In DANC there are presumably twenty-six figures, but the tale is called "Dancing Man" in the running title throughout in Baring-Gould's edition; in his first analysis, Holmes has a five-letter word, the second and fourth letters of which are, he hypothesizes, *e*; he concludes that the word might be *sever, lever,* or *never,* but it is just as likely to have been *seven, refer,* or dozens of others. *"Never,"* however, turns out to be right, giving him *n, v,* and *r.* Holmes's lucky solution of the code fails to save Cubitt's life; Holmes uses somebody else's code to summon that person DANC, REDC.

coffee FIVE, HOUN, SIGN, SIXN; and curaçao BRUC; *café noir* MUSG; clears Phelps's NAVA and Burnet's WIST brains; made over spirit-lamp NAVA; *see* **twine.**

coffins: Holmes opens one (a duplex) with several screwdrivers LADY, uses his pocket-jemmy on the other SHOS; *see* **box;** *"Gloria Scott."*

coin: Syracusan, Garrideb polishes 3GAR.

coiner: Holmes identifies by copper and zinc filings in cuff SHOS; *see* **counterfeiting machine.**

cold acknowledgment: Holmes's, of information that Watson has but he does not SUSS.

cold beef and a glass of beer: Holmes rings the bell for SCAN.

cold, frosty CHAS; cold sunshine ABBE; cold, damp reek VALL.

Coldstream Guards: Tangey's former regiment NAVA.

collar: Charpentier seizes Drebber by STUD; Hopkins seizes Neligan by BLAC; Holmes seizes Walter by, and throws him back into the room; Walter staggers and falls senseless to the floor BRUC; Watson awakens from his faint to find his collar-ends undone and the tingling aftertaste of brandy upon his lips EMPT.

collections, singular: paper, key, peg, string, metal discs MUSG; Pope's *Homer*, candlesticks, letterweight, barometer, twine REIG; apple, string, shilling map of London, photo SIXN; pipes, novels, pinfire revolver, guitar WIST.

colonels (various armies): *see* **Barclay, Colonel** and wife **Nancy (Devoy); Carruthers** (Colonel); **Dorking, Colonel; Emsworth** (Colonel); **Hayter, Colonel; Moran, Colonel Sebastian; Munro** (Colonel Spence); **Openshaw** (Colonel Elias); **Ross** (Colonel); **Stark** (Colonel Lysander); **Upwood, Colonel;**

Walter (Colonel Valentine); "**Warburton, Colonel, madness of**"; Wardlaw, Colonel.

Colonna, Prince of: Holmes traces pearl from prince's bedroom to the bust of Napoleon SIXN.

colors: red and black, Ross's racing SILV; green and white, San Pedro's WIST; blue and white, Priory School's PRIO; red streaks, violet sky; black smudge on silvered slope; green-splotched bog, russet slopes of moor HOUN; duns, drabs, and slate-grays of London SOLI; house is pitch-black against a slate-coloured sky WIST; black walls and broken water (chasm) FINA; for a peculiar use of *black, see* **Cushing** (Sarah) CARD; shades of red hair – straw, lemon, orange, brick, Irish-setter, liver, clay, flame REDH; titles of stories include black, blue, orange, red, scarlet, silver, and **yellow**, q.v. – perhaps Conan Doyle's favorite.

combinations: Holmes's word for his plans, methods, deductions (not his undergarments) STUD.

Come at once if convenient – if inconvenient come all the same. – S. H.: telegram to Watson CREE.

comet vintage: wine from a comet-year, thought to have superior flavor; Holmes savours the case like a STOC.

commissionaire: uniformed retired soldiers who act as messengers, guides, etc. BLUE, MAZA, NAVA, STUD; the one in STUD is a middle-aged, retired marine sergeant whom Watson addresses as My lad; *see* **Peterson; Tangey, Mr.; watchman.**

common, heathy: Melas dumped there GREE; Misprinted *healthy common* in Doubleday, first edition.

commonplace: little murder, says Holmes NAVA; *see* **absurdly simple.**

comparative anatomy: of Bushman and Hottentot: Mortimer spent many a charming evening discussing with Sir Charles HOUN; Morphy has chair of CREE; *see* ***Cuvier, Baron Georges Léopold Chrétien Frédéric Dagobert.**

compass: pocket, Holmes carries MUSG.

composer: of music, Holmes REDH.

condyle, upper, of human femur: Watson's possibly mistaken notion of anatomy; condyle = protuberance at end of a bone, and the femur does not have one on its upper end SHOS; *see* **bone.**

conjurer: Holmes is STUD; has air of NORW; *see* **charlatan; devil; magician; witchcraft.**

"Conk-Singleton forgery case": Holmes helped Lestrade with a forgery case STUD, possibly this one; he tells Watson to put away the pearl in his safe and to bring out the Conk-Singleton papers at the end of SIXN.

Conquerer: ship; Holmes suggests the name to elicit the true name of Browner's vessel CARD.

conscience, Holmes's: Roylott's death will not weigh heavily upon (perhaps echoing Hamlet's lack of concern for the deaths of Rosencrantz and Guildenstern) SPEC.

conseedar: (= *consider*) example of MacDonald's Aberdonian accent VALL; *see* **dialect.**

consistency: Holmes says, We must look for consistency. When there is a want of it we must suspect deception THOR.

constable: together with a sergeant, he good-humoredly throws Holmes and Watson out of the house LADY; *also see* **Cook.**

contempt: Holmes snorts his, for petty theft BRUC; *see* **snarl; sneer.**

continents: *see* **fair sex.**

contingencies: *see* **improbable.**

Continental Gazetteer: Holmes consults for Bohemian geography SCAN; *see* **gazetteer.**

Cooee!: Australian cry BOSC.

Cook: police constable, finds Openshaw's body FIVE; Cook's Tourist Office; actual company; Watson consults manager of Lausanne branch LADY.

cooks: mulatto; great goggle eyes; hideous; yellowish features of a pronounced negroid type; sleeps on a litter of straw in the kitchen (other servants sleep in the outhouse) WIST; new cook at 221B Baker Street ruins Holmes's eggs THOR; *see* **Turner.**

coolies: *see* **squealing, Sumatra.**

*Copernicus, Nikolaus (1473–1543): Polish astronomer; Holmes ignorant of his heliocentric theory STUD.

copper: McMurdo uses this term of opprobrium for police VALL.

"Copper Beeches" CREE.

"Coptic Patriarchs, two": the case engages Holmes's attention, so he must send Watson to investigate Amberley RETI; Coptic monasteries: Coram's research GOLD.

Coram, Professor: eyes glow like embers; Anna says she will not tell his name but shortly thereafter she calls him Sergius GOLD.

cord: Cairns's ankles lashed with BLAC; *see* **towel.**

Cormac, Tiger: vicious Scowrer VALL.

Cornelius, Mr.: Oldacre's pseudonym NORW.

Cornish: referring to Cornwall; language, related to Phoenician, Chaldean, Holmes wrongly conjectures; horror, Holmes's term for the tale; air makes flowers grow DEVI.

Cornwall: southwesternmost county in England; half the families ruined by failure of **Dawson and Neligan**, q.v.; setting for DEVI.

*Corot, Jean Baptiste Camille (1796–1875): French painter; one of his works in Sholto's collection SIGN.

correspondence: Holmes's, transfixed to mantel by jackknife MUSG.

coruscation: Holmes sarcastically asks Watson for one more – yet another brain-wave VALL; *see* **intellect.**

Cosmopolitan, Hotel: carbuncle lost there BLUE.

cotton wadding and carbolized bandages: Watson's treatment for severed thumb ENGR.

counterfeiting machine ENGR, 3GAR, VALL; the one in ENGR turns out half-crowns by the thousand; *see* **coiner.**

country: girl, incredible stupidity of the class (Coram, re Tarlton) GOLD; great service to his, Mycroft twice tells Holmes that a solution to the case will be BRUC.

course of true love (Sir Henry's and Beryl's) does not run smoothly: Watson, paraphrasing Shakespeare, *A Midsummer Night's Dream* HOUN.

courteous acquiescence: Holmes thanks Sterndale for, sarcastically DEVI.

*Cousin, Victor (1792–1867): French philosopher; *see* **art.**

cove: slang for "chap, fellow"; Merton twice calls Holmes a MAZA.

Covent Garden Theatre: Holmes and Watson hear Wagner performed there REDC.

Coventry: Sergeant (police), doubts Holmes's sanity THOR; city, Openshaw had factory in FIVE, Morton worked in SOLI.

cows, red: observed on journey to Devonshire HOUN; *see* **horseshoes.**

Cox & Co.: bank; Watson's dispatch-box, filled with records of Holmes's cases, kept there THOR; tin box CREE; Holmes has another tin box containing case records MUSG; dispatch-cases filled with documents; attempts have been made to get at and to destroy these papers VEIL.

Coxon and Woodhouse's: stockbrokers; old Coxon gives Pycroft a ripping good testimonial when he is dismissed from the firm STOC.

C. P. R.: Hopkins thinks they may be the initials of a stockbroker's client; Holmes says, Try Canadian Pacific Railway BLAC.

cravat: Holmes, in disguise, wears one BERY; Simpson, in country dress, wears one; it is red and black, by coincidence Colonel Ross's **colors,** q.v. SILV; Walter wears, over his mouth BRUC; Gregson, on surveillance, is muffled in a cravat and greatcoat REDC; *cf.* **muffler; ulster.**

Craven Street: location of the Mexborough Private Hotel HOUN.

crazy: *see* **lunatic; strait-jacket.**

credit, for solving cases: *see* **number.**

Crédit Lyonnais: French bank; Sylvius forged check on MAZA; Holmes thought Moriarty kept most of his fortune in VALL; Devine cashed check at Montpellier branch of LADY.

Cremona: Italian city, source of great violins STUD; *see* **Amati; Stradivarius.**

creosote: *see* **barrels.**

crib, to crack a: thieves' cant for breaking and entering or safe-cracking; Holmes uses REIG.

cries: *see* **child; cock-a-doodle; cooee; noise; scream.**

criminal: Holmes's remarks about: no crimes and no criminals these days STUD; man, or at least criminal man, has lost all enterprise and originality COPP; London criminal a dull fellow BRUC; London uninteresting since Moriarty's death NORW; I would have made a highly efficient criminal CHAS; criminal strain in Moriarty's blood FINA; in criminal investigation, first rule is to look for a possible alternative BLAC.

cripes!: Winter swears by ILLU.

cripple: Jack(y) Ferguson SUSS; partial, Wood CROO; fake, Boone TWIS.

Criterion Bar: Watson and Stamford meet at STUD.

croaker: McGinty calls Morris; = cowardly complainer VALL.

Crocker, Captain Jack: *see* **Croker, Captain Jack.**

Crockford: clerical directory RETI.

crocodile: nips off Small's leg in the Ganges SIGN.

crocus-bed: blooming beneath Adair's window (on March 30!) EMPT; flower-bed, trampled beneath window DANC.

Croker, Captain Jack: (*Crocker* in Doubleday edition) tall, golden-moustached, blue-eyed, tanned, springy step; re Brackenstall he says, Curse the beast! and calls him a drunken hound ABBE; *see* **lions; squirrel.**

"Crosby the banker, terrible death of": Holmes has solved the case GOLD.

cross: on the, Slaney's American slang for dishonest DANC; Abdullah Khan makes Small swear on the cross of the Christians SIGN.

cross-dresser: Adler, who dons her "walking clothes" to pose as a male youth SCAN.

Crowder, William: gamekeeper BOSC.

Crown Derby tea set: Maberley has nothing rarer than 3GAB.

Croydon: London suburb, scene of part of CARD.

crush: if Croker plays tricks, Holmes threatens to crush him ABBE; *see* **break.**

Cubitt: Hilton: tall, ruddy, clean-shaven; florid cheeks; great, earnest blue eyes; wife Elsie, née Patrick: as a widow, devotes herself to care of the poor and administration of her husband's estate DANC.

cuff, shirt: Mortimer scribbles on HOUN; Holmes makes note of time on, of enormous importance NAVA.

Cummings, Mr. Joyce: rising barrister THOR.

*Cunard, Samuel (1787–1865): founder of steamship line; *see* **Ruritania.**

cunning, innate: Watson's – Holmes speaks ironically, and cruelly VALL; *see* **intellect; scintillating; think.**

Cunningham: the J. P. and son Alec try to throttle Holmes REIG.

curled down: Holmes, with his pipe 3GAB; coiled, curled (or huddled) *up* elsewhere – e. g. CREE, DEVI, IDEN, REDH; *see* **relapse.**

curried: mutton SILV; chicken NORW.

curse, imprecation: *see* **bitter curse; brute!, the; Carey, Peter; Carruthers** (Bob); **cripes!; Croker, Captain Jack; damned; Gar!, by; George, by; Gibson** (wife); **God; Jingo!; Jove; Lord Harry!; Presbury** (Professor); **Ronder; Ross** (Colonel); **Selden; Small, Jonathan; Stackhurst, Harold; touts; Tut!; Von Bork; Williamson, Rev.** (?); **Woodley** (Jack).

curtains: Holmes and Watson hide behind CHAS.

Cusack, Catherine: Countess of Morcar's maid BLUE.

Cushing: Susan, a maiden lady of fifty; large, gentle eyes; works at an antimacassar; Sarah, brazen flirt; fine, tall woman – black and quick and fierce (says Browner); Mary, Browner's perfidious wife CARD.

cutlets: Coram eats large dish for lunch, shared secretly with Anna GOLD.

*Cuvier, Baron Georges Léopold Chrétien Frédéric Dagobert (1769–1832): comparative anatomist FIVE.

Cyanea capillata: lion's mane; more fully, an acraspedote tetramerous medusan, or jellyfish LION.

Cyclopides: butterfly variety, Stapleton pursues HOUN.

dagger: most formidable hornhandled, two-edged REDC; curved Indian SECO.

daintiest thing under a bonnet on this planet: Holmes's description of Adler SCAN.

d'Albert, Countess: one of Milverton's blackmail victims CHAS.

Damery, Sir James: gray Irish eyes; big, masterful aristocrat ILLU.

damned: old woman be, Holmes curses STUD.

Dane: rascally lascar's assistant at Bar of Gold TWIS.

Dangling Prussian: inn; Holmes threatens Von Bork that one of the village inns will be renamed this; covert threat that the German will be hanged LAST.

*Danton, Georges Jacques (1759–1794): French revolutionist VALL.

darbies, derbies: *see* **handcuffs.**

Darbyshire: *see* **Straker.**

dark lantern: lantern with hinged metal shields to occlude the light REDH, SIXN, SPEC; *see* **bull's-eye.**

"Darlington Substitution Scandal": Holmes used the "Fire!" ruse SCAN; *see* **Armsworth.**

Dartmoor: site of Baskerville Hall; desolate, lifeless; odour of decay and heavy miasmatic vapour; mire swallows Holmes waist-deep; *see* **pony** HOUN; site of King's Pyland SILV.

*Darwin, Charles Robert (1809–1822): English naturalist; theory of natural selection mentioned in a newspaper article, by Holmes at a concert STUD; Holmes alludes to the survival of the least fit – those who can afford monkey-gland injections CREE.

data: capital mistake to theorise before one has (Holmes) SCAN; data! data! data! I cannot make bricks without clay (Holmes) COPP; similar statements in ABBE, CARD, CREE, DEVI, SECO, SPEC, SUSS, VALL, WIST; *see* **facts; trifles;** *also see* **improbable.**

dates: it is frequently impossible to square dates in the stories with real time or with internal allusions; the author is often vague about days, months, and even years (e.g., it was in a year, and even in a decade, that shall be nameless SECO); Wisteria Lodge case is explicitly dated 1892 WIST, but in that year Holmes was thought to be dead at bottom of **Reichenbach Falls,** q.v.; the tales begin in each of the twelve months; April is most common: no date specified SPEC; fourteenth REIG, twenty-third SOLI, twenty-fourth FINA, twenty-seventh REDH. Conan Doyle also likes the third: of May FINA; of

last month EMPT; of December SIGN; *see* **Great Hiatus.**

*David, Uriah, Bathsheba: biblical characters; Holmes says the story is in the first or second of Samuel (actually, II Samuel 11) CROO.

Dawson: groom SILV; bookkeeper on indigo plantation; his wife eaten by jackals SIGN; Dawson and Neligan, West Country bankers, failed for a million (Holmes knows all about) BLAC.

deaf: somewhat, Allen VALL; rather, Barrymore HOUN; as a post, MacNamara VALL; very, Kirwan (Mrs.) REIG; absolutely, Holmes (rapt in thought) SILV; snakes are, but the swamp-adder responds to Roylott's whistle SPEC.

deal (unfinished fir or pine): box TWIS; table EMPT, REDH; floorboards REDC; chairs STOC.

deaths: avoidable, or probably so, occur due to Holmes's ineptness, slowness, or sloth: Milverton CHAS; Cubitt DANC; Openshaw FIVE; Trevor (old) GLOR; Anna GOLD; Kratides GREE; Selden HOUN; Gruner (acid burns, as bad as death) ILLU; Lady Frances LADY; McPherson, Murdoch LION; Mrs. Staunton (landlady's daughter) MISS; Brunton MUSG; Heidegger PRIO; Blessington RESI; Amberley (Mrs.) and Ernest RETI; Lady Beatrice SHOS; Tonga STUD; Edwards VALL; Murillo, Lopez WIST; faked: Oldacre, Douglas NORW, VALL; Watson describes death as that dark valley in which all paths meet GREE.

death sentence: Selden escapes because of doubts of his sanity; after his death, Watson says he deserved it HOUN; Slaney condemned at Norwich assizes; commuted to penal servitude DANC; Carruthers serves a few months for attempted murder of Woodley SOLI; Oberstein gets a fifteen-year sentence (for spying), though he murdered Cadogan West BRUC.

decanter: Brackenstall throws at Theresa Wright's head ABBE; for carafe, *see* **water.**

deerstalker: never so-called; referred to as close-fitting cloth cap BOSC, cloth cap HOUN, ear-flapped travelling-cap SILV.

De Jure inter Gentes: law book; Holmes buys; its date, 1642, is too late for it to have been printed in black letter STUD.

de Merville: General, of Khyber fame; once a strong soldier, he has become a weak, doddering old man; daughter Violet, has the ethereal, other-world beauty of some fanatic; will not listen to (Holmes's) reason, perhaps because of Gruner's **posthypnotic influence,** q.v.; ivory cheeks, abstracted eyes ILLU.

demon: *see* **devil.**

Dennis: name invented by Hope, or by his accomplice STUD.

***de Capus, Hugo:** alluded to as a real personage of the time of the first crusade, but not identifiable VALL.

***De Reszke, Jean (1850–1925) and Édouard (1855–1917):** Polish opera singers HOUN.

***De Quincey, Thomas (1785–1859):** English author FIVE, STUD, TWIS.

Desmond, James: in line for Baskerville inheritance; venerable appearance and saintly life HOUN.

dessert-spoon: Watson observes that animal's footprint might be nearly as large as CROO; *cf.* **egg-spoon; fish** (for spoon-bait).

detective: plain-clothes; tall, thin man with coloured glasses (never identified) EMPT; similarly attired (or disguised – actually Barker) RETI; private, Anna hires to take moulding of key GOLD; private, a class with whom Eccles has absolutely no sympathy; Holmes dismisses this judgment with a Quite so WIST; private, Armstrong does not approve of the profession; Holmes responds, In that, Doctor, you will find yourself in agreement with every criminal in the country; eminent specialist (the detective-dog Pompey) – Holmes introduces Watson to MISS; *cf.* **epithets.**

devil himself: Trevor calls Hudson GLOR, Sylvius calls Holmes MAZA; cunning fiend: Moran calls Holmes EMPT; Holmes exhibits demoniacal force SECO; *see* **human;** Holmes tells Brown that the devil tempted him (Brown) into horse-stealing SILV; Holmes exclaims that there is some devilry going forward in Mrs. Warren's house REDC;

Holmes says, There is something devilish in this, Watson; the *Aurora* is going like the devil; Small describes Indian mutineers as devil-worshipers and as two hundred thousand black devils SIGN; McGinty calls Morris an old devil; Holmes says that Moriarty's deviltry is responsible for Douglas's death; Barker says Moriarty is This king devil VALL; Walters says mulatto cook at the window might have been the devil himself; Baynes says If it were the devil himself a constable on duty should never thank God that he could not lay his hands upon him; later Baynes says that the cook is as fierce as the devil; Warner says Henderson (Murillo) sold his soul to the devil in exchange for money, later calls him a black-eyed, scowling, yellow devil; Burnet (Signora Durando) says that to San Pedrans there is no fiend in hell like Juan Murillo WIST; Theresa and Hopkins call Brackenstall a devil ABBE; Mrs. Lucca calls Gennaro a devil REDC; Tregennis calls the death and madness of his siblings devilish; Roundhay says Satan is in his devil-ridden parish DEVI; Mortimer thinks the hound is both material and diabolical; Holmes says, In a modest way I have combated evil, but to take on the Father of Evil himself would, perhaps, be too ambitious a task; says that a devil with merely local powers like a parish vestry would be too inconceivable a thing; says that the devil's agents may be flesh and blood; calls

Stapleton's plot devilish cunning; sees a lurking devil in eyes of portrait; Sir Henry says no devil in hell will keep him from his ancestral home HOUN; Prendergast is a raging devil GLOR; devil incarnate, Turner says McCarthy was BOSC; Holmes calls Openshaw's killers cunning devils FIVE; Holmes says that jewels are the devil's pet baits BLUE; Amberley is a misshapen demon RETI.

Devine: French sculptor SIXN; Marie (maid), engaged to head waiter at hotel LADY.

dialect: broad Western (American) accent, Sir Henry's HOUN; American (Evans, alias J Garrideb), but no eccentricity of speech; however, in his final remarks, he suddenly emits a spate of American slang 3GAR; Aberdonian accent (MacDonald); English/American (Douglas) VALL; northern English (nurse) YELL; foreign (lodger, an Italian) REDC; mincing (Russian, Coram) GOLD; curious, lisping (Spanish, Anthony) HOUN; Holmes, posing as Altamont, speaks fake American, good enough to deceive Von Bork LAST; though an American gangster, Slaney says, It was he that was hurt, not she DANC; for more American accents, *see* **Baldwin, Ted; Dixie, Steve; Doran** (Hatty); for German accents, *see* **Bohemia, King of; Shafter; Stark** (Colonel Lysander).

diamond: of the first water, in a setting of brass, metaphor for

Sholto's house SIGN; for flaw, *see*
Watson, John H.; *and see* **jewels.**

dibbs: Prendergast's slang for
money GLOR.

*****Dickens, Charles John Huffam
(1812–1870):** English novelist; *see*
Pickwick.

digestion: Holmes opines, What
your digestion gains in the way of
blood supply is so much lost to
the brain (explaining why he
starves himself) MAZA.

dig(s, -gings): slang for lodgings
STOC, STUD.

dingy, liver-coloured brick: Birlstone VALL.

dinner: excellent, Ivy Douglas eats,
the day after her husband's apparent murder VALL; Adler returns home each evening at
seven for SCAN; the Trelawney
Hopes dine at half-past seven
SECO; Holmes orders from Mrs.
Hudson, to be served as soon as
possible MAZA; after failing to
save his client, Holmes notes the
time of the next train and says, I
fancy we should be back in
Baker Street for dinner DANC;
Holmes and Watson eat a light
one before they enter Oberstein's
house BRUC; Holmes and Watson have time for a mouthful before they encounter Moran
EMPT.

Diogenes Club: Mycroft's; contains
the most unsociable and un-
clubable men in town GREE; *see*
club.

dip: *see* **Bannister.**

diseases: Tapanuli fever; black
Formosan corruption; coolie dis-

ease; rickets DYIN; typhoid
STUD, VALL; shattered nervous
system and diabetes BOSC; gout
MISS; dropsy SHOS; quinsy and
swollen glands IDEN; St. Vitus's
(sic) dance STOC; lumbago,
hæmorrhage (the **malignancy,**
q.v., is evidently temperamental,
not a tumor) CREE; weak spine
SUSS; spinal curvature VALL;
brain-fever CARD, COPP, CROO,
NAVA; violent headache
(stroke?) CARD; catalepsy RESI;
nervous depression (also CROO,
REIG); dyspnœa, cardiac exhaus-
tion; yellow fever (also YELL);
epidemic (illness unnamed) at
Stapleton's school, three boys
died; Sir Henry has delirium,
high fever HOUN; mitral valve
(misprinted *value* in Doubleday,
first edition); enlarged spleen,
weak heart SIGN; ichthyosis,
pseudo-leprosy BLAN; scorbutic
(scurvy); stitches, concussion, delirium, erysipelas ILLU; spinal
meningitis (canine) SUSS; enteric
fever STUD; consumption FINA,
HOUN, MISS; measles ABBE;
heart trouble, rheumatic fever
LION; rheumatism PREF; cataract
(also EMPT); epileptic fit; aortic
aneurism STUD; senile decay
LADY; diphtheria; apoplexy (also
CROO) GLOR.

disguises: Holmes's –*see* **aged
seaman; Altamont; Basil, Captain; bookseller; Escott; groom;
Harris; loafer; non-conformist
clergyman; old; ouvrier; priest;
registration agent; Sigerson;
workman;** he and Watson pose
as **architects** and as **fishermen,**
qq.v.; Watson poses as a clerk
STOC and is disguised as a

chauffeur and as **Barton, Dr. Hill,** qq.v.; see **Hope** (Jefferson); **make-up; masks; refuges; Silver Blaze; Wilson** (sham chaplain); **Windibank, James.**

dissipation: Holmes has a general air of SOLI.

diversionary tactics, Holmes's: *see* **cigarettes; hat; oranges; watering-pot.**

Dixie, Steve: bruiser; huge negro (inspector calls him the big nigger); speaks a travesty of Black American dialect, repeatedly calling Holmes Masser 3GAB; *see also* **head;** for other blacks, *see* **cook; Hebron** (John).

Dixon: Mrs., housekeeper SOLI; Jeremy MISS.

D. M. A. O. F.: *see* **Windle, J. W.**

Dobney, Susan: old governess LADY.

doctors: (physicians; thus Huxtable, a Ph.D., is omitted; the list also ignores the British distinctions among medical men with and without doctorates; many are simply Mister): *see* **Agar, Dr. Moore; Ainstree, Dr.; Anstruther, Dr.; Armstrong, Dr. Leslie; Barnicott, Dr.; Barton, Dr. Hill; Becher, Dr.; Bennett, Trevor; Ernest, Dr. Ray; Farquhar, Mr.; Ferrier** (Dr.); **Fisher, Dr. Penrose; Horsam, Dr.; Jackson** (Dr.); **Kent, Mr.; Meek, Sir Jasper; Mortimer** (James); **Oakshott** (Sir Leslie); **Richards, Dr.; Roylott, Dr. Grimesby; Saunders** (Sir James); **Sterndale, Dr. Leon; surgeon, local; Trevelyan,**

Percy; Verner, Dr.; Watson, John H.; Willows, Dr.; Wood (Dr.); some are friends who take over Watson's practice, some are scoundrels; Holmes says, When a doctor goes wrong he is the first of criminals SPEC; doctor reports Trevor's death to his son; another, a nervous little chap, discovers pistols in mutineer's bed GLOR.

documents: returned by surprise trick NAVA, SECO; *also see* **jewels.**

Dodd, James M.: stockbroker who consults Holmes; stern blue eyes, square jaw; from his address in Throgmorton Street, Holmes deduces that he was a soldier in the Middlesex Corps BLAN.

dog-cart, tall: Holmes drives seven miles to Kent in TWIS; *see* **vehicles.**

dog-grate: Garcia overpitches note into; it is found unburned WIST.

dog-kennel: covers a well in which two bodies are concealed RETI.

dog-lash: hangs on Roylott's bed; tied into a loop to snare the serpent SPEC.

dogs: *see* **Airedale terrier; bloodhound; bulldog; Carlo; foxhound; hound; lurcher; Pompey; retriever; Roy; sheepdogs; spaniels; staghounds; terrier; Toby; wolfhound;** McPherson's, dead LION; nonbarking nocturnally SILV (*cf.* CREE, where Roy the wolfhound does bark at night); coachman sets dog on Holmes MISS; Brown threatens to do so SILV; Sherman threatens to set forty-three of them on Watson SIGN; Rucastle threatens to throw Hunter to the mastiff COPP; Milverton has a beast of a dog that roams garden CHAS; Holmes runs around like one BOSC; Brown cringes alongside Holmes like a dog after its master SILV; Hope calls Drebber a dog STUD; Holmes calls Oberstein and Jones cunning old dogs BRUC; dog set on fire ABBE; dog eaten by Hound; Cartwright would have pined away as a dog does at his master's grave HOUN; dog thrown through window; Holmes remarks on beautiful, faithful nature of dogs LION; Holmes drops Toby over a wall; Tonga resembles a Newfoundland SIGN; dogs reflect the characters of their masters COPP (*cf.* children reflecting the characters of their parents CREE); *see* **Holmes Bibliography; Holmesisms; shiver.**

dog-whip: Henderson has lashed at folks with WIST.

Dolores: maid SUSS.

"Dolsky in Odessa": Holmes cites this case and that of **"Leturier in Montpellier,"** q.v., as examples of the forcible administration of poison STUD.

Don Juan: Brunton is a bit of a MUSG.

door: Holmes and others hide behind DANC; college doors are double 3STU.

dooties: pronunciation of *duties* by railway guard ENGR; similarly, dook (for *duke*) PRIO; vagabone (for *vagabond*), wiper (for *viper*) SIGN; Proosia (for *Prussia*) BLUE.

Dorak: Presbury's correspondent; suave Bohemian dealer; Holmes identifies name as Slavonic CREE.

Doran: Aloysius; daughter Hatty, speaks American dialect – e.g., I guess; real bad; *see* **dress** NOBL.

Dorking, Colonel: one of Milverton's blackmail victims CHAS.

Dost Akbar: one of the Four SIGN.

double bed: Holmes and Watson sleep in TWIS, VALL; *see* **relations.**

double valves with automatic self-adjusting slots BRUC.

Douglas: John (Jack), peculiarly keen gray eyes, democratic manners; wife Ivy, some twenty years younger; sad appealing eyes; after her husband's apparent death, Watson catches her and Barker laughing heartily in the garden VALL; see **Edwards.** (One would like to think that after Jack's murder the Widow Douglas emigrated to America and became a character in Mark Twain's novels, but the dates are not quite right.)

Dovercourt, Earl of: engaged to Lady Eva Blackwell CHAS.

Downing: policeman WIST.

"Dowson, Baron": hanged MAZA.

drag: large carriage drawn by four horses with seats inside and on top: Holmes and Watson ride in Colonel Ross's to watch the race SILV.

dreamland: Watson finds himself in, with Morstan's face looking down SIGN.

Drebber, Enoch J.: low forehead, blunt nose, prognathous jaw STUD; *see* ***Boccaccio, Giovanni.**

dress: men's: foppish – St. Simon, high collar, black frock-coat, white waistcoat, yellow gloves, patent-leather shoes, light-coloured gaiters NOBL; king of Bohemia, double-breasted coat with heavy bands of astrakhan slashed across sleeves and front, deep blue cloak lined with flame-coloured silk, brooch with flaming beryl SCAN; Lord Bracken-stall, foppish embroidered night-shirt ABBE; Sholto, long topcoat with astrakhan collar and cuffs, rabbit-skin cap with hanging lappets SIGN; Milverton, semi-military smoking jacket, claret-coloured, black velvet collar CHAS; Smith, velvet smoking-cap DYIN. **Gentlemanly** – Holmes affects a certain quiet primness of dress MUSG, tweed-suited and respectable SCAN; doctor, gentleman in black GLOR; Drebber, heavy broadcloth frock-coat and waistcoat, light-coloured trousers, immaculate collar and cuffs, well-brushed top-hat, patent-leather boots STUD; Damery, lucent top-hat, dark frock-coat, black satin cravat, lavender spats, varnished shoes ILLU; Kent, black coat and bowler hat BLAN; Merryweather, very shiny hat and oppressively respectable frock-coat REDH; Angel, black frock-coat faced with silk, black waistcoat, gold Albert chain, gray Harris tweed trousers, brown gaiters, elastic-sided boots IDEN; Holder, sombre yet rich style, black frock-coat, shining hat, neat brown gaiters, well-

cut pearl-gray trousers BERY; Pycroft, very shiny top-hat, neat suit of sober black STOC; lodger (Lucca, Gennaro), dark clothes, very smartly dressed – quite the gentleman REDC; cabman's fare (Stapleton), dressed like a toff HOUN; Trevelyan, black frock-coat, dark trousers, touch of colour about necktie RESI; Munro, dark-gray suit, brown wide-awake hat YELL; Watson and Adler, ulsters SCAN. **Formal** – Holmes and Watson don dress-clothes, posing as theatre-goers, but are actually burglars CHAS; Moran is in dress-clothes when he fires at Holmes EMPT; Watson and Sir Henry put on dress-clothes for their first dinner at the Hall HOUN. **Professional but slovenly** – Baker, rusty black frock-coat, no shirt BLUE; Mortimer, dingy frock-coat, trousers frayed HOUN. **Mixed professional and agricultural** – Roylott, top-hat, frock-coat, gaiters, hunting-crop SPEC. **Travelling** – Holmes, long gray travelling-cloak and close-fitting cloth cap BOSC. **Country** – Sir Henry, who has not had time to buy city clothes, ruddy-tinted tweed suit; Holmes, on the moor, tweed suit, cloth cap; Stapleton, gray suit, straw hat HOUN; Hatherley, who has just returned from a job in the country, heather tweed suit and cloth cap ENGR; Neligan, Norfolk jacket, knicker-bockers, cloth cap BLAC; Simpson, gray tweed suit, cloth cap, cravat; Ross, frock-coat and gaiters SILV; Peter the groom, leather cords and gaiters SOLI;

Lestrade, light brown dustcoat and leather leggings BOSC. **Schoolboy** – Saltire, Eton jacket, dark trousers PRIO. **Clerical** – Holmes in disguise, broad black hat, baggy trousers, white tie SCAN; Mount-James, rusty black, very broad-brimmed top-hat, loose white necktie, looks like a parson or an undertaker's mute, though he is neither MISS; Lawler, old black frock-coat, soft felt hat, looks like itinerant preacher but is actually an assassin VALL; Williamson, short surplice over light tweed suit SOLI. **Uniforms** – **commissionaire**(s) and **pages**, qq.v., wear them; railway porter wears a velveteen uniform STUD; detectives wear some kind of prescribed garments – Inspector Morton is in unofficial tweeds DYIN. **Peculiar**, possibly because American – Baldwin, heavy gray suit, reefer jacket, yellow overcoat, soft cap VALL; Slaney, gray flannel suit, panama hat DANC; Sir Henry (who has lived in America), tweed suit HOUN. **Loud**, in bad taste – Dixie, loud gray-check suit, flowing salmon-coloured tie 3GAB. **Exotic** – Sholto's khitmutgar, yellow turban, white, loose-fitting clothes, yellow sash SIGN. **Lodge regalia** – McGinty, flat black velvet cap, purple stole VALL. **Low-class** – common loafer (Holmes in disguise), shiny, seedy coat, red cravat, worn boots BERY; Wilson, a tradesman, baggy gray shepherd's check trousers, dirty black frock-coat, drab waistcoat REDH; *see* **lavender; pea-jacket; spats.**

Dress: women's: Bellamy fumbles in her dress LION; Dunbar apparently keeps her dresses on the floor of her wardrobe THOR; Hunter, electric blue, which she is forced to wear; a kind of beige (beige also = a fabric) COPP; Morstan, Watson much impressed by her garb: sombre grayish beige, untrimmed and unbraided; later, white diaphanous material with red at neck and waist SIGN; Mrs. St. Clair, mousseline de soie, pink chiffon at neck and wrists TWIS; Lady Brackenstall, sequin - covered dress ABBE; Sutherland, ridiculous Duchess of Devonshire hat; fairly well-to-do in a vulgar, comfortable way; black jacket with black bead trim; brown dress, rather darker than coffee-colour; purple plush at neck and sleeves; worn grayish gloves; gold earrings IDEN; Straker's mistress, dove-coloured silk with ostrich-feather trimming, at twenty-two guineas SILV; Doran, wedding dress, watered silk, white satin shoes, wreath and veil NOBL; Whitney, dark-coloured stuff, black veil TWIS; *see* **veils.**

dressing-gown: Holmes's, blue TWIS, purple BLAC, mouse BRUC, EMPT; Lady Brackenstall's, blue and silver ABBE; Douglas's, pink VALL; Harker's, flannel SIXN; Kratides', loose GREE; Roylott's long, gray SPEC; Alec Cunningham smokes a pipe in his, which has pockets REIG; Presbury does his ape-dance in his CREE; Cubitt dead in his, thrown over his night-dress DANC; Ivy Douglas sits in hers by the bedroom fire, just after her husband's death VALL.

drowning: *see* **suicides (real, apparent); water.**

drugget: carpet SECO.

drugs: *see* **bang; belladonna; cocaine, morphine; opium; paregoric;** Watson weans Holmes from drug mania; however, the fiend is not dead but sleeping MISS; in 1897 he is still guilty of occasional indiscretions; both Holmes and Watson sniff fumes of *radix pedis diaboli* DEVI; *see* **syringe; tissue; Presbury** (Professor); *also see* **make-up.**

drumming: brisk, Pinner's heels STOC; hollow, McFarlane's fists NORW; *see* **fingers.**

drunks: Baker BLUE; Brackenstall ABBE; Browner CARD; Carey BLAC; Drebber STUD; Falder SHOS; Hudson GLOR; Openshaw (Elias) FIVE; Ronder VEIL; Sholto (Sr.), Smith (Mordecai) SIGN; Tangey (Mrs.) NAVA; Toller COPP; (old) Trevor and Hudson GLOR; Turner BOSC; Watson's brother SIGN; Woodley SOLI; Hope feigns drunkenness STUD.

Dubuque, Monsieur: (*Dubugue* in Doubleday edition) Paris policeman NAVA.

duel, sporting: metaphorical, between Holmes and Milverton CHAS.

dull, foggy: weather DYIN, HOUN, SUSS; Holmes admits he is dull indeed BRUC; *see* **fool.**

Dulong: hotel in Lyons; Holmes ill in REIG.

du Louvre: hotel in Paris; Oberstein's address in France BRUC.

dumb-bell, one: the most important clue VALL.

Dunbar, Grace: Gibson's governess, with whom he is having a one-sided affair; her dark eyes have appealing, helpless expression of the hunted creature who feels the nets around it THOR.

"Dundas separation case": false teeth hurled at wife IDEN.

Dunlop: bicycle tyre PRIO; *see* **Palmer; unbreakable.**

Dupin, C. Auguste: Poe's detective; a very inferior fellow, says Holmes STUD; *cf.* **Lecoq.**

duplicate passages: *see* **repeated.**

Durando, Signora Victor: Italian form of title; one would expect *Señora*, since she is from a Spanish-speaking, Central American country; her husband is recalled and shot by Murillo WIST.

dust: Holmes identifies with low-power microscope SHOS.

dying mumbles, half-understood: a rat BOSC; lion's mane LION; speckled band SPEC; the professor, it was she GOLD.

Dynamics of an Asteroid, The: Moriarty's treatise; scientific press incapable of criticising VALL; *see* **binomial theorem.**

dynamite (blasting powder): used as a weapon (in America) REDC, VALL.

Eagle Commercial Hotel: Baldwin stays at VALL.

ears: pierced, man's (Spaulding's) REDH; woman's, man's, severed; both pierced for earrings CARD; Prince's prick up when he hears Lady Beatrice SHOS; Holmes pricks his up DANC, SILV; Holmes claps his to the ground HOUN; swamp-adder evidently provided with SPEC; flattened and thickened (= boxer) GLOR; left, jagged or torn; bitten in saloon fight (Shlessinger's) LADY; Dunbar covers hers and rushes away from Mrs. Gibson THOR.

earth on shoes: SIGN; mud on sleeve LADY, SPEC; clay and chalk on boots FIVE; splashes on trousers STUD: clues from which Holmes deduces much.

east wind: omen of coming changes, including war LAST.

E. C. (East Central): London financial district STOC.

écarté: card game; Mortimer and Sir Henry play HOUN.

Eccles, John Scott: WIST; *see* **detective; spats.**

Eckermann: *see* **voodoo.**

eclipses: Moriarty gives MacDonald a lecture on VALL.

ecliptic, obliquity of: Holmes discourses on GREE; but he knows nothing of astronomy STUD; *see* **equation.**

editions, differences (the first reading is from Baring-Gould, the second from Doubleday): "The Reigate Squires," "The Reigate Puzzle" REIG; "The Dancing Man" (running title), "The Dancing Men"; East Rust, East Ruston DANC; Royal Mal-lows, Royal Munsters CROO; from Isonomy stock, the Somomy stock; Capleton, Mapleton; briar, brier (pipe) SILV; derbies, darbies CARD; bhang, bang; dir, dis (German) SIGN; some eye might rest upon it, someone might rest upon it RETI; flat hand, fat hand GREE; Dubuque, Dubugue; jemmy, jimmy NAVA; (smallish,) blond, dark; gurgling, guggling STOC; Swedish, German VALL; arrest had been effected, affected WIST; reapers', reapers, 3GAR; Thrice, 'Thrice LADY; Holmes deduces Watson's musings: identical passages in CARD and RESI in Doubleday, not in Baring-Gould; What was the month? / The sixth from the first: omitted in Doubleday MUSG; for a couple of typographical errors, alter corrected, in Doubleday, first edition, *see* **healthy, s.v. common,** and **mitral value, s.v. diseases;** cf. **black-letter.**

Edmunds: Berkshire Constabulary; smart lad; thin, yellow-haired; later sent to Allahabad VEIL.

education: Holmes takes the case for the sake of his, not for a fee REDC; Hatty Doran's is from Nature, not the schoolmaster NOBL; *see* **game;** *and* **Board schools; public schools; schoolmaster; universities.**

Edwards, Birdy: real name of McMurdo, Douglas VALL.

eggs: hard-boiled by mistake THOR; Holmes eats four at high tea VALL; eggspoon, Watson points with STUD; Browner crushes Fairbairn's head like an egg CARD; *see* **pumpkin, rotten; scrambled eggs.**

egotism: *see* **admiration.**

EgPGt: Holmes deciphers this watermark as Egria Papier Gesellschaft and identifies Egria as a Bohemian place-name SCAN.

elbow: Gregson firmly elbows Leverton back REDC; *cf.* **facts; knees.**

electric: *see* **blue, electric; light, electric.**

elemental forces like untamed beasts in a cage FIVE; *see* **weather.**

Elementary: Holmes says CROO; but he never utters the mythical phrase Elementary, my dear Watson!; *see* **absurdly.**

Elise: mysterious, pretty German girl who tries to warn Hatherley of danger; later (perhaps) helps Ferguson to carry Hatherly to safety ENGR.

Elman, J. C.: vicar; Holmes forges his name to a telegram RETI.

Elrige's: Norfolk farm near Cubitts' DANC.

Elizabethan foundation, Victorian portico: Tuxbury Old Hall BLAN; *see* **Jacobean.**

emerald tie-pin: given to Holmes (presumably by Queen Victoria) BRUC.

Empire, British: *see* cesspool; *also see* **Australia; Canada; India; New Zealand; South Africa;** these possessions provide opportunities for advancement, investment, refuge, or "transportation" (of convicts).

Emsworth, Colonel: smoky skin and straggling gray beard; vulture's beak nose; two fierce gray eyes; was awarded the V.C. in the Crimea; wife, Mary, a gentle little white mouse of a woman; son, Godfrey, Dodd's friend BLAN.

Encyclopædia: American, Holmes consults FIVE; Britannica, Wilson copies REDH.

engaged (to be married): Holmes, to Agatha CHAS; *see* **relations;** for other engagements, *see* **Armitage** (Percy); **Blackwell, Lady Eva; Cadogan West** (Arthur); **Devine** (Marie); **Lomond, Duke of; Morphy** (Alice); **Woodley** (Elizabeth); *see* **Lestrade, G.,** for his engagement on what seems to be an unofficial, moonlighting job.

engine, racing: *see* **mind.**

England: for England, home, and beauty — martyrs on the altar of our country, says Holmes, after confessing burglary — his slightly sardonic variation of England, home, and duty BRUC; the English are not very hard to deceive; a more docile, simple folk could not be imagined (Von Bork's mistaken assessment) LAST; for remarks about British and English matters, *see* **Board schools; boxers; country; Empire, British; games; law; prejudice; Presbury** (Edith); **thorn; Wilson** (Jabez); **window-fasteners; women; workman.**

Englischer Hof: in Baden, Watson stays at LADY; in Meiringen, Holmes and Watson stay at FINA.

entrances: into Holmes's and Watson's rooms at 221B, many dramatic and disorderly, notably those of Holder BERY, Eccles WIST, Roylott SPEC, Huxtable PRIO, Dixie 3GAB, Moriarty FINA; some of these threaten Holmes's life, but he is, of course, imperturbable.

envelope: long, thin, blue, containing compromising letter SECO; blue, containing papers necessary for the conviction of Moriarty's gang FINA; Holmes withdraws from inside coat-pocket in Turkish bath ILLU; bulky, from Lestrade, containing Browner's confession CARD; with crest and/or monogram ABBE, NOBL.

epithets, for Holmes, hurled at him by scoffers: *see* **busybody; cocksure; jack-in-office; theorist;** *cf.* **clever.**

equation, personal: as the astronomers have dubbed it (says Holmes); he uses it to assess Brunton's intelligence, almost the equal of his own MUSG.

equinoctial gales FIVE.

Ernest, Dr. Ray: chess-playing adulterer RETI.

Escott: Holmes's pseudonym; plumber CHAS.

Escurial, Hotel (Madrid): Henderson (Murillo) and secretary murdered there WIST.

Esmeralda: ship on which Small had hoped to escape to the Brazils SIGN.

ether, injected: Watson's remedy LADY.

"Etherege, Mrs.": Holmes found her husband for her IDEN.

Eton and Oxford: Moran EMPT and Clay REDH educated there.

Euclid (flourished circa 300 B.C.): Greek geometer SIGN, STUD.

European: vogue, Moriarty's treatise on the binomial theorem FINA; reputation, Presbury's CREE.

evaluation of colleagues, Holmes's: most official police, including Lestrade and Gregson, are bumbling fools; incredible imbecility FIVE; Jones is an absolute imbecile REDH; Rance . . . you will never rise in the force STUD; you (Baynes) will rise high in your profession WIST; the official police may blunder in the matter of intelligence, but never that of courage REDC; occasional want of imaginative intuition down there (the Yard), but they lead the world for thoroughness and method 3GAR; Hopkins winces at Holmes's ironical comments about his work BLAC; foolish constables permit illegal visitors (beautiful, drunk) to enter crime scenes SECO, STUD; Holmes is annoyed when he and Watson are taken for the official police DANC; *see* **facts; imagination; jack-in-office; police.**

Abe; Smith (Culverton); **Stapleton; Sterndale, Dr.** Leon; **Teddy; Tregennis** (Mortimer); **Von Bork; Walter** (Colonel Valentine); **Watson, John H.; Wilder, James; Wilson** (Jabez); **wink; Wood** (Henry [Harry]); these include projecting; extraordinarily bright, though small; blazing; brooding; masterful black; large hazel; eagle-eyed; extraordinarily bright, though small; dim, glazed; devil's light in; bulldog; great goggle; glow like embers; gray Irish; great, earnest blue; large, gentle; dark, helpless; stern blue; fierce gray; peculiarly keen gray; glaring, wild-beast, arresting; dark Italian; troubled blue; curiously penetrating light-blue; cold; vivid black; glazed sunken; sullen; vacant gray; impudent; sidelong; dead, dull, malevolent, with a slight squint; very small, twinkling; steel-gray, cold, malignant; protruding brilliant; wide-opened blue (though dead); twinkling distrustful; blue Teutonic; keen gray; sparkling dark; peculiarly light watery gray; steel-gray, deep-set; bright (with fever); deeply sunken; timid; large blue, singularly spiritual; keen; coal-black; shifty, light gray; frightened; not very friendly; weak, watery blue; blazing black; bleared; sullen, menacing gray; averted; gray, dark eager; fierce; finest red; wild; furious; unresponsive; furtive; small fat-encircled; yellow-shot, bilious; tiny; ten gray, eight blue, four dark, three black, one hazel, one red; three keen, two blazing, two

bright, two great, two small; two peculiarly, one curiously, one singularly; in DANC, Cubitt's large blue eyes turn tired; his wife is wearing away before his eyes; a look in her eyes forbids doubt; Watson tells from Holmes's eyes that he is excited; one of Holmes's then turns vacant; then both inexorable eyes gleam; in turn, Slaney has a gleam of suspicion in his eyes; in HOUN, Sir Henry's blaze and within a couple of paragraphs Stapleton's are blazing with fury .

eyebrows: Holmes's, drawn (down) EMPT, PRIO, WIST; raises (in surprise, sardonically) HOUN, SHOS, STUD; heavy, tufted BRUC; knitted COPP, SILV; bushy, twitch with irritation VALL; Watson's express incredulity CARD, RESI; MacDonald's great, sandy eyebrows are bunched in a yellow tangle; Barker's, thick, strong, black; drawn low VALL; Rance knits his STUD; Lestrade's go up once or twice as Holmes explains NORW; Morstan's rise a little when Watson presents her with the treasure-chest SIGN; Steiler's quiver FINA; Sir Henry raises his thick ones when he finds that Holmes has no luggage HOUN; Turner's, outstanding, drooping BOSC; Sylvius's, heavy, threatening MAZA; Bellinger's, shaggy, gather into a frown SECO; Henderson's, great, bunched, black WIST; Cairns's, Coram's, thick, tufted, overhung BLAC, GOLD; Armstrong's, thatched MISS.

eyelids: Holmes's, droop; heavy-lidded; half-closed COPP, ENGR, RESI, RETI, SIGN, STOC; Whitney's droop TWIS; Mrs. Barrymore's, swollen; Sir Henry's shiver HOUN; Lady Frances's and Huxtable's quiver LADY, PRIO; *see* **wink.**

face: Holmes's, aquiline, dead-white tinge EMPT; pale and exultant HOUN; austere, gaunt, granite, gray (with anger and mortification), ascetic, haggard, wasted, grim, pale, sharp, keen, alert, eager, very white and grave BRUC, CHAS, DANC, DEVI, DYIN, MISS, NAVA, REDC, SILV, THOR, VALL; sharp, wizened (in disguise) EMPT; rigid CREE, SECO; darkening PRIO; like a clear-cut classical statue HOUN; throws himself on, examining cracks in boards SPEC; lies flat on STUD; over the brink EMPT; look of annoyance on DANC; shows that he is thoroughly taken aback by new development BLAC; Watson's, honest, twitching with anxiety MAZA; dour VALL; Garrideb's, dazed 3GAR; murderess grinds heel into Milverton's upturned CHAS; Brunton's distorted, liver-coloured countenance MUSG; Roundhay's ashy DEVI; Drebber's livid STUD; Joseph Openshaw's the colour of putty FIVE; Pinner's clay-coloured, with purple lips STOC; Murdoch's turns black LION; Stoner's drawn and gray SPEC; Anna's GOLD, McFarlane's NORW, Bannister's 3STU ghastly; Bannister's also twitches 3STU; Holdhurst's, wry NAVA; Lyons's, rigid, set – that of a desperate woman HOUN; Scowrers', seven pale, rigid VALL; Hopkins's, grows longer and longer during Holmes's speech; later, very red BLAC; Hudson's, red SIXN; Gilchrist 3STU, Slaney DANC bury theirs in their hands (Slaney's are manacled), Walter BRUC sinks his in his hands; Hayes's, heavy, unshaven PRIO; Hope's handsome, distorted with a spasm of despair; Lady Hilda's, pink with indignation; in an instant all colour is dashed from it; when it turns ashen, she stares at Holmes; then, beautiful again, it is wet with tears SECO; Sir Charles's, exhibits almost incredible distortion; Sir Henry's, strong, pugnacious HOUN; Barclay's, contorted in fear and horror; Wood's, worn and swarthy but at one time remarkable for its beauty CROO; Boone's, peels off like bark from a tree TWIS; Merton's, sallow, turns a shade whiter MAZA; Mount-James's, whiter than his neck-cloth; Armstrong's, dark, crimson with fury MISS; Moran's EMPT, Coram's GOLD, grim; Mary Browner's, lights up; fades; she is frightened by her husband's CARD; confession of guilt on Cunninghams' REIG; Trevelyan is taper-faced RESI; faces at windows BLAN, WIST, YELL; other faces include ape-like, baboon, bulldog, crumbling, hairless, hatchet, monkey, prize-fighter's, rat, slab-sided, twitching, vacuous, vulture, yellow.

facts: Holmes demands them from clients or police, with the (slightly varied) formula "Pray give me . . . exactly . . . ," often uttered with marked impatience BERY, BRUC, ENGR, FIVE, GOLD, MISS, MUSG, NOBL, REIG, RESI, SCAN, SECO, SIGN, SIXN, SPEC, STOC, YELL, when, at first, a client withholds facts, Holmes refuses the case; but he then deduces the facts ILLU, SECO; Watson meekly admits to Frankland that he had spoken without knowing all the facts HOUN; Holmes discards useless facts, which elbow out the useful ones STUD; Holmes says the authorities are excellent at amassing facts, though they do not always use them to advantage; there are too many facts, Holmes must pick out those that are relevant NAVA; Each fact is suggestive in itself. Together they have a cumulative force BRUC; *see* **data; improbable; trifles.**

faddy, fads, justifying eccentric behavior: Rucastle COPP, Klein 3GAB.

faint: Watson's first and last, when Holmes, thought dead, appears EMPT; Mrs. St. Clair faints at the sight of blood, but later says, I am not hysterical nor given to fainting TWIS; Lady Hilda feigns a faint SECO; Lady Mary faints twice, or so she claims ABBE; Richards falls into chair in a sort of faint; Porter faints with horror DEVI; old Trevor faints, his face in the nutshells GLOR; Nancy Barclay turns as white as death; prevented from falling by Wood CROO; in cab with Watson, Morstan turns faint, bursts into a passion of weeping; when Watson

tells her of Tonga's dart, she nearly faints again; Small confesses that he fainted when the crocodile nipped off his leg SIGN; Horner faints in court BLUE; Harker faints in the hall SIXN; Hatherley faints in the rosebushes when his thumb is cut off ENGR; Bannister nearly faints 3STU; Mary faints at sight of coronet BERY; Hatty Doran faints in America than almost faints in England NOBL; Huxtable falls prostrate and insensible PRIO; for Walter's faint, *see* collar; cf. **fit(s).**

Fairbairn, Alec: smart and curled; cowardly skunk CARD.

fair sex: your department (Holmes says to Watson) SECO; With your natural advantages, every lady is your helper and accomplice (Holmes to Watson) RETI; Watson boasts that his experience with women extends over many nations and three continents SIGN; *see* **women;** Watson says that Holmes has helped people throughout three continents (the same three?) REDH.

fake, false, feigned, phony (not including disguises, impersonations, or aliases): address REDH; bequest 3GAR; clumsiness DEVI, GOLD, REIG; cow-tracks, limp PRIO; death, disability, or illness (catalepsy, fit, sprained ankle, etc.) DYIN, NORW, PRIO, REIG, RESI, THOR, TWIS, VALL; dialect LAST; drunkenness STUD; expedition BLAC; fire-alarm NORW, SCAN; London ways ABBE; teeth IDEN; clergymen LADY, SOLI.

Falder: Lady Beatrice, Norberton's sister, drinks like a fish, has the bad grace to die before the Derby is run; Sir William and Sir Denis are her husband's eighteenth-century forebears SHOS; for her appearance, *see* **body.**

false London ways: Brackenstall's ABBE.

famous (along with great, well-known): frequent epithet for business firms or individuals: *see* **Castalotte, Tito; Gelder & Co.; "Harden, John Vincent"; Harding Brothers; Holder & Stevenson; Mawson & Williams'; Morton** (and Kennedy); **Moser, Monsieur; P-E-N; "Persano, Isadora, well-known journalist and duellist"; Venner & Matheson; Walter** (Sir James); **Westhouse & Marbank.**

"Farintosh, Mrs.": Holmes recovered opal tiara SPEC.

farm-lad: sent for doctor DEVI.

Farquhar, Mr.: Watson buys Paddington connection from STOC.

fauna (literal, metaphorical, alive or prepared for the table; there are individual entries for those of importance): mammals – dogs (by far the most numerous), baboon, cheetah, chimpanzee, beasts, horses, cats, jackal, coyote, lion, lynx, tiger, wolf, caribou, mongoose, cows, bulls, heifers, ox, sheep, mouse, fox, rat, ferret, mole, skunk, squirrel, stoat, badger, griffin [mythical], camel, llama, pig, boar; insects – glow-worm, spiders (technically, arachnids), flies and bluebottles, bees, beetles, butterflies; fish– pike, eels, dace, jack, shark, gudgeon, trout, oysters, sponge; birds– fowls, eagle, hawk, buzzard, vulture, raven, bittern, swan, gull or curlew, chicken, partridge, (cock-) pheasant, goose, cock, (carrion) crow, jay, grouse, flamingo, ostrich, plover, woodcock, canary, stormy petrel, stool pigeon; reptiles – crocodile, gila, cobra, serpent, snake, slow-worm; crustaceans – lobster, shrimp.

feeble projections: gables 3GAB; *see* **architecture;** in Sussex, Holmes's neighbor Stackman lives in a house called The Gables LION.

fees, Holmes's: *see* **money.**

feet: Holmes, distracted, stamps his on the ground HOUN; fidgets with them EMPT; Holmes's on Watson's shoulders PRIO; Holmes sticks his on corner of mantelpiece IDEN; bare, Arthur's, in snow BERY; bare, Blessington's (hanged) RESI; fairy, McMurdo says Ettie has VALL; *see* **foot.**

Ferguson: Mr., secretary to Stark; morose Englishman (*see* **Becher, Dr.**) ENGR; Mr., secretary to Gibson THOR; Robert, big Rugby three-quarter, wife, son Jack(y), baby SUSS; Captain 3GAB; Ferguson and Ferguson, tea-brokers SUSS.

Feringhee: Indian word for European; said to be an attempt at *Frank,* but surely *Frankie* is closer SIGN.

"Ferrers documents": Holmes occupied with this case (along with "Abergavenny"); Huxtable persuades him that his case is more important PRIO.

ferret-like: Lestrade STUD, Oldacre NORW.

Ferrier: John, (adopted) daughter Lucy STUD; Dr., Phelps's neighbor, takes charge of him because he (Phelps) is practically a raving maniac NAVA.

Ffolliott, Sir George: Garcia's neighbor WIST.

F. H. M.: by coincidence, initials of both Millar and Moulton NOBL; *see* **P. C.**

field-glass: Holmes instructs Watson to bring along his excellent SILV; *see* **night-glasses.**

fiend: *see* **devil; drugs.**

Fifth Northumberland Fusiliers: Watson's regiment, after the Berkshires STUD.

Fighting Cock: forbidding and squalid inn where Saltire is kept PRIO.

fine but chilly CREE.

fine rain BLAC.

fingers: Holmes's, clotted, from ghastly pool issuing from crushed skull HOUN; long, white, nervous, pick up cocaine bottle, three times a day SIGN; quivering; cold, thin — close on Watson's wrist; tap on wall EMPT; tap rapidly on arms of chair LADY; drum on cushions THOR; tap or drum on table, on furniture BLUE, BRUC, STUD; twitch on coverlet DYIN; long thin, on lady's shoulder REDC, wave in time to music REDH; quick, nervous MISS; clasp round his

long, thin shins NAVA; long, thin forefinger shakes at Hopkins BLAC, points to hole DANC, checks off points on palm of left hand SILV, taps pipe YELL; inserting two forefingers in his mouth, Holmes gives a **whistle** (q.v.) TWIS; whistles without fingers 3GAB; Holmes deduces that writing on wall was done with man's forefinger dipped in blood STUD; from Mortimer's forefinger, Holmes deduces that he rolls his own cigarettes; Sir Charles's fingers are dug into the ground HOUN; Sawyer's, nervous, shaky STUD; ink smear on Sutherland's IDEN, on St. Simon's, which are later tapped on table NOBL; Garcia's, drum on table WIST; Ryder's, quivering BLUE; Elise holds up one shaking finger ENGR; *see* **antennæ; blood; body; feet; hand; nails; touch.**

fingertips: Holmes's, together, meditatively COPP, FINA, FIVE, IDEN, NORW, REDH, SIGN, VALL; from Smith's spatulate finger-ends, Holmes deduces that she is a musician or a typist; her spirituality causes him to decide on the former SOLI; *cf.* **sleeves.**

fire: Holmes reports that Moriarty's gang has set fire to 221B; later Watson compares the spray at Reichenbach to smoke from a burning house FINA; when Holmes awakens him at 7:15 A.M., Watson asks, What is it then — a fire? A couple of paragraphs later, Holmes says, I am glad to see that Mrs. Hudson has had the good sense to light the fire SPEC; fire alarm, false NORW, SCAN; the "Fire!" ruse: Holmes says that when a woman thinks her house is on fire, she rushes to the thing she values most SCAN; *cf.* **"Armsworth Castle"; "Darlington substitution scandal"**; for trousers on fire, *see* **buttons.**

firelock: flintlock rifle; *see* **Achmet.**

fish: Lady Beatrice drinks like a; Holmes prates of pike, eels, dace; claims he has forgotten the spoon-bait for jack SHOS; Small, like some evil fish, is dragged from mud by Holmes, Watson, and police; Jones has caught one fish (Small) SIGN.

Fisher, Dr. Penrose: Watson offers to summon DYIN.

fishermen: Watson's and Holmes's disguises; they actually catch trout SHOS.

fishing-rod: Holmes uses in trigonometric calculations (did he bring it with him to Hurlstone?) MUSG; Holmes and Watson have fishing equipment with them, including rods SHOS.

fist: great knotted, Gibson raises to threaten Holmes THOR.

fit(s): Holmes falls into feigned REIG; of laughter, both Holmes and Watson break out into SIGN; of laughter, Holmes's boded ill HOUN; hearty, of laughter, Holmes's TWIS; hilarity, sudden burst of; sudden frivolity, Holmes's BRUC; in train station, Phelps's NAVA; hot, Elias Openshaw's FIVE; queer, Presbury's CREE; of blackest depression – and of splendid energy and vigour, Holmes's SIGN; *cf.* his black melancholy DANC, melancholy

philosophical mood RETI; more depressed and shaken than I (Watson) had ever seen him FIVE; *see* **laughter; spasm.**

"five orange pips" (= FIVE) WIST.

fixed point: Holmes says Watson is the one in a changing age LAST; *see* **stormy petrel.**

flame: -coloured, Wilson's hair REDH; -like, Holmes's intuitions CREE; *see* **Winter.**

flamingo: *see* **cloud.**

flask: Holmes carries NAVA; Sholto offers to open his; Holmes offers his to Small, and Jones asks for a pull SIGN; Lestrade carries HOUN; *see* **spirits.**

flat-chested, respectable, and most unromantic: dwellings SIXN; narrow-chested houses SECO; flat-faced, pillared, porticoed BRUC; sombre, flat-faced RESI; *see* **architecture.**

flattery: *see* **admiration.**

*Flaubert, Gustave (1821–1880): French novelist REDH.

flies and bluebottles: drone like a harmonium around Carey's corpse BLAC.

flint instruments: Garrideb collects 3GAR; *cf.* **celts.**

flora (omitting vegetable products such as drugs, tobacco, wine; there are individual entries for those of importance): sickly plants; rotting vegetation; rank weeds and lush, slimy waterplants; melancholy half-grown pines; melancholy dripping garden; dripping moss; faded, fading, fleshy hart's-tongue ferns;

gorse; brambles; yellow leaves; scrub-oak; lichens; lichen-blotched (-spotted); cottongrass; pollarded elms; firs; oaks; chestnuts; trees (stunted and nipped); flowers (Cornish, Bellamy); crocus; grass; greensward (in a glade); honeysuckle; rhododendron; rose; oranges; orchid; *radix pedis diaboli;* laurels; yew; most of these allusions are gloomy and unpleasant, occasioned in part by the many descriptions of the moor in HOUN.

Florida: charming climate, Holmes remarks (has he been there?) FIVE.

flowers: *see* **crocus; rose.**

Flowers, Lord: note from, in Hope's dispatch-box SECO.

flush: on Holmes's sallow cheeks FIVE; Bennett answers with a CREE; pink, on Miss Turner's face; later, a quick blush BOSC; Wilson flushes up to the roots of his flaming head REDH, Gregson up to the roots of his flaxen hair STUD; a flush steals over Sutherland's face IDEN; Croker ABBE, Soames 3STU flush with anger; *see* **cheeks.**

flying creature: Holmes says he has never seen a crime committed by; sarcastic retort to Hopkins,

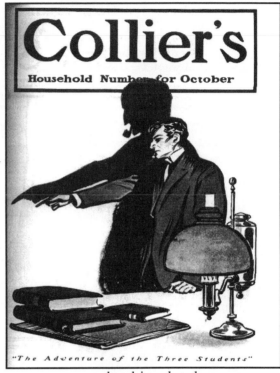

Collier's
Household Number for October

"*The Adventure of the Three Students*"

who claims that there were no footprints at crime scene BLAC.

fly-paper: this word, along with *hen-pheasant,* at first confuses Holmes as he wrestles with secret code GLOR; *see* **pig's bristles.**

fog COPP, REDC; dense yellow; later heavy brown swirl (it plays a role in the tale and is mentioned half a dozen times) BRUC; dense white, serious (important in the tale) HOUN; yellow; dense, drizzly SIGN; *see also* **dull; opalescent; thick.**

"Folkestone Court": burglary (q.v.), probably perpetrated by Stapleton HOUN.

food and drink: *see* **Beaune; beef; beer;** beeswing (s.v. **bees**); **brandy; breakfast; butter; champagne; chianti; chicken; claret; cocoa; coffee; cold beef and a glass of beer; curried** (chicken and mutton); **cutlets; dinner; eggs; flask; gasogene; gin; green peas; grouse; half-and-half; ham and eggs; hot water** (and lemon); **loaf; luncheon; meals; meat; milk; Montrachet; mutton; oranges; oysters; partridge; pâté; port; rashers and eggs; ribston pippin; roast beef sandwich; rum; sandwich; scrambled eggs** (cold); **sherry, brown; spirits; supper; tea;** tinned meats (s.v. **loaf**); **toast; Tokay; trout; whisky (and soda); wine; woodcock;** drugged food SILV, WIST.

fool: Holmes calls himself HOUN, SOLI, TWIS; *see* **ass; dull;** Browner calls himself a besotted fool CARD.

foolscap: size of writing paper, 13 x 16 inches; so named not because it was made into dunces' caps but because paper makers used a jester's cap and bells as a watermark; Wilson fills sheet of REDH; Holmes tells Watson to get foolscap and pen and begin narrative of how they saved the State BRUC; Harker's pen travels shrilly over SIXN; Browner's statement typed on CARD; Holmes rises from bed with a long document written on 3GAR; the lodger's notes are written on slips of REDC; police inspector pulls folded sheet of from his notebook 3GAB.

foot: Beryl Stapleton taps ground impatiently with; Holmes strikes door with flat of his HOUN; Holmes puts his on Cunningham's pistol REIG; Holmes jams Shlessinger's door with his LADY; St. Clair limps on one, when he is disguised as Boone TWIS; Holmes fakes a limp PRIO; club-foot, *see* **"Ricoletti of the club foot and his abominable wife";** *and see* **feet.**

footman CHAS; machine-like 3GAB; helps butler eject Millar NOBL; footmen ILLU.

footprints: Holmes cannot recognize Watson's HOUN; the ground is iron-hard – no footsteps THOR; blurred, vague – Holmes can make nothing of them NAVA; clues BERY, BOSC, CROO, DANC, DEVI, FINA, GOLD, HOUN, LION, PRIO, REDC, RESI, SIGN, SILV, STUD; Mortimer: Mr. Holmes, they were the footprints of a gigantic hound! HOUN; Holmes says he hears fairy footsteps of Merton MAZA; *see* **flying creature; tiptoe;** *also see* **Holmes Bibliography.**

foot-race: Holmes first, Watson second, Lestrade third HOUN.

Forbes: detective; small, foxy man with a sharp but by no means amiable expression; accuses Holmes of taking credit for professionals' work NAVA.

Ford: car, Altamont's LAST; *see* **vehicles.**

Fordham: lawyer FIVE; doctor GLOR.

forehead: Holmes's, with discoloured lump SOLI, wrinkled with speculation VALL; clammy (Holmes's and Watson's) DEVI; splendid; sunk on edge of box (Brunton's) MUSG; acid-splashed (Clay's) REDH; all crinkled (Rucastle's) COPP; mopped with handkerchief (Walters's) WIST.

Foreigners (there are individual entries for those of importance): Americans (North, Central, South, native), Andaman Islanders, Australians, South Africans, Austrians, Bohemians, Chinese, Danes, Frenchmen, Germans, Ghazis, Greeks, gypsies, Hungarians, Indians, Italians, Malays, Pathans, Russians, Swedes: they, especially the men, are almost always scoundrels or inscrutable; Eccles is uneasy, surrounded by foreign host, footman, cook WIST; the Irish, Scots, and Welsh (e.g., McMurdo, MacDonald, Howells) are volatile and peculiar – i.e., non-English; *see* **Stepney; Latin; women, exultant over death, dancing, singing, clapping hands, springing in air.**

foreign languages: spoken by Holmes, French: Un sot trouve toujours un plus sot qui l'admire (A fool always finds a greater fool to admire him) STUD; Il n'y a pas des sots si incommodes que ceux qui ont de l'esprit (There are no fools so annoying as those with some spirit) SIGN; L'homme c'est rien – l'oeuvre c'est tout (The man is nothing – the work is everything) REDH; Nous verrons (We shall see) BOSC; affaire de cœur (love affair); voilà tout (behold all [that is everything]) IDEN; German: Wir sind gewohnt daß die Menschen verhöhnen was sie nicht verstehen (We are used to people sneering at things they don't understand); Schade daß die Natur nur *einen* Mensch aus dir schuf, Denn zum würdigen Mann war und zum Schelmen der Stoff (It is unfortunate that Nature created only *one* person of you, where there was material for a worthy man and for a knave); SIGN; Latin: Populus me sibilat, at mihi plaudo Ipso domi ac nummos contemplar [error for *contemplor*] in arca (People hiss at me, but I congratulate myself because at home I have so many coins in my treasure-chest) STUD; risus sardonicus [*see* **Hippocratic smile**] SIGN; Omne ignotum pro magnifico (Everything unknown is considered a marvel) REDH; Vox populi vox Dei (The voice of the people is the voice of God) ABBE; locus standi (position) COPP; Italian: pericolo, vieni (danger, come), Holmes translates, but *see* **attenta** REDC; Hindi: shikari (hunter) EMPT; Sholto speaks French: Le mauvais goût méne au crime (Bad taste leads to crime) SIGN; McMurdo speaks Irish: acushla VALL; Wood speaks strange tongue, probably Hindi CROO; Baker uses Latin phrase: disjecta membra BLUE.

foreign potentate: *Kaiser Wilhelm II (1859–1941 [reigned 1888–1918])? SECO.

foresight: Holmes deduces from what is left of a hat-securer on Baker's billicock BLUE.

forgery: *see* **"Conk-Singleton forgery case."**

formulas: pairs of contrasted men – one a (royal, noble, well-born) cad, the other a (lower-class, sometimes a little tarnished) hero (e. g., Brackenstall and Croker) ABBE, CARD, CROO, GOLD, LADY, REDC, SCAN, SOLI, STUD, VALL, VEIL, WIST; *see also* **lover; revenge**; plot line: It is foggy and cold. Holmes and Watson are smoking after breakfast. They are interrupted by the sudden appearance of a troubled client whom Holmes calms with a cigarette, coffee, or brandy. He demands the facts and listens with eyes closed and fingertips joined. When the client leaves, Holmes casts off his lethargy and consults good old index for more data. He then energetically hauls Watson into a hansom, which rattles off to a train station. Arriving at the scene of the crime, they find a bumbling professional policeman in charge. Holmes investigates the minutiae of the problem, crawling about with lens and tape measure. He solves the problem in a dramatic way but lets the professional get the credit. Holmes and Watson return to Baker Street for a post-mortem of the case. Watson expresses wonderment and admiration, which Holmes dismisses with a deprecatory wave of his long, thin fingers. The case was, after all, absurdly simple, he says.

Forrester: Mrs. Cecil, Morstan is governess in household of; Holmes helped her unravel a domestic complication SIGN; Inspector, keen-faced REIG.

Fortescue: scholarship, in Greek; very valuable 3STU.

Fournaye: Henri, Lucas's alias; Madame Henri, Lucas's French wife SECO.

Fowler, Mr.: eventually marries Alice Rucastle and gets a government appointment in the island of Mauritius COPP.

fowls, solemn: in Sherman's menagerie SIGN.

foxhound: Holmes compared with BRUC, DEVI, STUD; *see also* **dogs; hound; retriever.**

fragment: torn, of message; writing of extraordinary interest REIG; in dead hand THOR; torn from diary (KKK records) FIVE; pages torn from Carey's logbook BLAC; *see* **handwriting.**

Frankland: litigious Baskerville neighbor; Frankland vs. Morland cost him two hundred pounds, but he got his verdict; Lyons is his daughter; he is burned in effigy HOUN; *see* **law.**

*Franz Josef (1830–1916): Austrian emperor, reigned 1848–1916 LAST.

Fraser: Annie, Peters's so-called wife LADY; consumptive tutor at Vandeleur's (Stapleton's) school HOUN; Mary, *see* **Brackenstall.**

freckled like a plover's egg: Hunter's face COPP; freckles start out on Lyons's face HOUN.

Freebody, Major: Joseph Openshaw visited on the day of his death FIVE.

"French government case" FINA; "French president; Legion of Honour" GOLD; these two are perhaps the same case; for France, French, *see* **chemistry; Devine; foreign; Le Brun; music; ouvrier; *Vernet, Émile Jean Horace.**

frequency of letters in English words: Holmes knows (E, T, A, O, I, N, S, H, R, D, L) DANC.

friends: except for Watson, Holmes has none; he does not encourage visitors FIVE; but *see* **Trevor.**

"*Friesland*": Dutch steamship; shocking affair, which nearly cost us (Holmes and Watson) both our lives NORW.

frivolity: *see* **fit(s).**

frock-coat: St. Simon thrusts hand into breast of, to express offended dignity NOBL; also worn by Drebber STUD, Damery ILLU, Merryweather and Wilson REDH, Angel IDEN, Holder BERY, Trevelyan RESI, Baker BLUE, Mortimer HOUN Roylott SPEC, Ross SILV, Lawler VALL; the frock-coat was a necessity for gentlemen's city wear; *see* **dress.**

frou-frou: dwindling, of skirts SECO.

fuller's earth: crooks claim to be mining it; they are actually counterfeiters ENGR.

furnace: central-heating, at Norberton's house; condyle (bone) discovered therein SHOS; *see* **Harvey.**

furniture: Holmes moves nervously about, tapping it BRUC; *see* **fingers;** *cf.* **hands** (Murdoch's). For other furniture, *see* **chair; deal** (for table and chair); **double bed; drugget; hearthrug; hiding places** (for Japanese cabinet); **key** (for locked drawer and bureau); **lamp; light** (for Lady Hilda's chair); **mantel; McMurdo** (for the chair into which he pushes his fiancée); **press; safe; side by side** (for couches); **Wilson** (for the chair into which Holmes shoves him).

gables: *see* **feeble.**

*Gaboriau, Émile (1832–1873): French novelist; creator of Lecoq STUD.

Gabriel: archangel VEIL.

gaiters: sometimes the equivalent of **spats,** q.v.; but strictly speaking, gaiters cover the calf, spats the arch of the foot, over the shoe BERY, IDEN, NOBL, SILV, SOL, SPEC; *see* **dress.**

gale: hurricane GOLD; severe, blows up-channel, heaping the seas to the base of the cliffs and leaving a lagoon at the turn of the tide (and bringing in *Cyanea capillata*) LION.

game: is afoot, Holmes wakes Watson, remarking thus— quoting Shakespeare, *Henry V* ABBE; game afoot: Holmes's brightened eyes assure Watson that it is WIST; Holmes: I play the game for the game's own sake BRUC; Holmes to Watson: you have never failed to play the game

MAZA; MacDonald re Holmes: he plays the game; Holmes: I would play the game; I do not think it a fair game; Marvin re McMurdo: shoot him if he tries any games VALL; *see* **art; education; work;** Watson says the game is hardly worth the candle, re Holmes's cocaine injections SIGN.

game-shots: Moran EMPT, Sylvius MAZA.

games, sports (there are individual entries for those of importance): backgammon and draughts, billiards, bowling, boxing, cards, chess, cricket, écarté, fishing, hunting, poker, polo, rowing, rugby, whist, yachting; *see* **boxers; racing; single-stick; view-halloa; big-game shooting; game-shots;** Staunton is a sportsman to the marrow; Holmes says amateur sport is the best and soundest thing in England; it is free from betting, but outside betting does go on among the public MISS.

Gar!, by: McGinty swears repeatedly; so does McMurdo VALL.

Garcia: Aloysius WIST; Beryl, *see* **Stapleton** HOUN.

gardener: Trevor gives Hudson job as GLOR; *see* **Mortimer; Warner.**

Garrideb: John, arresting eyes; Nathan, good old fossil, ends up in a nursing-home in Brixton; Alexander Hamilton, Kansas [!] lumber king; Howard, constructor of agricultural machinery – the last two are invented by John (i.e., Evans) 3GAR; *see* **Evans** (Kil-

ler"); **Morecroft; Winter** (James).

gas: Holmes tells Watson to light it; asks Smith to turn it up (signal) DYIN; Holmes turns it up himself, to view coffin LADY; used as deadly weapon RETI; gas-light shows that every vestige of colour has left Ryder's face BLUE; a mere point of light in Oberstein's house BRUC; *see* **lamp; light, electric.**

gasfitters' ball: Sutherland meets Angel at IDEN.

gasogene: siphon-bottle MAZA, SCAN.

gasp: loud, Neligan's BLAC.

gazetteer: first volume, just being published, Holmes consults for Andaman geography SIGN; *see Continental Gazetteer.*

Gelder & Co.: Stepney sculpture-works, a well-known house SIXN.

gems: *see* **jewels; treasure.**

genetics, faulty: Effie (white) and Hebron (light-skinned black) produce a child far darker than her father YELL.

genius: Holmes says it is an infinite capacity for taking pains (a bad definition, he adds) STUD; *see* ***Carlyle, Thomas;** a supreme manifestation of Holmes's, says Watson, is a tense, far-away expression THOR; *see* **face.**

genius loci: pervading spirit of a place; Holmes believes in VALL.

gentleman: courteous, red-faced, represents railway company BRUC; I call him a gentleman by courtesy, but he was quite a common-looking person (St. Simon, re Moulton) NOBL; when he discovers that Walter has betrayed his country, Holmes remarks, How an English gentleman could behave in such a manner is beyond my comprehension BRUC; Watson says that Cubitt is a (country) gentleman; Holmes calls him an honourable gentleman DANC; *cf.* **honour.**

George: by, Lestrade BRUC and Leverton REDC exclaim; *George II (1683–1760), king of Great Britain and Ireland, reigned 1727–1760 VALL; *George III (1738–1820), king of great Britain and Ireland, reigned 1760–1820, alluded to by Holmes NOBL.

Georgian: early 3GAR; half Tudor, half Georgian THOR.

German: war (World War I) PREF; Ocean (Baltic) DANC; language: Holmes says that, though unmusical, it is the most expressive LAST; *for references to German and Germans, see* **foreign; Gruner; Heidegger; Klein, Isador; manager; music; *Rache;* sailors; Shafter; Stark** (Colonel Lysander); **verbs; Von Herder; Von Bork; waiter;** English editions of VALL changed the Shafters from Germans to Swedes because English readers in 1914–1915 would not easily accept sympathetically portrayed Germans.

Ghazis: murderous STUD.

Gibson: Neil, the Gold King; cold eyes; wife, née Maria Pinto, shrieks curses at Dunbar THOR .

Gilchrist: tall (taller than Holmes), flaxen-haired; troubled blue eyes; plays rugby, cricket; practices the long-jump when he should have been studying Greek; father, Sir Jabez 3STU.

gin: Rance lusts for a four of gin hot (fourpence worth of gin with hot water and lemon); Drebber patronizes a gin-palace STUD.

girl: Mrs. Warren's maid REDC; of fourteen (years), does simple cooking for Wilson REDH; small servant CARD; ethereal slip of a – , Holmes's description of Morrison CROO.

glade: lovely, of greensward; setting for forced marriage and shootings SOLI.

glass: magnifying, and tape-measure: beginning with STUD, Holmes uses these basic tools in many of his cases, especially those that take him into the field. Even those problems that are solved in his Baker Street rooms sometimes require them. In IDEN, for instance, Holmes has probably used his glass to identify the peculiarities of the type-bars on Windibank's typewriter, though we do not actually see the Master at work with his lens; powerful convex lens SIGN; *see* **microscope;** Blue Carbuncle cuts glass as though it were putty BLUE.

glasses (spectacles): worn by Johnson (Sidney) BRUC, Garrideb (Nathan) 3GAR, Tregennis (Mortimer) DEVI, Kemp GREE; Mortimer HOUN and Eccles WIST wear gold-rimmed; Presbury wears horn(-rimmed) CREE; Rucastle wears a pair on his nose COPP; Angel IDEN, Barker RETI, and Sherman SIGN wear tinted; Heidegger wears, one lens knocked out PRIO; Ross wears an eye-glass (monocle) SILV; *see* **detective; pince-nez.**

gloomy: weather MISS.

"Gloria Scott": ship, rat gutted, mouldy old coffin of a Chin China coaster GLOR, MUSG, RESI, SUSS.

glove: black kid (its significance is never explained; it must have been Gennaro's, though why he should wear gloves – and leave one by his victim – is a mystery) REDC; Holmes asks Phelps if he looked for a dropped glove NAVA; Sutherland's, torn; gloves, Windibank drops his IDEN; Gilchrist leaves his on tutor's chair; he has evidently worn them to practice jumping 3STU; Watson notes that Morstan is well-gloved SIGN.

glow-worm, enormous: Holmes resembles SIGN.

glue: Holmes identifies with low-power microscope SHOS; *see* **scales**; uses gum-brush to glue clippings in index REDC.

God: -forsaken: the moor, according to Watson; he exclaims, My God, those screams! HOUN; My God! Watson whispers SPEC; Holmes exclaims, What has become of any brains that God has given me! LADY; Holmes ex-

claims, You're not hurt, Watson? For God's sake, say that you are not hurt! 3GAR; many characters use His Name – e. g. Johnson BRUC, Prendergast GLOR; *see* **religion.**

"Godno, in Little Russia, analogous incidents in, in the year '66": spelled thus in Doubleday edition; spelled correctly as Grodno in Baring-Gould edition; Grodno is in Russia, not Little Russia, as Holmes says HOUN.

gods, unclean: voodoo worshipers propitiate – Holmes, quoting Eckermann's *Voodooism and the Negroid Religions* WIST.

***Goethe, Johann Wolfgang von (1749–1832):** great German writer; two quotations from SIGN; *see* **foreign languages.**

Goldini's: restaurant, garish Italian; Holmes summons Watson to BRUC; *see* **Marcini's.**

golf: Neligan, wearing knickerbockers, arrives with the pretense of playing; true motive, to clear his father's name BLAC; Holmes discourses on golf clubs GREE.

good old index: Victor Lynch filed under *V,* as is the Voyage of the Gloria Scott SUSS; index IDEN, SCAN; great scrap-book REDC; row of formidable scrap-books EMPT; huge book of references BRUC; index books CREE; huge (commonplace) books VEIL; Holmes also consults **Encyclopædia** (American); *Bradshaw; Crockford;* **gazetteer;** *Lloyd's* **Register of Shipping;** *London* (big map of); *Out of Doors;* red-covered volume; *Whitaker's Almanac,* qq.v.

*Gordon, Gen. Charles George "Chinese" (1833–1885): British military hero, killed at Khartoum; Watson had a picture of CARD, RESI.

Gorgiano, Giuseppe: devil and monster; glaring, wild-beast eyes; at the bottom of fifty murders REDC.

Gorot, Charles: his name and Huguenot extraction put him under suspicion NAVA.

gorse: flowering, on Charlington Heath SOLI; *see* **hiding-places.**

gossip: *see* **Lucas** (Eduardo); **Pike, Langdale; pubs.**

governesses: *see* **Burnet, Miss; Dobney, Susan; Dunbar, Grace; Hunter, Violet; Morstan** (Mary); **Smith** (Violet).

governor: Victor calls his father kindly, charitable good old governor; he also calls him the dad GLOR.

Grafenstein, Count Von und Zu: Von Bork's uncle; Holmes saved him from the Nihilist **Klopman,** q.v.

grammar: *he* changes to *my* MAZA.

gramophone MAZA.

grasp: *see next entry.*

grass him: *grasp* in American edition; = knock him down; Holmes does it to Joseph Harrison twice NAVA.

gravel: red, thrown by Sterndale DEVI; *see* **pebbles.**

*Greathead, Col. William Wilberforce Harris (1826–1878): British army officer SIGN.

Great Hiatus: May 1891-April 1894, when Holmes is thought dead but is actually touring Europe and Asia and doing a little **chemistry,** q.v.

Great Orme Street: location of Mrs. Warren's house [the London Street Guide lists no such street, but Great Ormond Street is in the right location]; Howe Street intersects, says Watson [but it, too, does not exist] REDC.

greed: *see* **motives.**

green baize door 3STU, WIST; baize = fabric with nap resembling that of felt.

Green Dragon: inn; Holmes and Watson stay at; *see* **Barnes.**

Green, Hon. Philip: looks like a bearded ruffian; Vibart calls him *un sauvage – un véritable sauvage;* son of Admiral Green, the commander of the Sea of Azof fleet LADY.

green peas: landlady babbled of, Holmes says, paraphrasing Shakespeare, *Henry V* 3STU.

Gregory, Inspector: policeman; tall, fair man with lion-like hair and beard, curiously penetrating light-blue eyes SILV; *see* **imagination.**

Gregson, Tobias: policeman; fair-haired; gallant, and, within his limitations, capable GREE, REDC, STUD, WIST; muffled in a cravat and greatcoat; strikes stick on ground to summon cabman (actually Leverton) REDC; upsets his whisky and water STUD; *see* **bulldog.**

***Greuze, Jean Baptiste (1725–1805):** French artist; Moriarty owns a painting by VALL.

"Greyminster, Duke of": = Holdernesse (PRIO) BLAN.

"Grice Patersons in the Island of Uffa": 1887 case; we are told only that they had singular adventures FIVE.

griffins: heraldic, atop posts at Shoscombe Old Place SHOS; *see* **heraldic; lions.**

Griggs, Jimmy: little clown VEIL.

***Grimm, Brothers:** Jacob (1785–1863) and Wilhelm (1786–1859), German philologists, collectors of fairy tales SUSS.

grin: Clayton the cabman grins at Holmes HOUN; Holmes himself grins – *see* **laugh;** grinned and gibbered: Presbury; perhaps an echo of squeak and gibber, *Hamlet* CREE; *cf.* **gurgling, gargling.**

groan: *see* **whistle.**

grocer: village; also serves as postmaster HOUN.

groom: out-of-work, drunken (Holmes's disguise) SCAN; Perkins HOUN.

Grosvenor: Hotel, Holmes's and Watson's Swiss host, Steiler, has been a waiter there FINA; Mansions, St. Simon's residence; "Grosvenor Square furniture van" NOBL; Klein has house in Grosvenor Square 3GAB.

grotesque REDC, WIST; there is but one step from the grotesque to

the horrible (says Holmes) WIST; singular, not to say grotesque SIXN; grotesque and bizarre SOLI; the more outré and grotesque an incident is the more carefully it deserves to be examined HOUN; grotesquely curved and long nose (Holdernesse) PRIO; grotesque criminal (Beppo) SIXN.

grouse: *see* **oysters.**

Gruner, Baron Adelbert: Austrian murderer; beastman; vivid black eyes; looks thirty but is forty-two; murderer's mouth; collects Chinese porcelain ILLU; *see* **book.**

guaiacum: test for blood, superseded by the Sherlock Holmes's test STUD.

guess: No, no, I never; it is a shocking habit – destructive to the logical faculty (says Holmes) SIGN; *see* **exceptions; imagination.**

gurgling, gargling: (*guggling, gargling* in Doubleday edition) Pinner makes these sounds when he is hanging himself; his heels also drum on the woodwork, which Pycroft mistakes for knocks at the door STOC; *cf.* **grin.**

guy: = fellow, chap; Evans calls himself a soft-hearted guy – American slang 3GAR.

gypsies: wretched SPEC; shuffling and lying PRIO; wandering HOUN, SILV; gypsy horse-dealer (Murphy) HOUN; gypsy pierced Spaulding's ear REDH; spelled *gi-* in Baring-Gould edition.

habits: Holmes a man of narrow and concentrated habits, one of which is Watson; others are the violin, shag tobacco, old black pipe, index books – and others perhaps less excusable CREE; in his personal habits one of the most untidy men MUSG; but *cf.* **dress.**

*Hafiz (fourteenth century): Persian poet IDEN; *see* **Persian.**

Haines-Johnson: auctioneer and valuer 3GAB.

hair: Holder plucks at his BERY; Hope's hands tear at his SECO; Hunter cuts hers COPP; Woodley's is plastered down SOLI; Drebber's is crisp, curling STUD; snaky locks of grizzled hair curl down from under Amberley's old straw hat RETI; Blessington's thin, sandy hair bristles up RESI; Bannister turns white to the roots of his 3STU; Milverton has a shining patch of baldness CHAS; Sholto has bristle of red around bald dome SIGN; Von Bork has a broad, bald head LAST; Wilson's and Archie's are rich red REDH; Boone wears red (orange) wig (black – for some reason – on the TV series) TWIS; under his microscope, Holmes identifies hairs as threads from a tweed coat SHOS; policemen have yellow, flaxen, fair, lion-like; white occurs in disguises.

hairpin: Holmes asks Phelps if he looked for a lost NAVA.

half-and-half: ale and porter; Holmes drinks, but only when disguised as a drunken groom SCAN.

*Hallé, Charles (1819–1895): German-born British pianist STUD.

Halliday's Private Hotel: Stangerson murdered in STUD.

ham and eggs NAVA, SIGN.

hammer: not a weapon (no stains); Douglas was using it to hang pictures VALL.

"Hammerford will case": Damery negotiates with Sir George Lewis in this case ILLU.

Hampstead: northwestern metropolitan borough of London; Milverton (CHAS), Pycroft (STOC), Barker (VALL) lived there; 443 miles above sea level (*sic* in Baring-Gould's note 34) VALL.

hand(s): Holmes's, cut (knuckles burst) FINA, NAVA; Phelps kisses Holmes's; clutches Annie's to detain her NAVA; Holmes waves one towards some papers on a chair; lays one on each of Watson's knees; Mrs. Gibson's left one clutches a short note THOR; Holmes holds one of Watson's; then one of Holmes's steals into Watson's CHAS; Watson clasps Holmes's in silence WIST; Holmes holds stone in one, revolver in other MAZA; strikes knee with impatient gesture; puts hand to forehead HOUN; Milverton's murderess's hand is buried in her bosom CHAS; Neligan makes angry gesture with clenched hand BLAC; Munro passes his over his forehead twice, then makes a fierce gesture with his closed hand YELL; Watson throws his out EMPT; Holmes leans chin upon hands and stares into fire SPEC; sinks head into hands REIG; puts hands in pockets (with a negligent air) COPP, NAVA; rubs hands because the case is entirely to his heart NAVA, SIGN; leans chin upon hands to study mud; disregards Brown's trembling hand (refusing to shake it); chuckles and rubs together SILV; head on hands, in thought; brightens and rubs thin hands together REIG, VALL; jaw resting on two fists TWIS; long hands twitch and jerk DYIN; rubs his long, nervous hands together; raises one as signal for Watson to throw smoke-bomb; refuses to shake King of Bohemia's SCAN; heavy, on Watson's shoulder; rubs his thin hands together, showing avidity PRIO; shakes his clenched hands in the air FIVE; takes Smith's ungloved SOLI; pats Holder's BERY; pats St. Clair TWIS, MacDonald VALL on shoulder; claws at the floor SECO; raves in the air (presumably with his hands) FIVE; Morstan raises a gloved hand; Watson's and Morstan's instinctively seek for each other SIGN; Trevelyan lays his thin, white hand on Holmes's mantelpiece RESI; Brown's shake until his hunting-crop wags like a branch in the wind SILV; Browner's CARD, Armstrong's MISS heads sunk on; McMurdo's shaky from excesses of previous evening VALL; J Stoner has charred stump of match in her right, matchbox in her left, and simultaneously gropes for help SPEC; Sylvius's dark, hairy ones clenched in a convulsion of re-

strained emotion MAZA; Brackenstall's two clenched ones raised in air; Croker's clenched; one of Croker's sunburned ones strikes leg ABBE; Sir Henry rubs his with pleasure in anticipation of stalking Barrymore; asks Watson to feel his – they are as cold as a block of marble; Beryl makes quick little movements with hers; Watson's is inert, grasping his pistol HOUN; St. Simon's hand in **frock-coat**, q.v.; coldly grasps Hatty's NOBL; palms of Mrs. Ronder's push great, steaming, blood-stained jaws away; Holmes pats one of hers and raises his in a gesture of pity and protest VEIL; Milverton's is no niggard hand CHAS; Overton's brawny one slaps knee; he presses both of his to his head MISS; one of Wilson's is larger than the other, from which Holmes deduces manual labour; Clay's, with writhing fingers, emerges from floor; he says to Jones, I beg that you will not touch me with your filthy hands REDH; Sholto's thrown up SIGN; Damery throws up his kidgloved; Gruner claps his two to his face, paws with burning hands ILLU; Ames's wrung in hall; Barker's great, strong ones are clasped convulsively (cf. Cubitt, below); Barker beats head with clenched fist; Mrs. Douglas's head sunk in her finely moulded ones; McGinty's hairy as a gorilla's; McMurdo's clenched in agony; Scowrers' clap McMurdo on the back VALL; drumming of Brunton's frenzied ones MUSG; Johnson's twitching BRUC; Von Herling's fat ones clap LAST; leper's, like brown sponges BLAN; Mycroft's broad, flat (*fat* in Doubleday edition), like the flipper of a seal GREE; Gregson's fat STUD; mysterious lodger's (E Lucca's) two thin ones dart out for tray REDC; M Tregennis's thin ones clasp convulsively together; later his fingers are contorted; Sterndale's great ones open and shut DEVI; Cubitt's great, strong ones clasp and unclasp DANC; Bellinger's thin, blue-veined ones are clasped over ivory head of umbrella; lays one kindly on Hope's shoulder; Lady Hilda's white-gloved ones clasp and unclasp; outstretched; I would cut off my right one, she says SECO; Leverton strikes his together with vexation REDC; Presbury shakes his two in a furious passion CREE; Stark presses Hatherley's in a cold, dank grasp ENGR; Holder jerks his up and down BERY; Holdernesse claws with his, then sinks his face in them PRIO; Gilchrist buries face in his 3STU; Murdoch claws with bony ones at the furniture LION; Amberley claws into the air with bony ones RETI; Moriarty claws air EMPT; Trevor claps both his to his head, begins running round in circles; his son sinks his face into his shaking ones GLOR; Hopkins lays one of his upon Anna's arm to claim her as his prisoner GOLD; Gregson lays one of his upon E Lucca's sleeve with as little sentiment as if she were a Notting Hill hooligan REDC; Beppo snaps at one of Watson's SIXN; always look at

the hands first, Watson, says Holmes CREE (he says the same thing about **knees,** q.v.); Holmes has published a monograph upon the hands of slaters, sailors, cork-cutters, compositors, weavers, and diamond-polishers SIGN; *see* **Holmes Bibliography.**

handcuffs: Holmes recommends special design to official police; they are clapped on Hope STUD; Jones's clatter upon Clay's wrists REDH; Lestrade puts darbies on Browner CARD; Holmes deftly fastens on Cairns's wrists BLAC, on Beppo's SIXN; click on Smith DYIN; click on criminals MAZA; Martin slips on Slaney DANC.

handkerchief: Watson wears in sleeve, betraying his military past CROO; in Dodd's sleeve BLAN; large, red silk, Mycroft uses to brush away wandering grains of snuff GREE; gypsies wear spotted ones, which Stoner thinks may explain her sister's dying words SPEC; Jones mops face with red bandana; one of the Irregulars waves his as a signal to Holmes SIGN; Sterndale mops forehead with DEVI.

handwriting: Greek *e*, *p*'s, tails of *g*'s, *i*-dots; Holmes deduces writers' ages; and also that they were members of the same family REIG; Greek *e* and twirl of final *s*; then Holmes reads character from long letters SIGN; Greek *e* with flourish; the writer's (Porlock's) terror makes it almost illegible VALL; writer is female WIST; writer is a woman of character NAVA; scrawling, feminine hand LION; thick pen

VALL; St. Clair has two hands, his wife says: writes in his hurried one TWIS; illiterate handwriting (Presbury's correspondent) CREE; legal twist about it (William Whyte's); *a* printed in German fashion STUD; document written on train, Holmes deduces NORW; long and short *s*, alternated, from which Holmes dates document at a glance (he's off by twelve years); Holmes deduces that an agitated but educated man, writing with a hotel pen and ink, tried to make his writing look uneducated; Barrymore deduces that writing on envelope was a woman's HOUN; distinctly masculine printing, misspelling (*i* for *y*) tells Holmes that the writer was a man of limited education CARD; lodger prints messages to disguise (woman's) hand REDC; Holdernesse writes a peculiar stiff hand PRIO; Mycroft also shows what he can do: letter was written with a J pen on royal cream paper by a middle-aged man with a weak constitution GREE; *see* **manuscript; palimpsest; pen.**

hangings: rope RESI, braces STOC.

"Harden, John Vincent": well-known tobacco millionaire; subjected to peculiar persecution; Holmes is immersed in the case when Smith asks for his help SOLI.

Harding Brothers: great emporium SIXN.

Hardy: Sir John, plays cards with Moran EMPT; Sir Charles, letter from in Hope's despatch-box SECO; Mr., foreman who ac-

companies Sutherland and mother to gasfitters' ball IDEN.

*Hare, John (1844–1921): actor SCAN.

Hargrave: alias of Baldwin; spelled Hargrove in some editions VALL.

Harker, Horace: journalist; at Doncaster when the (horse-race) stand fell; too shaken to write about it SIXN.

harmonium: Stark sets lamp on; it is an anomaly in the house – ostensibly a fuller's earth mill but actually a counterfeiting machine ENGR; *see* **flies.**

Harold, Mrs.: probably murdered by Sylvius MAZA.

harpoon: *see* **Allardyce's, umbrella, weapons.**

Harraway: Scowrer secretary; vulture-faced VALL.

Harringby, Lord: Garcia's neighbor WIST.

Harris: under this pseudonym, Holmes claims to be an accountant STOC.

Harrison: Joseph; sister Annie, dark Italian eyes; from her handwriting, Holmes deduces that she is a woman of rare character, exceptional nature; the Harrisons are children of an ironmaster NAVA; *see* **clever.**

Harris tweed: trousers IDEN.

Harrow Weald: Maberley's address 3GAB.

Harvey: furnace-runner SHOS.

hatchet-face: Leverton REDC; *see* **aquiline.**

Hatherley, Victor ENGR.

hats: Holmes's tilted over his **nose, q.v.** CARD; he knocks his own hat off the hall table in order to bring his nose near the tar-scented gloves BLAN; *see* **billy-cock; cap; daintiest thing under a bonnet on this planet; deerstalker; dress; Scotch bonnet; velvet smoking cap; wide-awake.**

Hayes: Reuben, rude publican; squat, dark, elderly man with sullen eyes; and wife; Holmes, faking a sprained ankle, complains, But I can't walk; Hayes retorts, Well, then, hop. Spelled *Hays* in some editions PRIO.

Hayling, Jeremiah: hydraulic engineer; missing, presumably murdered ENGR.

Hayter, Colonel: Holmes's and Watson's host in the country, while Holmes recuperates REIG.

Hayward: crook RESI.

head: well-shaped, Huxtable's PRIO; woolly, Dixie's 3GAB; whirling, Phelps's NAVA; swims, Anna's GOLD; horribly mutilated, Adair's, by bullet EMPT; smashed to a pulp, Garcia's WIST; crushed, West's BRUC; Holder beats his against the wall BERY; Hope drops his on his chest SECO; Cubitt's is massive DANC; Small's sunk on his breast SIGN; Holmes's sunk on his breast on the drive to Kent TWIS; I use my head, not my heart, says Holmes; later it is girt with bloody bandages ILLU; Holmes raises his with a sudden jerk BRUC; Windibank's masquerade is more creditable to his head than to his heart, says Holmes IDEN; *cf.* **heart;** *also see* **skull;** *and see* **hand(s),** since heads are often sunk upon them.

heart: great, Holmes's 3GAR; *see* **best and wisest;** noble, Lady Hilda calls her husband's SECO; aching, one must do something to ease, says Amberley; so he paints the room where he has murdered his wife and her lover RETI; cold hand seems to close round Phelps's NAVA; broken, Sir James's, kills him BRUC; great metallic, boat's engines whiz and clank like SIGN.

hearthrug, tiger-skin ABBE; *see* **bearskin hearthrug in 221B.**

Hebron: John, black lawyer; formerly married to Effie Munro; daughter Lucy YELL.

hedge: Holmes and Watson hide behind MISS.

heeled: Slaney's slang for armed, with a pistol DANC.

He! he! You are a funny one!: Bradstreet, to Holmes TWIS.

Heidegger: German master; Holdernesse suspects that "this German" may have aided and abetted the escape of Saltire PRIO.

heifers: Mormons' term for their wives STUD.

height: Holmes's, rather over six feet STUD; his legs must be very long — observe what he can do with his **feet, q.v.;** man's, calculated from his stride BOSC,

SIGN, STUD; Holmes says it is a simple calculation enough STUD; the heights of Gilchrist, Ras, and McLaren are of some importance 3STU; that of King of Bohemia elicits Watson's comment; *see* **rate.**

Henderson: *see* **Murillo** (Don Juan) WIST.

heraldic emblems: mouldering, atop pillars at Charlington Hall SOLI; *see* **coat; griffins; lions.**

Hercules: the son of the cataleptic Russian patient has chest and limbs of RESI, as does King of Bohemia SCAN.

Hereford Arms: inn, Holmes and Watson stay BOSC.

hiding places: beneath floor NAVA, REDH, SECO, 3GAR, VALL; behind wall GOLD, NORW, VALL; secret panel by bell-pull SCAN; dressing-gown pocket REIG; back drawer of Japanese cabinet GLOR; writing-desk SECO; for jewels: goose crop BLUE, overcoat pocket MAZA, under ground MUSG, bust of Napoleon SIXN; Henderson hides in gorse bushes WIST; Holmes, sometimes with others, hides behind or in **laurel bush; rhododendron bush; curtains; door; hedge; rocks; shadows,** qq.v.; ladies hide things in their **bosom,** q.v.

high, thin, yellow brick: house REDC.

Hill, Inspector: coincidentally, expert on Saffron Hill and Italians SIXN.

Hippocratic smile SIGN.

hist!: cries Holmes when he hears the Hound approaching HOUN.

history: of crime, Holmes knows, and cites – especially in the early tales STUD, SIGN; in middle and later stories he seldom calls on this knowledge, though he does so in HOUN, NOBL.

"Hobbs, Fairdale": Mrs. Warren's lodger, for whom Holmes arranged an affair REDC.

Hoffmann Barcarolle: from *The Tales of Hoffmann*, by Jacques Offenbach (1819–1880); wailing notes, whining music; spelled *Hoffman "Barcarole"* in Doubleday edition MAZA.

Holborn: restaurant STUD.

Holder: Alexander; niece Mary – a sunbeam; calls his son Arthur villain! thief! blackguard! BERY; John, Small's sergeant SIGN.

Holder and Stevenson: second largest private bank in the City BERY.

Holdernesse: Duke of, former Cabinet minister, grotesquely curved and long nose; wife, Lady Edith, the daughter of Sir Charles Appledore; son, Lord Saltire, a charming youth BLAC, PRIO.

Holdhurst, Lord: Foreign Minister, future premier, with an honourable record; nonetheless, Holmes leaves open the possibility that Holdhurst himself might have destroyed the treaty NAVA.

"Holland, reigning family of": Holmes has solved a case for SCAN.

Hollis: traitor LAST.

Holloway and Steele: house-agents 3GAR.

Holmes Bibliography: (adapted from Vincent Starrett, *The Private Life of Sherlock Holmes* [Chicago: University of Chicago Press, 1960], pp. 96-101) his "trifling" monographs: 1. *Upon the Distinction Between Ashes of the Various Tobaccos* STUD; 2. *Upon the Tracing of Footsteps* SIGN; 3. *Upon the Influence of a Trade upon the Forms of the Hand* SIGN; 4. *The Book of Life* STUD; 5. *On the Typewriter and Its Relation to Crime* IDEN; 6. *Upon the Dating of Old Documents* GOLD, HOUN; 9. *Of Tattoo Marks* REDH; 10. *On Secret Writings* DANC; 11. *On the Surface Anatomy of the Human Ear* CARD; 12. *Early English Charters* 3STU; 13. *On the Polyphonic Motets of Lassus* BRUC; 14. *Chaldean Roots in the Ancient Cornish Language* DEVI; 15. *Malingering* DYIN 16. *Upon the Use of Dogs in the Work of the Detective* CREE; 17. *Practical Handbook of Bee Culture, with Some Observations on the Segregation of the Queen* LAST; never – or not yet – printed in full are his account of his travels under the name of Sigerson EMPT and his study of the Whole Art of Detection ABBE; for his first-person accounts of his cases, *see* **write them yourself.**

Holmes, Mycroft: eyes, peculiarly light, watery gray GREE; steel-gray, deep-set; occasionally he *is* the British government; salary four hundred and fifty pounds a year; specialism is omniscience; uncouth physical inertia; absolutely and indignantly refuses to climb railings; fidgets in his seat BRUC; calls Holmes Sherlock and my dear boy BRUC, GREE; despite his torpor, he acts as Watson's brougham-driver, disguised in a dark cloak FINA; keeps rooms at 221B Baker Street intact during the Great Hiatus EMPT.

Holmes, Sherlock: nom de guerre used by Stapleton HOUN; Adler, in disguise, ill-advisedly says, Good night, Mister Sherlock Holmes SCAN; brother **Holmes, Mycroft,** q.v.; sister? COPP; son? BERY; forebears were country squires but include French artist Vernet GREE; in his feigned illness DYIN, raves of **battery; half-crowns; oysters,** qq.v.; for his appearance, *see* **chin; eyes; face; finger; glow-worm; hands; height; nose; phlegmatic; saturnine; skull;** *also see* **admiration; avidity; friends; languor; sarcasm; vices.**

Holmesisms: Only one important thing has happened in the last three days, and that is that nothing has happened SECO; The curious incident of the dog in the night-time: the dog did nothing in the night-time; that was the curious incident (*see* **dogs**) SILV; amateur domiciliary visit (euphemism for **burglary,** q.v.) BRUC; truncated fowling piece (sawn[sawed]-off shotgun, *see* **weapons**) VALL; for others, *see* **data; facts; knees.**

Home Secretary MAZA.

honour: very sensitive, Sir James Walter's BRUC; debt of, Trevor embezzles in order to pay GLOR; Phelps kisses Holmes's hand and exclaims, God bless you! You have saved my honour! NAVA; Holmes asks how Gilchrist, an honourable man, could have copied the examination 3STU; Norberton is of honourable stock, will live to an honoured old age SHOS.

Honours List: *see* **knighthood.**

*Hood, General John Bell (1831–1879) FIVE.

Hope: Jefferson, avenger; though a stranger in the city, he gets a job as London cab-driver (highly unlikely!); for his disguise, *see* **old** STUD; Trelawney, Right Honourable, endowed with every beauty of body and of mind; Lady Hilda, daughter of Duke of Belminster, bright eyes (brightness of fever); draws in her breath sharply SECO.

hopeless: Watson says, I knew that the case was hopeless – referring to his desire to keep Holmes, who is supposed to be vacationing and recuperating, from investigating the murder REIG.

Hopkins: Ezekiah, American philanthropist, invented by Clay REDH; Stanley (police) ABBE, BLAC, GOLD, MISS; Holmes says (ABBE) that he has helped Hopkins in seven cases, all of which have, he fancies, found their way into Watson's collection; but there are only four in the canon.

*Horace (Quintus Horatius Flaccus, 65–8 B.C.): Roman poet and satirist BLUE, IDEN, PRIO, STUD.

Horner, John: plumber, falsely accused BLUE.

horny, far from: hands of suspect SIGN.

horror: when there is no imagination, there is none (Holmes) STUD; brutal preliminary shadows forth strange and inexplicable horror CARD; Sir Henry's hands raised in HOUN; scream vibrates with frenzy of SOLI; Holmes, Watson, M Tregennis look with horror after black carriage taking O and G Tregennis to insane asylum; freezing horror takes possession of Watson DEVI; Harker is frozen with SIXN; the faces of Barclay CROO, Drebber STUD, Gilchrist 3STU, Sholto SIGN, B Tregennis and Holmes himself DEVI register horror; *see* **Cornish;** *cf.* **terror.**

Horsam, Dr.: summoned by Peters LADY.

horses: noble chestnuts with glossy haunches CHAS; splendid, high-stepping, gray SHOS; fresh, glossy chestnut ENGR; a very gregarious creature, says Holmes SILV; Carruthers threatens to put a bullet into Holmes's and Watson's SOLI; pair of beauties @ a hundred and fifty guineas apiece SCAN; pair of cobs HOUN; two rough-haired, unkempt PRIO; breathless trotter VALL; foaming, Holmes's and Watson's LADY; Elise's eyes like those of a frightened horse ENGR; mulatto cook is strong as a cart-horse WIST; speed: one-horse carriage, ten miles in an hour ENGR; a pair of grays, twenty to twenty-four miles in three hours MISS; wild moor-ponies stupidly permit themselves to be engulfed in mire HOUN; Holmes identifies the number of horses by the sound of their hoofs – since there are only two, it is not a particularly dazzling exhibition of his deductive powers SCAN; *see* **Prince; Silver Blaze;** *cf.* **children.**

horseshoes: to simulate cow-tracks; old shoes but new nails PRIO; Holmes fits shoe to trace SILV.

hotels: *see* **Anerley Arms; Bentley's; Black Swan Hotel; Brambletye Hotel; Claridge's; Cosmopolitan, Hotel; Dulong; du Louvre; Eagle Commercial Hotel; Grosvenor Hotel; Halliday's Private Hotel; Langham Hotel; Mexborough Private Hotel; National Hotel; Northumberland Hotel; Plymouth; Strand;** *for inns, see* **Alpha Inn; Bull Inn; Chequers Inn; Dangling Prussian; Englischer Hof; Fighting Cock; Green Dragon; Hereford Arms; Railway Arms; Westville Arms** (some of these are pubs – e. g., the Alpha).

Hotspur: ship; rescues mutineers, takes them to Australia GLOR.

hot water: Barrymore has provided, in Watson's and Sir Henry's rooms HOUN; and lemon GOLD.

hound: selfish, drunken – Croker's metaphors ABBE; murderess calls Milverton a hound CHAS; Charpentier calls Drebber a hound STUD; old – Holmes is like DEVI; old – Holmes and Watson are two PRIO; good hounds run silent MAZA, 3GAB; Holmes says

that hounds like the Stockdales will bite the hand that feeds them 3GAB; Douglas tries to throw hounds (Scowrers) off his track; McMurdo calls policemen hounds VALL; hound : detective :: wolf : crook STUD; bloodhound-mastiff mix; witnesses to its existence include hard-headed countryman, farrier, moorland farmer; Holmes asserts that a hound will not bite a dead body; Watson calls it a bogie [*sic*] hound HOUN; *see* **footprints.**

house-agents: realtors SOLI, 3GAR.

housekeeper: the Roylott household has one (not named), but the Stoner sisters always get what they want for themselves SPEC; *see* **Bernstone, Mrs.; Dixon; Lexington, Mrs.; Marker, Mrs.; Porter, Mrs.; Pringle, Mrs.; Saunders, Ikey; Turner, Mrs.**

Howe Street: location of the house from which Gennaro sends signals REDC; *see* **Great Orme Street.**

Howells, Rachel: house-maid; excitable Welsh temperament; disappears after suffocating Brunton; at first thought to be drowned in mere or lake, but body not found MUSG.

Hudson: blood-sucking criminal GLOR; Morse, shopkeeper SIXN; Mrs., Holmes's and Watson's landlady BLAC, BLUE, DYIN, EMPT, LAST, LION, MAZA, NAVA, SIGN, SPEC, WIST; longsuffering DYIN; cuisine a little limited NAVA; Holmes makes her walk on her knees EMPT; replaced by new cook? THOR; by Turner? SCAN; some like to think that Holmes's old housekeeper in Sussex LION, and Martha, who works with Holmes in the Von Bork case LAST, is Mrs. Hudson, but there is no evidence for this assumption.

Huguenot: *see* **Gorot** *and* **Les Huguenots.**

human: Hopkins ABBE and Holdernesse PRIO say that Holmes's powers are hardly ABBE, PRIO; *see* **automaton; devil.**

humour, Holmes's sense of: limited, somewhat perverted MAZA; offensive to Watson LADY; mischievous gaze which was characteristic of his more imp-like moods THOR; *see* **pawky; practical.**

Hunter: Ned, groom SILV; Violet, governess; Holmes is much impressed by her; to Watson's disappointment, Holmes shows no further interest in her once the case is solved COPP.

hunting: Holmes is a master huntsman; Holmes and Watson are hunters, seeking Moran, who himself is a big-game hunter EMPT; Gregson and Baynes hunt together WIST; Watson has coursed many creatures in many countries in his checkered career SIGN; *see* **game-shots; games, sports; view-halloa.**

hunting-crop: Brown's wags like a branch in the wind SILV; Sir Henry armed with HOUN; loaded, Holmes's favourite weapon SIXN; threatens Windibank

with IDEN; hits Clay's wrist with REDH.

"Huret, boulevard assassin": Holmes solves case, for which he receives an autograph letter from the French President and the Order of the Legion of Honour GOLD.

Huxtable, Thorneycroft: M.A., Ph.D., etc.; vacant gray eyes; he mentions one of his books, *Huxtable's Sidelights on Horace*, to establish his credentials PRIO.

Hyams: Oldacre's tailor NORW.

Hyde Park: *see* **park.**

Hynes Hynes, Mr., J. P.: Garcia's neighbor WIST.

hypnosis: *see* **mesmerism, post-hypnotic.**

hysterics, violent: Holmes's reappearance throws Mrs. Hudson into EMPT.

ideas: Holmes admits his are quite wild (he does not mean it) ABBE; Watson's are limited but exceedingly pertinacious, says Holmes BLAN; *see* **intellect; mind.**

idiot: *see* **lunatic.**

illustrators: Sidney Paget (1860–1908) for the *Strand Magazine* in Britain and Frederic Dorr Steele (1874–1944) for *Collier's* in the United States, from whose drawings we get many of our impressions of Holmes and Watson; Paget, who used his brother Walter as the model for Holmes, drew the detective so often that the portraits of other characters came to resemble him – e.g., that of Jim Browner in CARD.

imagination, Holmes's views of: he values it; it is the one quality which Gregory lacks; if he (Gregory) were gifted with it, he would rise to great heights in his profession SILV; often the mother of truth VALL; claims scientific use of HOUN; tells Lestrade he lacks it NORW; *see* **guess; horror.**

imbecility (of police): *see* **evaluation; inspector.**

impossible: Watson objects: Holmes, this is impossible. Holmes retorts (sarcastically): Admirable! A most illuminating remark PRIO; *see also* **improbable.**

improbable: when you have eliminated the impossible, whatever remains, however improbable, must be the truth (and similar formulas by which Holmes describes his logic) BERY, BLAN, BRUC, SIGN; *see also* **data, facts.**

inconvenient: *see* **come.**

Indians: (including Afghans; the author does not always distinguish them) *see* **Abdullah Khan; Chowdar, Lal; Dost Akbar; Mahomet Singh; Rao, Lal; Ras, Daulat; Ghazis; Khalifa; Nana Sahib; Pathan;** enteric fever, the curse of our Indian possessions STUD; Indian settings CROO, SIGN; *see* **native Americans.**

inhuman: Holmes's effect on Watson GREE; *see* **automaton.**

initials, of significance in the tales: *see* **A D P; C. A. M.; C. C. H.; C. P. R.; D. M. A. O. F.; E. C.;** **EgPGt; F. H. M.; J. A.; J. H. N.; KKK; L. L.; M. R. C. S.; P. C.; V. C.; V. R.;** *see also* **NN** *and* **P-E-N**, though they are not initials.

ink, violet: on Sutherland's finger IDEN; *cf.* **fingers,** on which ink is sometimes smeared; *see also* **handwriting; pen.**

inns: *see* **hotels.**

Inquisition of Seville STUD; *see* **secret societies.**

inspector: unnamed, rubicund 3GAB; unnamed; pips are a joke, he says, at which Holmes exclaims, Incredible imbecility! FIVE; *see* **Bradstreet, Inspector; Gregory, Inspector; Gregson, Tobias; Jones** (Peter); **Lestrade; Macdonald, Alec;** *see also* **police.**

instinct: *see* **analytic.**

intellect: Holmes's magnificent, babbling like a foolish child DYIN; Machiavellian, Holmes calls Watson's, speaking ironically VALL; *see* **coruscation; mentality; scintillating.**

intercourse: McMurdo's with Ettie VALL.

intuition: *see* **analytic.**

iodoform: Watson smells of SCAN.

irascibility: Holmes arouses in others, e.g., **Armstrong; Breckinridge; Brown; Gibson; Presbury; Ross; Roylott; Sterndale.**

Irish: -American criminals VALL; -American traitor; secret society; civil war (England has stirred up); Holmes gives serious trouble to the constabulary in Skibbareen (usually spelled *Skibereen*)

LAST; *see* **Altamont; Damery, Sir James; MacNamara, Widow; McGinty, Black Jack; McMurdo, Jack; Scowrers.**

iron: strike while hot: Holmes's platitude CARD.

irony: *see* **sarcasm.**

***Irving, Washington (1783–1859):** American writer; *see* **Sleepy Hollow(s).**

Italians: associated with **restaurants** and the **Mafia,** qq.v.; old, cruel Italian spirit (Klein's phrase) 3GAB; *cf.* **Latin;** *and see* **Beppo; Gorgiano, Giuseppe; Lucca.**

ivy: upon wall, Saltire and Heidegger climb down PRIO; Presbury climbs up and down CREE; yeoman's daughter climbs down to escape Hugo Baskerville HOUN; Ivy is Mrs. Douglas's first name VALL; Ivy Plant, pub where MacPherson goes for brandy to revive curious lady (Hilda Trelawney Hope) SECO.

J. A.: *see* **tattoos.**

Jack: common nickname, even for men whose true names are not John: Bennett (Trevor), James, Ferguson, Croker, Douglas, McMurdo, McGinty, Munro (Grant), Pendergast, Smith, Stapleton, Woodley.

The cover of *Collier's Magazine;* this issue heralded the return of Sherlock Holmes.

jackal: Watson equates criminals with jackals and tigers BLAC; jackal : lion :: Porlock : Moriarty; jackals eat Dawson's wife SIGN; *see* **fauna.**

jack-in-office, Scotland Yard: Roylott's insult; Holmes is piqued because Roylott confuses him with the official police SPEC.

Jackson: Dr., takes Watson's practice CROO; *General Thomas Jonathan, "Stonewall" (1824–1863) FIVE; Prize, for comparative pathology, Mortimer has won HOUN.

Jacobean: Birlstone, Douglas's manor VALL; High Gable, Henderson's house WIST; *see* **architecture.**

Jacobs: servant (butler?), Lady Hilda's SECO.

Jacobson's: shipyard where Smith hides the *Aurora* SIGN.

James: postmaster's son HOUN; Jack James, traitor LAST; Watson called this by his wife (although it has been established that his first name is John) TWIS; given name of both brothers Moriarty, the professor and the colonel FINA; *James I (1566–1625), king of Great Britain, reigned 1603–1625 (as James VI of Scotland, reigned 1567–1603) VALL, WIST.

jarveys: Holmes uses this slang term for cab drivers STUD.

jay: like a; Slaney's American slang for like a **fool,** a **sucker,** qq.v. DANC.

"Jefferson Hope murder": = STUD: SIGN.

jemmy: burglar tool; Evans uses to pry up flooring 3GAR; also called *jimmy* NAVA; for Holmes's, *see* **burglary.**

jewels: yellow diamond, returned to pocket by trick MAZA (*see* **hiding**); Black Pearl of the Borgias SIXN; Blue Carbuncle BLUE; "brilliant" (diamond, Holmes's ring) IDEN; emerald snake ring (Holmes refuses) SCAN; emerald (Holmes's) BRUC; old-gold snuffbox, with amethyst (Holmes's) IDEN; flaming beryl (Bohemia's) SCAN; pebbles, lustreless stones, actually long-hidden royal treasure MUSG; pearls in bosom (Morstan's) and Agra treasure SIGN; gold pin, bull-dog head, ruby eyes (Drebber's) STUD; Spanish silver, diamonds (Lady Frances's) LADY; pearl pin (Damery's) ILLU; shining pin, glittering rings (Sylvius's) MAZA; rough nugget and twisted snake rings (Douglas's); several diamond pins (McGinty's) VALL; little gilt earrings (Susan Cushing's) CARD; silver locket (Effie's) YELL; Milverton advises lady to turn diamonds into paste; diamond tiara worn by Milverton's murderess in photo CHAS; opal tiara: *see* **Farintosh;** *and see* **treasure, Agra.**

Jews: moneylenders SHOS; peddlers STUD; pawnbroker CARD; jew's harp, Parker performs remarkably on EMPT; *see* **sheeny.**

Jezail: a long, heavy Afghan rifle (OED); for Jezail bullet, *see* **wound.**

J. H. N.: Neligan's initials on notebook containing lists of stocks BLAC.

Jingo!: Carruthers swears by the living SOLI.

John: Holmes's dog-cart driver TWIS; Adler's landau driver SCAN; pompous butler MISS; Spencer John, gang leader 3GAB; for other Johns, including Jacks and foreign cognates, *see* **Baskerville** (John); **Bennett, Trevor; bull; Clay, John; Clayton, John; Cobb, John; Croker, Captain Jack; Douglas** (John [Jack]); **Eccles, John Scott; Edwards, Birdy; Ferguson** (Jack[y]); **Garrideb** (John); **"Harden, John Vincent"; *Hare, John; Hebron** (John); **Holder** (John); **Horner, John; James; Mason** (John); **McFarlane** (John Hector); **McGinty, Black Jack; McMurdo, Jack; Mitton, John; Morland, Sir John; Munro** (Grant); **Murdoch, Ian; Murillo** (Don Juan); **Neligan, John Copley; Openshaw** (John); **Prendergast** (Jack); ***Richter, Jean Paul; Sloane, Hans; Small, Jonathan; Stapleton; Straker** (John); **Turner** (John); **Watson, John H.; Woodley** (Jack). *Also see* **Jack; James.**

Johnson: Shinwell, nicknamed Porky; scorbutic; former convict, but Holmes's valuable assistant ILLU; Sidney, unpopular with his colleagues BRUC; Theophilus HOUN; with Morton, one of the Oxford flyers, Staunton's rugby opponents MISS.

Joint, the: not prison, but an American gangsters' secret society DANC.

joke: Holmes complains, It is no joke when a tall man has to take a foot off his stature for several hours on end EMPT; *see* **practical;** for Watson's frequent You are joking! *see* **repetitions.**

Jones: Athelney (called Anthony in some American editions), fat police detective, red-faced, burly, plethoric, very small twinkling eyes; downcast when no reward is forthcoming SIGN; Peter, Scotland Yard inspector REDH, REIG; *see* **police.**

José: one of Henderson's servants WIST.

journeys end in [with] lovers' meetings: Holmes, quoting Shakespeare, *Twelfth Night* EMPT, REDC.

Jove: Watson swears by STUD; Holmes twice swears by MISS; as does Hayter, whistling REIG.

junk: Trevor uses this seaman's term for salt-beef GLOR.

Jupiter, descending: Holmes announces Mycroft's visit thus BRUC.

*Kaiser: *see* **foreign potentate.**

Kansas: lumber-producing state 3GAR.

*Keats, John (1795–1821): English poet; Holmes, quoting, says that Klein is the *belle dame sans merci* of fiction 3GAB.

keg: Holmes sits on MUSG.

Kemp, Wilson: small, mean-looking, middle-aged; wears glasses; giggles; steel-gray eyes, glistening coldly, with malignant, inexorable cruelty GREE.

Kensington: London borough; one of Watson's surgeries is there EMPT, NORW, REDH; as is Holmes's bookshop on **Church Street,** q.v.

Kent, Mr.: surgeon BLAN.

Keswick: respectable paper-hanger STUD.

key: Lady Hilda takes impression of, thrusts in her bosom SECO; by chance dropped in Hope's cab; he takes moulding of it; shakes it in Drebber's face STUD; Beddington obtains mouldings of locks, presumably to make keys STOC; Cadogan West's office opens with one; three needed for theft; Walter takes an impress of them BRUC; Evans uses stolen one to enter house 3GAR; Anna hires private detective to take moulding of; leaves scratches around keyhole in wood GOLD; scratches around keyhole of watch STUD; from Presbury's watch-chain, Holmes uses to open his mysterious box CREE; Openshaw (E) produces an old rusty one to open brass box FIVE; small penknife used instead of, leaves scratches in paint BLAC; wire used instead of RESI; chisel or strong knife used instead of REIG; missing: room locked from within CROO; Watson assumes that Mrs. Amberley has duplicate key to strong-room, since seven thousand pounds in securities are gone RETI; Rucas-

tles hide hair from Hunter in locked drawer but provide her with keys; she later locks Mrs. Toller in the wine-cellar COPP; lock forced REIG; stable-door locked when boy chases Simpson; important point, says Holmes, who sends a telegram to ascertain if door was locked; Holmes asks if Simpson has duplicate key in his possession SILV; Arthur Holder says that any old key will fit the bureau wherein the coronet is locked; I myself have opened it with the key of the box-room cupboard BERY; lodger demands key to house, later locks self in room REDC; Stapleton's bedroom locked; Holmes strikes door just over lock with the flat of his foot HOUN; Bannister leaves his duplicate in Soames's green-baize door 3STU; Carey has the only one to his sixteen-by-ten-foot cabin BLAC; Adair locks himself in, lest the ladies surprise him EMPT; gypsies under lock and key PRIO; Small throws treasure-chest key into Thames SIGN; curious, old-fashioned key in treasure-box lock MUSG; Stapleton turns key in lock of doghouse door HOUN; Stark locks Hatherley in a room that is actually a huge hydraulic press ENGR; Miss Harrison locks bedroom from outside and takes key; her brother uses a key, but for the servants' door NAVA; Bradstreet uses key to unlock Boone's cell TWIS; Von Bork has a small key on his watch-chain that unlocks his large safe LAST; *see* **burglary; Chubb; scratch;** in five tales there are mouldings or impressions or impresses; in three there are duplicates. A figurative key (to the affair): Holmes says that it is in the bathroom.... Oh, yes, I am not joking TWIS.

Khalifa: at Khartoum, Holmes visits during the hiatus EMPT.

khitmutgar: Hindi for butler; Sholto addresses his servant thus SIGN.

kid: bones of WIST; tethered EMPT; *see* **child.**

King, Mrs.: cook DANC.

kings: *see* **James I; George II; George III;** *see also* **Stuart.**

Kirwan, William: a good servant – actually a blackmailing coachman, dead; half-witted mother REIG.

KKK FIVE; *see* **secret societies.**

Klein, Isadora: Spanish; married to German sugar king 3GAB.

Klopman: Nihilist LAST.

kneecap: Staunton once slipped one MISS; *see* **artificial.**

knees: Holmes says the first thing to examine in a man is the knee of the trouser IDEN (he says the same thing about hands CREE); Holmes examines Clay's; Watson asks, And what did you see? Holmes responds, What I expected to see – they are worn, wrinkled, stained REDH; bent CROO, NOBL; one of Croker's leaves an impression in the dust ABBE; Lady Hilda on hers to plead with Holmes SECO; Ryder clutches Holmes's BLUE; Gibson's bony ones almost touch

Holmes's THOR; Holmes falls upon his, on the floor REDH; elbows on FINA, TWIS; Holmes instructs Mrs. Hudson to walk on hers to move wax-figure EMPT.

*Kneller, Sir Godfrey (1646–1723): German-English painter HOUN.

knickerbockers: *see* **dress; Neligan, John Copley.**

knife: white-hafted REDC; very small pen BLAC; (great) clasp BLAC, SIXN; long-bladed NAVA; long, deadly, sheathed VALL; cataract SILV; sealing-wax GOLD; multiplex ABBE; jack MUSG; large LION; very blunt 3STU; not very sharp RESI; *see* **weapons.**

knighthood: Holmes refuses 3GAR; Holmes smiles at Honours List BRUC; but *see* **Legion of Honour.**

knocked up: Watson and Mrs. Hudson SPEC; Watson, by Hatherley ENGR; You are knocking yourself up, old man (Watson to Holmes) SIGN.

knots: sailor's, Holmes recognizes ABBE, CARD.

knuckles: Presbury's, thick and horny CREE.

Kratides, Paul: protruding brilliant eyes; sister Sophy GREE.

lackey: rejoicing PRIO.

lady: in stately Court dress, photo of CHAS; consumptive English, asks for Watson's medical service (she does not exist; fabricated by Moriarty) FINA; certain gracious BRUC; *see* **Queen.**

Lady Day: the Feast of the Annunciation, March 25; Trevelyan moves in with Blessington on RESI.

lamp: oil TWIS; Holmes buys, fills, burns to time how long it lasts; the original lamp had been lit in broad daylight, Holmes concludes DEVI; Holmes moves one to read a fragment of the Klan papers FIVE; Hatherley takes one to illuminate the hydraulic press; it later catches the house afire ENGR; gas GREE, MISS; red (Barnicot's) SIXN; in the fashion of a silver dove SIGN; *see* **ashes.**

Lancaster: Gate, Moran has rented a house there NOBL; James, seaman; ribston-pippin of a man, ruddy cheeks, fluffy white sidewhiskers; given a half-sovereign and sent on his way BLAC.

landladies: *see* **Charpentier; Hudson; Merrilow; Warren;** *also see* **green peas.**

landlady's daughter: Staunton marries; her rough-looking father informs Staunton of the impending death of; she lies dead with wide-opened blue eyes MISS.

Langham Hotel: large, ostentatious; Green LADY, King of Bohemia SCAN, and Captain Morstan SIGN stay there, though not at the same time.

languor, infinite, Holmes's: extreme, to devouring energy, the swing of his nature, says Watson IDEN, REDH; laziness, fits of splendid energy and vigour SIGN.

Lanner: police inspector, smartlooking RESI.

lantern: little pocket, Holmes's SIGN; he lights it to observe size-twelve footprints WIST; lights crypt SHOS; lights Oberstein's massive door BRUC; Stark has one in one hand, cleaver in the other ENGR; Baxter lights her way with one, carrying drugged mutton SILV; Barrymore lights one to search for Sir Charles HOUN; Musgrave lights a large one MUSG; grooms and employees carry them to investigate circus accident VEIL; Sir Robert's stable-lantern lights his heavily moustached face SHOS; Sholto detaches a side-lantern from his carriage to light to way to Pondicherry Lodge SIGN; *see* **bull's-eye; dark lantern.**

La Rothière, Louis: agent BRUC, SECO.

lascar: East Indian sailor; rascally; lascar scoundrel TWIS.

*Lassus, Orlandus (died 1594): German composer; Holmes analyzes his polyphonic motets BRUC; *see* **music.**

Latimer, Harold: young, powerful; rasping, menacing voice GREE.

Latin countries: countries of assassination (Holmes says) BRUC; *cf.* **Italian;** *and see* **foreigners.**

laughter: rare fit (Holmes's) HOUN; Holmes seldom laughs MAZA; Holmes's explosion of, at Lestrade; Holmes's hearty, at himself; Holmes's merry, expressing confidence in his violin-playing STUD; Holmes's hearty, at Lestrade NOBL; Holmes's hearty, noiseless BLUE; Holmes's hearty, when he hears that cab-fare has given his name as Sherlock Holmes; Holmes laughs and dances over dead body (Selden's, which appeared to be Baskerville's) HOUN; Holmes laughs heartily at his own (mis)adventures SCAN, SOLI; Holmes's roar of, at Wilson REDH; Holmes quivers with silent EMPT; Holmes bursts out laughing when threatened by Armstrong MISS, at St. Simon NOBL, Lestrade SECO, and Brown SILV; Holmes grins TWIS, chuckles SIGN at Watson's surprise; Holmes chuckles and wriggles REDH; Holmes chuckles (smiles) and claps (rubs) hands together (softly) IDEN, SILV, WIST; Holmes points with a chuckle at a house REDC; Holmes chuckles at missing bones SHOS; Holmes chuckles when Watson says he thinks Mycroft has some small government office; sudden burst of hilarity when things go his way BRUC; Holmes grins when Watson describes him as a self-poisoner FIVE; Holmes laughs softly to himself BOSC; Hayes's mouth loosens into a false laugh PRIO; ripple of, from Klein 3GAB; Coram bursts into insincere, high-keyed laughter GOLD; Pinner ill-advisedly laughs, exposing his badly stuffed tooth STOC; Kemp's little giggling laugh strikes fear into Melas GREE; Scowrers greet tale of murder with cries of delight and shouts of laughter VALL; Howells emits shriek after shriek of, as she falls back against the wall MUSG; *see* **fit; shout; shriek.**

laurel bushes: branches twisted and snapped BRUC; Holmes's body crashes through ILLU; Holmes crouches behind a screen of VALL; woman's scream bursts from SOLI; lawn is laurel-clumped NORW; *see* **shrubbery.**

lavender spats ILLU; *see* **spats.**

law: Frankland's hobby HOUN; Holmes has good practical knowledge of STUD; magnificent fair play of British criminal law DANC; Holmes says it is his business and that of every other good citizen to uphold the law SHOS; Holmes asks Watson, You don't mind breaking the law? Watson responds, Not in the least SCAN; Holmes says, I suppose that I am commuting a felony, but it is just possible that I am saving a soul BLUE; Holmes readily admits to false arrest, kidnapping, and theft LAST; Holmes acts as judge, Watson as jury, to acquit Croker; English divorce laws: monstrous! (Lady Brackenstall) ABBE; deplorable English divorce laws DEVI; laws prevent Lyons from suing for divorce HOUN; rigid British law becomes human and elastic ILLU; Douglas tries to dodge British law VALL; Windibank knows the law cannot touch him IDEN; *see* **burglary; warrant;** for Holmes's mistrust of juries, *see* **theory.**

Lawler: Scowrer assassin; a total abstainer VALL.

leader: = British term for what Americans would call a newspaper editorial HOUN, STUD.

Le Brun: French agent, crippled by Apaches in Montmartre ILLU.

Lecoq: Émile Gaboriau's detective character; a miserable bungler, says Holmes STUD.

*Lee, General Robert E. (1807–1870): Confederate military commander FIVE.

leetle, vell, vish, vas, vould: Shafter's German dialect; it remains the same in English editions, where Shafter's nationality is changed to Swedish VALL.

"Lefevre of Montpellier" STUD.

left-handed: Holmes deduces that Munro is, from the way he lights his pipe YELL.

leg: *see* **limb.**

Legion of Honour: French; Holmes accepts GOLD.

Leonardo: circus strong man; drowns near Margate VEIL.

Les Huguenots: opera by Giacomo Meyerbeer, German composer (1791–1864) HOUN.

Lestrade, G.: Scotland Yard inspector BOSC, BRUC, CARD, CHAS, EMPT, HOUN, LADY, NOBL, NORW, SECO, SIXN, STUD, 3GAR; rat-faced STUD (*see* **Ryder**); bulldog features SECO; thin and austere BRUC; ferret-like BOSC, CARD, STUD (*see* **Oldacre**); small, wiry bulldog HOUN; in a fog; no chicken; old hound STUD; obtuse but resolute CARD; best of the professionals HOUN; advises Holmes to abandon case; grossly triumphant manner NORW; conjectures that iconoclast murderer was rattled

and bustled SIXN; Holmes tells him that three undetected murders in one year won't do [error for "unsolved murders" or "undetected murderers"?] EMPT; though an official Scotland Yard detective, he is engaged by Miss Turner et al. to defend McCarthy BOSC; the last syllable of his name is pronounced to rhyme with *odd* or *aid;* his first initial is G. (CARD), but we are never told what it stands for.

Lesurier, Madame: milliner SILV.

let in: = let down, betray(ed); Cambridge or Cockney slang MISS, STOC.

letters: incriminating, indiscreet CHAS, SECO; Porlock's to Holmes is perhaps indiscreet; Moriarty's to Holmes, Dear me, Mr. Holmes. Dear me! VALL; strike terror into recipients – or change their lives BOSC, COPP, DANC, FIVE, GLOR, HOUN, PRIO, SIGN; Holmes's include one from a fishmonger, another from a tidewaiter NOBL; Holmes writes Watson from Narbonne, Nîmes FINA; writes to City firm and to Windibank IDEN; Elsie throws letter from America into fire DANC; letters, papers, or notes in fire, partially or totally burned CHAS, FIVE, HOUN, THOR, 3GAB, WIST; *see* **foreign potentate; photo;** *and cf.* **telegram.**

"Leturier in Montpellier" STUD; *see* **Dolsky.**

Leverstoke, Lord: son is at the school PRIO.

Leverton: Pinkerton agent; hero of the Long Island Cave mystery REDC.

lewd: and bloodthirsty tyrant (Murillo) WIST.

"Lewis, Sir George" ILLU; *see* **"Hammerford will case."**

Lewisham: London suburb; monotonous brick streets, weary suburban highways RETI.

Lexington, Mrs.: housekeeper, side-long eyes NORW.

lichen: several old houses are lichen-blotched or -spotted; *see* **architecture.**

lies: Holmes says, It is usually better to tell the truth VEIL; great, big, thumping, obtrusive, uncompromising lie VALL; rigmarole of lies 3GAR; absolute fabrication ABBE; Holmes says that Watson has added fibbing to his other vices MAZA.

life-preserver: = blackjack BERY, BRUC, GREE.

light: in visitor's face, both Holmes BLAN and Moriarty VALL arrange interviews thus; Lady Hilda chooses a chair so that the light is at her back and in Holmes's and Watson's faces SECO.

light, electric: CHAS, 3STU; pink 3GAB; tinted DYIN; Sir Henry plans to install at Baskerville Hall HOUN; *see* **gas; Swann and Edison; yellow.**

limb: artificial RETI, SIGN; one-legged newsvendor ILLU; one-legged greengrocer (Prosper) BERY.

lime-cream: unguent for hair BLUE.

*Lincoln, Abraham (1809–1865): U.S. president (1861–1865); Gibson resembles, but keyed to base uses THOR.

linen: *see* **chin.**

linoleum: in Watson's house TWIS; Watson's, with nail-marks from British workman CROO; in Phelps's office NAVA; *cf.* **cocoanut matting.**

lion(s): rampant atop pillar at Birlstone VALL; Sterndale DEVI, Sylvius MAZA hunt; Croker is as strong as ABBE; hound as large as a small lioness HOUN; crouching lion on seal (on envelope) SECO; *see* **griffins; heraldic; Sahara.**

lip(s): Holmes gnaws STUD; Holmes's cut SOLI; McPherson bites through LION; McMurdo bites VALL; looseness of (*see* **eye**) HOUN; fallen, Joseph Openshaw's FIVE; pendulous, Sholto's SIGN; thick, hanging (the Hapsburg lip?), King of Bohemia's SCAN; Holmes ridicules Dixie's 3GAB; Holmes, in disguise – doddering, loose-lipped senility TWIS; Holmes's firm lips shake 3GAR; Holmes's tighten BRUC; Holmes's compressed; puts them to Watson's very ear EMPT; Milverton's twitch; his murderess has a deadly smile on hers CHAS; Windibank IDEN, Tregennis DEVI, and Morstan SIGN are white to theirs; Nancy Barclay's tremble when she meets Wood CROO; Turner's are blue-tinged (as are corners of his nostrils) BOSC; Melas and Kratides are blue-lipped and insensible GREE; Ryder passes tongue over his parched BLUE; from Mrs. Lucca's there pour forth a thousand pretty Italian exclamations REDC.

list slippers: = slippers made of list, a kind of cloth NAVA.

literature: Watson notes that Holmes's knowledge of is nil STUD; *but see* *Alcuin; *Balzac, Honoré de; *Boccaccio, Giovanni; *Boswell, James; *Carlyle, Thomas; *Chaucer, Geoffrey; classical references; *De Quincey, Thomas; *Dickens, Charles; *Flaubert, Gustave; foreign languages; *Gaboriau, Émile; *Goethe, Johann Wolfgang von; *Grimm, Brothers; *Hafiz; *Irving, Washington; *Keats, John; *Macchiavelli, Niccolò; *Meredith, George; *Murger, Henri; *Poe, Edgar Allan; *Pope, Alexander; *Reade, William Winwood; *Richter, Jean Paul; *La Rochefoucauld, Duc François de; *Sand, George; *Shakespeare, William; *Spenser, Edmund; *Thoreau, Henry David.

litmus-paper NAVA; *see* **chemistry.**

L. L.: initials on letter received by Sir Charles before his death; they stand for **Laura Lyons,** q.v. HOUN.

llama, head EMPT; error for *lama;* corrected in some editions.

Lloyd's Register of Shipping: Holmes pores over FIVE.

loaf: Holmes tears piece from, devours FIVE; and tinned tongue, tinned peaches – Holmes's provisions on the moor, along with a flask of spirits HOUN.

loafer: vagabond; Holmes's disguise BERY.

lobster: tenacious as (Jones) REDH.

lock: *see* **key.**

locked room: secrets in BLAN, COPP, FIVE; death in CROO, RETI; stable-door locked SILV; Holmes locks door after Milverton's death CHAS.

locket: Munro draws from her bosom YELL; St. Simon opens to show Holmes the ivory miniature of Doran NOBL.

Lomax: sub-librarian, London Library, St. James's Square; Watson's friend, who supplies him with a volume on Chinese pottery ILLU.

Lomond, Duke of: engaged to Klein 3GAB.

London: population, 4 million STUD; 5 million CARD, RESI; University of, Trevelyan RESI and Watson STUD have M.D.s from; Holmes makes a hobby of having an exact knowledge of EMPT; Holmes knows its byways REDH; in cab, Holmes mutters names of squares and streets, exhibiting his intimate knowledge of SIGN; Holmes consults big map of BRUC; shilling map of, found in Venucci's pocket; Holmes and Watson pass through fashionable district of, followed by hotel, theatrical, literary, commercial, and maritime districts SIXN; telephone directory for 3GAR; for representative allusions to, *see* **awful;**

cesspool; colors; criminal; false; Lewisham; slavey; Stepney; Upper; worst; for landmarks, districts, squares, and streets, *see* **Big Ben; Bloomsbury; British Museum; Covent Garden; Hyde Park; St. Paul's; Thames; Brook Street; Charles Street; Church Street; Craven Street; Great Orme [Ormond] Street; Montague Street; Northumberland Street; Regent Street; The Strand; Tottenham Court Road; Wigmore Street; Berkeley Square; Grosvenor Square; St. James's Square; Croydon; Holborn; Kensington; Lewisham; Notting Hill; Paddington; St. Pancras; Whitehall;** *also see* **Baker Street**.

Lone Star: ship; name given to one of the States, Holmes says; Texas, I think, Watson adds FIVE.

"Long Island Cave mystery": truly a mystery, since there are no caves on Long Island REDC.

Lopez: secretary, probably murdered in Spain, where he has assumed the name Signor [*sic*] Rulli; *see* **Lucas** WIST.

Lord: Holmes swears by the Lord Harry ILLU; Great Lord of mercy, Peterson swears BLUE; Holmes swears, By the Lord, if you had killed Watson . . . 3GAR.

love: Holmes's for Watson BRUC, 3GAR; Holmes says, But love is an emotional thing, and whatever is emotional is opposed to that true, cold reason which I place above all things SIGN; Jack

throws his arms round his father's neck with the abandon of a loving girl SUSS; *see also* **passions, softer; relations.**

lover, wife, or husband, long-lost: returns, often for vengeance ABBE, CROO, DANC, DEVI, GOLD, ILLU, NOBL, NORW, STUD.

Lowenstein, H.: ape-serum shipper CREE.

Lucas: Eduardo, spy, alias Henri Fournaye; a student of international politics, an indefatigable gossip, a remarkable linguist, and an untiring letter-writer; his taste is luxurious to the verge of effeminacy SECO; Mr., pseudonym of Lopez; chocolate brown, wily, suave and cat-like, with a poisonous gentleness of speech WIST.

Lucca, Gennaro: wife Emilia REDC; for her Italian exclamations, *see* **lip(s).**

luggage: Holmes's and Watson's sent to Paris to decoy Moriarty; evidently never retrieved FINA.

lumber-room: room in which assorted items are stored; a boxroom; *see* **Baker Street; mind.**

lunatic, idiot: Holmes calls himself VALL; Watson thinks Holder is a madman BERY; Phelps is almost a raving maniac NAVA; Persano is found stark staring mad, gazing at a match box THOR; Lestrade and Lady Hilda (twice) say that Holmes is mad NOBL, SECO; king of Bohemia admits that he was mad – insane SCAN; Mason says Norberton has gone mad; he later thinks Holmes is another lunatic SHOS; *see* **strait-jacket;** *cf.* **ass; beetle; fool; mole.**

luncheon: Holmes and Watson eat a hasty luncheon at the railway-station buffet; later Holmes invites himself and Watson to luncheon with Phelps NAVA; Holmes and Watson snatch a hasty one at a restaurant SIXN; Holmes often winds up his investigation in time for.

lurcher: breed of dog; *see* **Toby.**

Lyceum Theatre: third pillar, rendezvous for Holmes, Watson, Morstan, and coachman SIGN.

"Lynch, Victor": *see* **"Victor Lynch, the forger."**

lynx: Hope has ears of STUD.

Lyons, Laura: Frankland's daughter; equivocal reputation; intimate with Stapleton HOUN; *see* **eye; freckled.**

Maberley: Mary; husband Mortimer; son Douglas, novelist 3GAB.

MacDonald, Alec: Scotland Yard inspector; Holmes calls him Mr. Mac, tells him he has not got the first idea what it is that he is investigating VALL; *see* **dialect.**

mace: stone-headed, wooden handle; one of Tonga's weapons SIGN.

*Machiavelli, Niccolò (1469–1527): Italian political philosopher; *see* **intellect.**

machine: *see* **automaton.**

MacKinnon, Inspector: policeman; Holmes, with a tolerant smile, says he is a good fellow RETI.

MacNamara, Widow: McMurdo's landlady after Shafter kicks him out; easy-going old Irishwoman; true as steel and deaf as a post VALL.

MacPherson: big constable, very hot and penitent SECO.

mad(man): *see* **lunatic.**

Mafia SIXN; *see* **Venucci.**

magician: Watson says Holmes is a RETI; *see* **charlatan(ism); conjurer; wizard.**

magnifying: *see* **glass.**

Mahomet Singh, one of the Four SIGN.

maid: RESI, SECO; scullery HOUN; smart, the only modern thing in the house SUSS; Holmes's BRUC, STUD; the Watsons' (Mary Jane?) BOSC, RESI.

maids: *see* **Agatha; Alice; Baxter** (Edith); **Devine** (Marie); **Dolores; Evans** (Carrie); **Mary; Mary Jane; Oldmore's; Parr** (Lucy); **Saunders; Stewart** (Jane); **Susan; Wright** (Theresa); *also see* **servants.**

Maiwand: site of battle STUD.

make-up: Holmes's, pile EMPT, heap SIGN of white hair; Holmes's, vaseline, belladonna, rouge, beeswax DYIN; Holmes's, black cassock and hat FINA; Holmes's, worker's blue smock LADY; St. Clair's, pigments, red wig, flesh-coloured plaster TWIS; Windibank's, tinted glasses, false moustache and whiskers IDEN; *see* **beards**; *cf.* **disguises.**

Malay: sallow attendant at Bar of Gold TWIS.

malignancy: extraordinary, on Presbury's face; a tumor? No, an evil expression CREE.

Malplaquet: battle; Cunninghams' house has the date (1709) on its lintel REIG.

*Malthus, Thomas Robert (1766–1834): English economist STUD.

man, Holmes and Watson comment on: a strange enigma; a soul concealed in an animal; the individual is an insoluble puzzle, in the aggregate a mathematical certainty SIGN; some of this is from ***Reade, William Winwood,** q.v.

manager: Harding Brothers; big blond German; blue Teutonic eyes SIXN.

"Manor House Case": Holmes has solved case, but Mycroft knew all along that it was Adams (we are not told his crime) GREE; manor houses: *see* **Abbey Grange; Baskerville Hall; Birlstone; Charlington Hall; High Gable; Hurlstone; Pondicherry Lodge; Riding Thorpe; Stoke Moran; Thor Place; Tuxbury Old Hall.**

man-servant, confidential WIST.

mantel, in 221B: littered with pipes, tobacco-pouches, syringes, penknives, revolver-cartridges, and other debris DYIN; jackknife impales Holmes's correspondence there MUSG; envenomed ivory box DYIN and small box containing Ming saucer ILLU rest there;

Holmes rests his feet on IDEN; Trevelyan lays his thin, white hand on RESI.

manuscript: Maberley's book; a calcined mass 3GAB; Holmes dates Baskerville manuscript at a glance; he is only off by twelve years HOUN; Musgrave says the that the spelling of the original ritual is mid-seventeenth century MUSG; *see* **palimpsest.**

"man with the twisted lip": (=TWIS) BLUE, COPP.

maps, charts: mentioned or reproduced BRUC, GOLD, HOUN, NAVA, PRIO, SIGN, SIXN; Shlessinger claims to be preparing a map of the Holy Land LADY.

Marcini's: restaurant HOUN; *see* **Goldini's.**

Marengo: battle; for Napoleon, it began in defeat but ended in victory, as do Holmes's deductions in ABBE.

"Margate, woman at" SECO.

Marker, Mrs.: Coram's housekeeper GOLD.

marriage: Watson's, Holmes says he cannot congratulate him SIGN; Mortimer's, Holmes says, Dear, dear, that's bad HOUN; *see* **women;** for Adler's, *see* **noon.**

"Marseilles, intricate matter from": referred to Holmes IDEN.

Martin, Inspector DANC.

Martini bullet: from the Martini-Henry rifle (OED); Holmes would rather face than one of Tonga's darts SIGN.

Marvin, Captain Teddy: policeman VALL.

Marx and Company, High Holborn: clothiers to Garcia WIST.

Marys: *see* **Brackenstall; Browner; Cushing; Emsworth; Fraser; Holder; Maberley; Morstan; Pinto (Maria); Sutherland;** maids FIVE, MAZA, SCAN, 3GAB.

masks: actual: King of Bohemia SCAN; Watson says, I can make a couple out of black silk [for himself and Holmes] CHAS; figurative: stoicism (Lady Mary ABBE, Small SIGN); aristocratic (Bellinger) SECO; jovial (McGinty) VALL.

Mason: platelayer BRUC; John, trainer SHOS; White, policeman VALL; Mrs., nurse; sour, silent SUSS; "Mason of Bradford" STUD.

Masonic: tie-pin REDH; breast-pin RETI; ring STUD; Holmes says, There is a wonderful sympathy and freemasonry among horsy men SCAN.

Massa: *see* **Dixie, Steve.**

masterpiece: *see* **Bruce-Partington;** LeVillard calls Holmes's work a *coup-de-maître* SIGN; Holmes says that if Moriarty had second-guessed him it would have been a *coup-de-maître* FINA; Holmes says that if he is successful in this case, it will certainly represent the crowning glory of his career SECO.

match: -seller, ostensible TWIS; Holmes lights Selden's body with HOUN; Mason lights crypt with SHOS; Musgrave lights lantern with, to explore ancient cellar MUSG; Lestrade strikes: with dramatic suddenness NORW, on his boot STUD; Holmes orders from Watson, to light his cigarette FINA, to light some form of tobacco REDC, to illuminate scratches GOLD; lodger prints *match* instead of *matches;* shortness of burnt end shows they were used to light cigarettes; Watson strikes to light Gregson's lantern REDC; Garrideb (Evans) strikes a match, lights a candle-stump, and disappears from view 3GAR; *see also* **vesta.**

mate: Hudson addresses young Trevor with this low-class term GLOR.

mathematics: Moriarty (EMPT, FINA, ILLU, LAST, MISS, NORW, VALL) and Murdoch (LION) practice; for Holmes's knowledge of, *see* **rate; trigonometry.**

"Mathews": he knocked out Holmes's left canine in the Charing Cross waiting-room; he and Morgan (along with Moran) have entries in Holmes's index EMPT.

"Matilda Briggs": ship, associated with **rat,** q.v. SUSS.

Maudsley: Ryder's convict accomplice BLUE.

"Maupertuis, Baron": most accomplished swindler in Europe; Holmes has defeated his colossal schemes REIG.

Mawson & Williams's: famous financial house; Pycroft does not show up for his job there STOC.

May Day: Browner's ship CARD.

Maynooth: Earl of; Lady; their daughter, Hilda EMPT.

MAZA: also exists in the form of a performed (1921) but unpublished play, *The Crown Diamond: An Evening with Sherlock Holmes;* the story was apparently written after the play.

McCarthy: Charles; son James (not quick-witted, says Holmes) BOSC.

McCauley, Paramore, and Swain: not a law firm, but men disciplined by the Ku Klux Klan in Florida; Holmes refers to them as A, B, and C FIVE.

McFarlane: Mr. and Mrs.; son

" I AM DELIGHTED THAT YOU HAVE COME DOWN, MR. HOLMES."

John Hector; Holmes calls Mrs. McFarlane a little, fluffy, blue-eyed person NORW.

McGinty, John: Nickname Black Jack; Scowrer bodymaster; dead, dull, malevolent eyes, with a slight squint; diamond pins VALL.

McHardy: foreman IDEN.

McLaren, Miles: five foot six; his height is important to Holmes (*cf.* **Gilchrist**); nearly expelled from university over a card scandal 3STU.

McMurdo: former boxer, servant of B Sholto; once fought against Holmes; *see* **boxers** SIGN; Jack, alias of Birdy Edwards; hot Irish blood; a fine tenor, sings "I'm Sitting on the Stile, Mary" and "On the Banks of Allan Water"; calls Ettie *acushla*, but his courtship is awkward: disengages her hands, kisses her, and gently pushes her back into a chair; later he makes a tiger-spring at her; *see* **Douglas; Edwards; intercourse** VALL.

McPherson, Fitzroy: science master; glazed sunken eyes LION.

meals: eaten at least three times a day, sometimes five times; breakfast usually includes toast and coffee, sometimes eggs (Holmes's breakfast is untasted VALL); (high) tea is a substantial meal; dinner is followed, later in the evening, by supper HOUN, TWIS; *see* **food.**

meat, raw: Tonga eats SIGN; carried to Sahara King in a zinc pail VEIL.

medal: size of a soup-plate; Evans should have for killing Prescott 3GAR.

medical: instruments in wicker basket RESI; stethoscope in top-hat SCAN; students, Sarah Cushing's: noisy, irregular habits CARD; treatment, Watson's: *see* **brandy; ether; castor oil; cotton; morphine; oil; strychnine**; he reads the *British Medical Journal,* q.v.

mediæval pottery: Holmes discourses on SIGN.

Meek, Sir Jasper: doctor; Watson offers to summon DYIN.

meerschaum: never mentioned; *see* **pipe, smoking, and tobacco.**

melancholy: *see* **fit(s).**

Melas, Paul: interpreter in many languages; his English is perfect; sparkling dark eyes; olive face and coal black hair proclaims his Southern origin GREE.

Melville: brewer, friend of Eccles WIST.

memory: Presbury's is much more nimble than Holmes thought CREE; evil, Prescott's 3GAR; *see* **"Merridew, of abominable memory."**

*Mendelssohn-Bartholdy, Jacob Ludwig Felix (1809–1847): German composer STUD.

mentality: Watson's, has a certain methodical slowness (Watson's own estimate) CREE; he says, I am all in the dark TWIS; Holmes has remarkable mental qualities WIST; *see* **intellect; mind.**

Mercer: Holmes's utility man CREE; mutinous second-mate GLOR.

*Meredith, George (1828–1909): English writer BOSC.

meretricious: effect of Watson's stories, says Holmes CROO; *see* **Watson.**

Merivale: of the Yard; policeman SHOS.

"Merridew, of abominable memory": he is *remembered as* abominable; his powers of recollection were presumably in good order EMPT.

Merrilow, Mrs.: elderly, motherly woman of the buxom landlady type VEIL.

Merrow, Lord: letter from, in Hope's despatch-box SECO.

Merrywether: banker who misses his rubber REDH.

Merton: County, agricultural area in Gilmerton region of U.S., near Vermissa Valley VALL; Sam, boxer; large and ugly; stupid, obstinate; faithful, fatuous; slab-sided face MAZA.

mesmerism: Holmes has an almost hypnotic power of soothing when he wishes REDC; *see* **post-hypnotic.**

messages: coded, telegraphed, typed, written, play a role in many cases – e. g., BRUC, CHAS, COPP, DANC, FINA, GLOR, HOUN, IDEN, ILLU, MISS, PRIO, REIG, STUD, TWIS.

messenger: express, Holmes tells Watson to ring for one SIXN; district, dispatched with message for Gruner ILLU; government, Mycroft sends Holmes a note by BRUC; *see* **post; telegram.**

method: in (Holmes's) madness, Watson quotes Shakespeare,

Hamlet REIG; you know my methods, Watson (says Holmes) BLUE, CROO, DEVI; Hopkins knows Holmes's methods BLAC; Baynes has his own system, his own little ways WIST.

Meunier, Oscar: of Grenoble, maker of wax-works EMPT; *see* **Tavernier.**

Mexborough Private Hotel: Craven Street, Stapleton's hotel in London HOUN.

Meyer, Adolph: agent BRUC.

Meyers: Toronto bootmaker HOUN; *see* **Canada.**

Michael: stable-hand SUSS.

microscope: low power SHOS; *see* **dust; glue; hairs.**

Middlesex Corps: regiment in which Dodd and Emsworth served BLAN.

Miles, Hon. Miss: one of Milverton's blackmail victims CHAS.

milk: -boy, sees Hope after Stangerson murder STUD; -man, catches sight of Ronder, drops tin, milk all over front garden VEIL; -train: brings MacDonald report of crime VALL; and a biscuit, revive Huxtable; *see* **claret** PRIO; Holmes adds to terrier's poison-and-water STUD; cook's skin-colour: clay with a splash of –WIST; Small says he has learned not to cry over spilled – he has just thrown the Agra treasure into the Thames SIGN; *see* ***Thoreau, Henry David.**

Millar, Flora: *danseuse* NOBL.

Milner, Godfrey: Moran and Ronald Adair win four hundred and twenty pounds from him and Lord **Balmoral,** q.v., at whist EMPT.

Milverton, Charles Augustus: blackmailer; calls himself an agent; keen gray eyes; a plethoric sleeper (Holmes says); his murderess has a curved nose; worst man in London CHAS; *cf.* **Spaulding, Vincent,** the fourth smartest man in London.

mind: Watson's: utterly submerged EMPT; befogged SIGN; paralyzed HOUN; Holmes's and Watson's, absolutely blank CARD; Holmes's: like a crowded box-room LION, a lumber-room STUD, or attic carefully furnished and not crowded FIVE; gone DYIN; like a racing engine, tearing itself to pieces WIST; cold, precise, but admirably balanced SCAN; Watson is a whetstone for CREE; Holmes claims that he has watched the mind of a child (Edward Rucastle COPP) CREE; Holmes says, Suspicion, vague and nebulous, was now beginning to take outline in my mind; some dim perception that the matter was vital rose in my mind; in Stackhurst's mind also suspicions were forming LION; Holmes, sarcastically, to Gregson: to a great mind, nothing is little STUD; Holmes, sarcastically, to Watson: your reflection, though profound, had already crossed my mind MISS; Mycroft's is dominant BRUC; scheming, *see* **chess;** *cf.* **brains; genius; mentality.**

Ming: *see* **box.**

miniature: *see* **locket.**

mining: fortunes made from gold GLOR, ILLU, NOBL, STUD, THOR, VALL; coal and iron VALL; silver STUD; neolithic man mined tin upon Dartmoor; hound concealed in old tin mine in Grimpen Mire HOUN; tin mined in Cornwall since prehistoric times DEVI; fuller's earth – a subterfuge ENGR.

minutiæ: you have an extraordinary gift for (Watson to Holmes) SIGN; *see* **trifles.**

miracle plays: Holmes discourses on SIGN.

mirror: Hunter uses to spy on Fowler COPP; Holmes and Watson use to spy on lodger REDC; Holmes uses a silver-plated coffee-pot to spy on Watson HOUN; huge, heavily-gilt ones in McGinty's saloon VALL; Lady Frances's breath dims one LADY.

mitral valve: Sholto worries about his SIGN; *see* **disease.**

Mitton, John: valet of Eduardo Lucas; arrested for Lucas's murder but released SECO.

modesty: *see* **admiration.**

Moffat: bank robber RESI.

moidores: Brazilian coins; Small pictures himself coming home with pockets full of SIGN.

mole: he has been blind as a, Holmes says of himself TWIS; *see* **ass; beetle.**

"Molesey mystery": Holmes tells Lestrade that he (Lestrade) handled it fairly well in Holmes's absence EMPT.

money: the pound sterling was (and is) the basic British monetary unit; in the late nineteenth century it was equivalent to about $4.87 U.S.; today the exchange rate varies, but the pound usually = approximately $1.50 U.S.; the Victorian pound = 240 pence (the singular of *pence* is *penny;* today British money is on the decimal system, so one pound = 100 pence); farthing = 1/4 penny; shilling = 12 pence (thus, 20 shillings = 1 pound); florin = 2 shillings; half-crown = 2½ shillings; sovereign = gold coin worth 1 pound; guinea = 21 shillings. Slang: tanner = sixpence; bob = shilling; quid = pound; fiver, tenner = 5, 10 shillings, respectively; **equivalence:** in today's purchasing power, the late-nineteenth-century pound = about $183.00 U.S.; e.g., Moulton's hotel bill: room 8*s.* [i.e., 8 shillings], breakfast 2*s.* 6*d* [i.e., 2 shillings sixpence], lunch 2*s.* 6*d.*, cocktail 1*s.*, glass sherry 8*d.*; in modern American money = room $73.20, breakfast $22.88, lunch $22.88, cocktail $9.15, glass of sherry $6.10; from the charges for the room and sherry Holmes deduces that the hotel is an expensive one NOBL; **nineteenth-century American references:** seven dollars for a week's board and room (McMurdo's) at Shafter's VALL; seven thousand dollars: Ferrier has saved over twelve years; he is rich STUD; fifteen million dollars: Garrideb bequest (phony) 3GAR; **pay rates:** Holmes's fees: on a fixed scale, save when he remits them altogether THOR; five hundred pounds LAST; one thousand pounds SCAN; five thousand pounds 3GAB; twelve thousand pounds PRIO; *cf.* **education; game; work;** four pounds a month, a good wage COPP; sixty pounds a year, a nice income for a single lady IDEN; five hundred [pounds] a year, a very good salary for a clerk STOC; seven or eight hundred [pounds a year], hop-merchant's income, comfortably off YELL. **Some smaller amounts mentioned:** farthing, Holder won't give Arthur BERY; evening halfpenny newspaper HOUN; one-penny printed account of Birlstone Manor VALL; Mount-James screams that he will not spend a penny MISS; Stapleton swears he will spend his last penny to obtain divorce for Lyons HOUN; twopence per typewritten sheet IDEN; twopence a word for international telegrams LADY; fourpence worth of gin STUD; sixpence, chip on bridge not larger than THOR; six-penny packet of envelopes (expensive); Small and Tonga earn a hatful of pennies for their day's work SIGN; one-shilling map of London SIXN; one shilling per day for Cartwright HOUN; one shilling per day for Wiggins and each Irregular SIGN; Smith chucks shillings to the men at Jacobson's SIGN; uncle never gave Staunton a shilling in his life MISS; half-a-crown fee for Holmes's driver John TWIS; half a crown for a packet of notepaper SCAN; three bob and a tanner,

Wiggins asks Holmes for, to pay for Irregulars' (bus or Underground) tickets SIGN; five shillings, reply for telegram WIST; six shillings, wholesale for a plaster bust, retail for twelve to fifteen shillings (Holmes buys one for ten pounds) SIXN; Holmes bribes Rance with half-sovereign STUD; half-sovereigns for sailors BLAC and for cabman HOUN; Watson's disability pay is eleven shillings and sixpence per day STUD; Norton offers cabman half a guinea, Holmes offers cabman half a sovereign, Adler offers her driver half a sovereign to get to church in twenty minutes; Adler gives Holmes a sovereign for witnessing wedding, so he is ahead ten shillings SCAN; Holmes tries to hire bicycle from Hayes with a sovereign PRIO; **Large amounts:** value of Holmes's Stradivarius five hundred guineas (£750), for which he paid fifty-five shillings CARD; one thousand pounds in Elsie's hand-bag DANC, in King of Bohemia's chamois-leather bag SCAN; five thousand pounds for round-the-world trip for Maberley 3GAB; seven thousand pounds for blackmail CHAS; seven thousand pounds, Worthingdon bank robbed of RESI; fourteen thousand pounds, Openshaw estate FIVE; twenty thousand pounds, value of Blue Carbuncle (one-thousand-pound reward for its return) BLUE; thirty thousand pounds, bank loot REDH; forty thousand pounds, Moriarty's Greuze worth VALL; fifty thousand pounds, Prince of Wales needs loan of (banker gives him fifty one-thousand-pound notes) BERY; eighty thousand pounds, Norberton's Derby winnings SHOS; one hundred thousand-pound robbery MAZA, STOC; two hundred thousand pounds, Prescott's counterfeit notes 3GAR; nearly a quarter of a million [pounds], Prendergast amasses through fraud GLOR; half a million [pounds] sterling, value of Agra treasure SIGN; seven hundred and forty thousand pounds, value of Baskerville estate HOUN. **miscellaneous sums, often important to the plot:** 5 half-crowns in Watson's pockets – too few, says Holmes DYIN; four hundred and twenty-one pennies, two hundred and seventy half-pennies in Hugh Boone's pockets; he earns more than seven hundred pounds a year begging TWIS; four pounds a week, Wilson earns copying the encyclopædia REDH; eight pounds a month, salary asked for by Cairns, an expert harpooner BLAC; seven pounds thirteen [shillings], in Drebber's pocket STUD; two guineas, Stapleton gives cabman for a day's hire; five hundred pounds, one thousand pounds, Sir Charles's bequests to Barrymores and Mortimer, respectively HOUN; £1,100 a year, Mrs. Stoner's bequest; through fall in agricultural prices now worth not more than £750 SPEC; four thousand seven hundred [pounds], plumbing business sold for IDEN; thirteen guineas, doctor's fee MISS;

twenty-two guineas for dress for Straker's mistress SILV; fifty-pound wedding-present, Lady Frances to Devine; one hundred pounds, Shlessinger claims Lady Frances owes him; a sovereign, Holmes offers undertaker's man (calls him, my man) if the coffin-lid comes off in a minute LADY; fifty guineas for a night's work ENGR; bad florin – actually a rupee CROO; two hundred pounds, Arthur needs to repay gambling debt; one thousand pounds redemption, per beryl BERY; five [shillings] and threepence, Trevelyan's one-quarter share of each guinea earned RESI; five sovereigns, interpreter's fee GREE; fiver, Holmes wagers with Breckinridge, but it is raised to a sovereign BLUE; tenner, Mount-James offers, to bear expenses up to MISS; ten-pound note, Holmes sends Porlock an occasional; Moriarty pays Moran six thousand pounds a year VALL; ten pounds, Holmes's bribe for Susan 3GAB; ten-pound note, Simpson's intended bribe for stablehands; mistaken for a paperful of opium SILV; four hundred and twenty pounds, Moran wins at card-game EMPT; fifty shillings a week for room and board; lodger offers five pounds REDC; five hundred pounds, Von Bork pays supposed Irish-American traitor LAST; one pound a day for board and room at Charpentier's STUD; one thousand pounds for every body thrown into Thames from the Bar of Gold TWIS; twenty-seven pounds ten [shillings], Hatherley earns in two years' practice ENGR; fifty guineas, Watson's brother's watch worth SIGN; eightpence an ounce for Grosvenor mixture (tobacco); good pipe for seven [shillings]-and-sixpence; four thousand five hundred pounds, Effie's capital; eighty pounds, annual cost for Munro's villa YELL; Holmes suggests that Cunningham offer a fifty-pound reward for killer REIG; securities worth seven thousand pounds missing RETI; **foreign (other than American):** moidores SIGN, napoleons REDH, rupees CROO, SIGN.

mongoose: *see* **Teddy.**

monkey: *see* **ape; baboon; Teddy; voodoo.**

monocle: *see* **glasses.**

Montague Street: Holmes's rooms in, before Baker Street; near the British Museum MUSG.

Montgomery, Inspector: policeman CARD.

Montalva, Marquess of: *see* **Murillo.**

Montpellier: city in France (misspelled *Montpelier* in some editions); Holmes does chemical research there EMPT; Watson seeks Devine there LADY; site of cases involving Lefevre and Lesurier STUD.

"Montpensier, Mme": accused of murdering Carère; one of the two cases that Holmes solves after the conclusion of the Baskerville affair HOUN.

Montrachet: wine VEIL.

moon: Holmes says that if the earth travelled round the sun or the moon it would not make a pennyworth of difference to him or his work STUD; insanity not due to phases of, Holmes says CREE.

moor: word in note to Sir Henry printed in ink, not cut out of newspaper HOUN; *see* **Dartmoor.**

Moorhouse: Staunton's rugby team-mate MISS.

Moran: Patience, daughter of lodge-keeper BOSC; Col. Sebastian, second most dangerous man in London; old *shikari* (hunter); thin, projecting nose; high, bald forehead; huge, grizzled moustache EMPT, ILLU, LAST, VALL; *see* **nose,** *and cf.* **Spaulding.**

Morcar, Countess of: owner of gem BLUE.

Morecroft: *see* **Winter.**

"Morgan, the poisoner" EMPT; *see* **Mathews.**

Moriarty, Professor James: the Napoleon of crime; foul spider; oscillating head; deeply sunken eyes EMPT, FINA, ILLU, LAST, NORW, VALL; his gang is in the hands of the police in FINA but is back at full strength in EMPT; Holmes says the formidable Armstrong could take his place MISS; Colonel James, his brother, oddly bears the same given name FINA; another (younger) brother, station-master in the west of England VALL; *see* **arms; binomial; Dynamics; serpent.**

Morland, Sir John: Frankland wins suit against him for shooting in his own warren HOUN.

morocco case: square, black, lined with flesh-coloured velvet, containing the coronet BERY; neat, containing Holmes's hypodermic syringe SIGN; *see* **cocaine; syringe.**

morphine: Holmes's alternative to cocaine SIGN; Oakshott injects Holmes; Watson injects Gruner ILLU; Murdoch cries for morphia LION; *see* **cocaine; opium.**

Morphy: Professor; daughter Alice, Presbury engaged to CREE.

Morris: Brother, reluctant Scowrer; his poor little woman and children make him a coward; McGinty calls him a skunk VALL; William, one of Archie's aliases REDH.

Morrison: Annie, ethereal slip of a girl with timid eyes and blonde hair CROO; Morrison, Morrison, and Dodd, solicitors SUSS.

Morstan: Captain Arthur SIGN; daughter Mary, Mrs. Watson CROO, ENGR, FIVE, FINA, SIGN, STOC, TWIS; large, blue, singularly spiritual eyes; well-gloved SIGN; does needlework; calls Watson James TWIS; Holmes is persuaded to accept occasional invitations *chez* Watson ENGR, but there are no accounts of these *visites à trois;* she is often conveniently absent, allowing Watson to go off on cases with Holmes; when Holmes asks about her and Watson replies, She is away upon a visit, Holmes's response, Indeed! You are alone? is both

insulting and suggestive FINA; her mother is dead in SIGN but is mysteriously resurrected to explain Mary's absences – e.g., she is on a visit to her mother's FIVE; Mary dies during the **Great Hiatus,** q.v., and Holmes consoles Watson EMPT; for her possible successor(s), *see* **wives,** s.v. **Watson, John H.**

Mortimer: James, M. R. C. S., long nose like a beak, gold-rimmed glasses; his wife (of whom we know nothing, Holmes says) never appears, and at the end of the case James Mortimer and Sir Henry Baskerville take a world tour, apparently leaving her at home alone on the desolate moor HOUN; Coram's gardener, who also helps him to dress GOLD.

Morton: Cyril, electrician SOLI; Inspector, policeman, in unofficial tweeds; eyes gleam when told of Holmes's illness (*cf.* Smith, who smiles when told of it) DYIN; one of the Oxford flyers, Staunton's rugby opponents MISS; and Kennedy, famous Westminster electricians SOLI; and Waylight, where Warren is timekeeper REDC.

Moser, Monsieur: well-known hotel manager LADY.

mothers: *see* **old** (women).

motives: they are sometimes difficult for the reader – or even for Holmes – to determine; but one may say that revenge is the motive in almost a third of the stories (e.g., ABBE, BLAC, STUD); and greed plays a role in almost

half (e.g., BERY, BLUE, BRUC); *cf.*
prisoners.

Moulton, Francis Hay: called
Frank by his wife; kidnapped by
Apaches, q.v. NOBL.

Mount-James, Lord: unpleasant,
miserly peer; one of the richest
men in England; old and gouty
MISS; *see* **bus; chalk.**

mouse: *see* **dressing-gown; Emsworth.**

moustaches: *see* **beards.**

mouth: of a murderer; cruel, hard
gash (Smith's) DYIN; cruel, vicious (Shlessinger's) LADY; cruel,
thin-lipped (Sylvius's) MAZA;
cravat covers Walter's BRUC;
petulance about St. Simon's
NOBL; sensitive, tight and drawn
(Lady Hilda's) SECO; weak, sensitive (McFarlane's) NORW; for
Holmes's, *see* **toast.**

M. R. C. S.: Member Royal College of Surgeons; *see* **Mortimer.**

mud: Holmes studies BOSC, SILV;
see **earth;** -coloured clouds SIGN.

muffler, shepherd's check: Brunton's, tied to iron ring MUSG; *cf.*
cravat.

"Muller, the notorious" STUD.

mummy: head and a few bones of
SHOS.

Munro: Grant, hop-merchant;
called Jack by his wife, Effie; she
has a daughter (*see* **genetics**),
Lucy, from her former marriage
to Hebron YELL; Colonel
Spence, Hunter's former employer COPP.

Murcher, Harry: Rance's fellow
policeman STUD.

murderers: (including those who
attempt it and those who act in
self-defense or out of vengeance)
see **Amberley** (Josiah); **Apaches;
Beppo; Biddle; Browner, Jim;
Cairns, Patrick; Calhoun,
Captain James; Cunningham;
Dixie, Steve; Douglas** (John);
**Gruner, Baron Adelbert; Har-
rison** (Joseph); **Hayes** (Reuben);
Hayward; Hope (Jefferson);
Howells, Rachel; Lucca (Gen-
naro); **Moffatt; Moran** (Colonel
Sebastian); **Moriarty** (Professor
James); **murderess** (anony-
mous, Milverton's); **Oberstein,
Hugo; Roylott, Dr. Grimesby;
Shlessinger, Dr., and wife;
Scowrers; Selden; Silver Blaze;
Smith** (Culverton); **Stangerson,
Joseph; Stapleton** (Jack); **Stern-
dale, Dr. Leon; Sylvius, Count
Negretto; Tonga; Tregennis**
(Mortimer); **Turner** (John);
these include three women;
Holmes was the intended victim
of six – the Cunninghams, Moran, Moriarty, Roylott, Smith,
and Sylvius; among those who
would probably have liked to
murder him are Agatha (the
maid he jilted) CHAS, and (sometimes) Mrs. Hudson (his landlady), and Watson; *cf.* **blackmail;
thieves.**

**murderess (anonymous, Milver-
ton's)** CHAS.

Murdoch, Ian: hurls dog through
plate-glass window; coal-black
eyes; lives in a high, abstract region of surds and conic sections;

insists upon an algebraic demonstration before breakfast LION.

*Murger, Henri (1822–1861): French author; Watson skips over the pages of his *La Vie de Bohème* while waiting for Holmes to return STUD.

Murillo, Don Juan: Tiger of San Pedro (imaginary Latin American country); step of a deer, air of an emperor, yellow and sapless; enormously rich; uses the name Henderson in England; two daughters, ages eleven and thirteen; as the Marquess of Montalva, he is probably murdered in Spain WIST; case apparently referred to as "the papers of ex-President Murillo" NORW; *see* **dog-whip.**

Murphy: Major, Barclay's fellow officer CROO; one Murphy, gypsy horse-dealer HOUN.

Murray: Watson's orderly STUD; Mr., plays cards with Moran EMPT.

Musgrave, Reginald: Holmes describes him: exceedingly aristocratic type, thin, high-nosed, and large-eyed, with languid and yet courtly manners MUSG.

music: of the Middle Ages, Holmes's hobby BRUC; Holmes prefers German to Italian or French REDH; *see* **Brunton, Richard; *Chopin, Frédéric François; composer; *Lassus, Orlandus; *Mendelssohn-Bartholdy, Jakob Ludwig Felix; *Norman-Néruda, Wilhelmine; *Offenbach, Jacques; *Paganini, Niccolò; *Peace, Charlie; piano; polyphonic; *Sarasate y Na-**

vascués, Pablo Martín Melitón; Smith (James, Violet); **violin; *Wagner, Richard;** for Irish songs, *see* **McMurdo, Jack.**

mutton: curried, drugged SILV.

muzzle: cold, of revolver, Watson presses to Cairns's head BLAC.

nails: Holmes bites BRUC, STOC; tears at floorboards with SECO; Lyons's pink ones turn white with the pressure of her grip HOUN; Garcia gnaws his WIST; *see* **fingers.**

name: first, Holmes and Watson never call each other by; Mycroft and Sherlock use first names (naturally enough) BRUC, GREE; surprisingly, Sherman calls Holmes Mr. Sherlock SIGN; Watson's, *see* **James; problems;** MacDonald refers to Watson as your friend here, evidently having forgotten Watson's name VALL; Smith forgets Watson's name DYIN; some gems bear names: the Great Mogul SIGN; the Black Pearl of the Borgias SIXN; the Countess of Morcar's Blue Carbuncle BLUE; the Mazarin Stone MAZA; *cf.* **Americans;** *and see* **John; Mary; Violet.**

*Nana Sahib (circa 1820–): Indian rebel; real name Dandhu Panth SIGN.

*Napoleon I (1769–1821): last name Bonaparte; French emperor (1804–1815); busts of SIXN; gold coins named for, spelled with lower-case *n* REDH; Holmes calls Moriarty the Napoleon of crime FINA.

nark: informer; not, as in the U.S. word *narc,* from *narcotics* [agent] but from Romany word for *nose;* Johnson has never been one for the police ILLU.

National Hotel: Lausanne, Watson stays at LADY.

native Americans: Hope is as sharp as a Washoe hunter STUD; Apaches allegedly kill (actually kidnap) Moulton NOBL; Holmes is a red Indian – stoical CROO, NAVA.

nature: Holmes has no appreciation for CARD, RESI, SILV; but he retires to the soothing life of LION; Holmes says that when one tries to rise above nature one is liable to fall below it CREE; Holmes proposes a stroll in the sunshine, but it is a pretext NORW; Nature's iron grip on London; Holmes and Watson loiter the morning away in the garden GOLD; solitary country walks, on one of which Holmes buys a lamp DEVI; It is very pleasant to see the first green shoots upon the hedges and the catkins on the hazels once again WIST; Holmes and Watson go for a walk in the Park, where the first green shoots are breaking out upon the elms, and the sticky spear-heads of the chestnuts are just beginning to burst into their five-fold leaves; but when they return home and Holmes discovers that he has missed a client, he exclaims, So much for afternoon walks! YELL; *see* **flora; moor; rotting.**

"Naval Treaty" (= NAVA) FINA.

Navy: it costs Mrs. Charpentier a great deal to keep her son Arthur in STUD.

needlework: appropriate for ladies: *see* **Cushing** (Susan); **Hudson** (Mrs.); **Morstan** (Mary).

needle(s): Irregulars as sharp as STUD; for the apocryphal Quick, Watson, the . . . , *see* **quick.**

negro: Newton's horse is named The Negro SILV; *see* **black fellows; cook; Dixie, Steve; Hebron** (John); **Openshaw** (Elias); **voodoo.**

__Neill, General James George Smith__ (1810–1857): British army leader in India CROO.

Neligan, John Copley: son of absconding, dead, banker father; an anæmic youth; frightened eyes; wears knickerbockers BLAC.

Nepal: Wood taken there by his captors CROO.

neolithic man: remains of on moor HOUN; *see* **celts.**

nerves: Sir Henry's quiver, says Watson HOUN; Hunter's overstrung nerves fail her and she runs COPP; Moran a man of iron nerve EMPT; Green's like live wires LADY; Holmes soothes others' nerves with **cigarettes; cigars; coffee,** qq.v.

net(s): Holmes's frequent metaphor for his plans to trap a criminal; in HOUN, for instance, it is used at least four times; also uses *toils* FINA, *web* FIVE.

"Netherland Sumatra Company": the case has required

immense exertions from Holmes REIG; *see* **rat.**

newspapers: Holmes reads them all, especially the *Times* and the *Evening Telegraph*, makes huge balls of them BOSC; crumpled piles BLUE, TWIS; bundle of fresh SILV; Watson makes into a cloud, a bundle NOBL; *Times* seldom found in hands but those of the highly educated, Holmes says HOUN; Holmes uses its files to determine the date of Sholto's death SIGN; some are incredibly quick with their reports of crime NORW; advertisements placed in BLAC, BLUE, BRUC, ENGR, GREE, IDEN, NAVA, REDH, STUD, 3GAR, WIST; letters cut from HOUN; *Journal de Genève* carries account of Holmes's demise FINA; cutting from Buda-Pesth paper tells of stabbing deaths of two Englishmen GREE; Wilson pulls out a dirty, wrinkled newspaper from pocket REDH; Breckinridge carries the Pink 'Un, a sporting paper BLUE; Pike contributes to the garbage papers that cater to the general public 3GAB; Kent reads the *Spectator*, from which Holmes draws unexplained inferences BLAN; *see* **agony column; leading article; type-faces.**

Newton, Heath: his horse entered in race SILV.

New York: Holmes has some knowledge of, though he appears to believe that there are caves on **Long Island,** q.v. REDC; does he go there to solve the Montpensier case? HOUN.

New Zealand: Sutherland gets 4 1/2 % from stocks IDEN.

Niagara: inferred from drop of water STUD; whizzing and buzzing in Browner's ears CARD.

nick: subcutaneous and undetectable, on horse's ham (Holmes's phrase) SILV.

nickel and tin: amalgam used by counterfeiters ENGR.

nicknames: Baldy (*see* **Simpson**); *see* **boots; buttons;** growler (*see* **cab**); Holy (*see* **Peters, Henry** ("**Holy**"); Jem (*see* **Ryder**); Porky (*see* **Johnson**); *see* **Scowrers;** Tadpole (*see* **Phelps**); Tiger (*see* **Cormac**).

night: *see* **vigil.**

night-glasses: binoculars; Holmes uses SIGN; *see* **field-glass.**

nightmare: architectural, Gruner's house ILLU.

nightshirt: Heidegger dies in his, with a coat thrown over it PRIO.

Nihilism: murder in Spain attributed to WIST; *see* **Anna; Klopman; Von und Zu Grafenstein, Count.**

nitrite of amyl: Trevelyan uses to revive cataleptic patient RESI; *see* **chemistry;** *cf.* **Watson's medical prescriptions.**

NN: from these two remaining letters, Holmes deduces pencilmaker 3STU; *see* **P-E-N.**

"Noble Bachelor": (= NOBL) COPP

noise: creak and crackle (Holmes's and Watson's footsteps); long, whirling (whirring?), grinding; clang, click, whiz, tinkle, whistle

EMPT; fire crackles and snaps; thin, crisp, continuous patter; curious scuffling; sharp click of a cocking pistol HOUN; sharp snick CHAS, click LAST of electric-light switch; sharp snap of a twisted key; squealing (of dying coolies) DYIN; guggling, gargling, heel-tapping STOC; postman's rat-tat SIGN; door gives way with a snap SIGN; sharp crack of pistol hitting parapet THOR; sharp metallic snap of a key 3GAR; sharp metallic snick; creaking of key NAVA; creak of a turning key REDC; metallic scraping and clinking; snap and creak of hinges BLAC; whiz and clank (police boat's engines); pant and clank (*Aurora's* engines) SIGN; creaking of train brakes; heavy thud, as of a body striking the railway line; door flies open with a sharp crash BRUC; gentle, soothing sound, like steam from a kettle (it is actually a snake's hiss) SPEC; shuffling sound, then two sharp taps with the knocker BRUC; Von Bork's great car shivers and chuckles LAST; drone of misery and despair MISS; *see* **clang; Hoffmann Barcarolle; screams; skirts; violin; whining; whistle; women** (for ululation, whimpering).

non-conformist clergyman: Holmes's disguise SCAN.

"Nonpareil Club" HOUN; *see* **Upwood, Colonel.**

noon: marriage must be performed before SCAN.

Norah Creina: ship, lost off Oporto, taking with her Biddle, Hayward, and Moffatt, Blessington's murderers RESI.

Norberton, Sir Robert: violent, penurious man of the turf; when his Derby winnings pay off debtors, police and coroner give him only a mild censure for hiding the death of his sister SHOS.

Norlett, Mr. and Mrs.: rat-faced actor, impersonates dead woman; she acts as maid under maiden name Evans SHOS.

Norman Conquest: ancient oak was at Hurlstone before MUSG.

*Norman-Néruda, Wilhelmine (1839–1911): violinist; name misspelled Norman Neruda; married to **Hallé, Charles,** q.v. STUD.

North America: central portion an arid and repulsive desert STUD; *see* **Pacific slope.**

Northumberland Hotel: Sir Henry stays there HOUN (located at no. 11 Northumberland Street; now Sherlock Holmes Pub).

Norton, Godfrey: lawyer, weds Adler SCAN.

Norway: Holmes poses as Norwegian named Sigerson EMPT; banker Neligan's yacht founders off the coast of; as the tale concludes, Holmes suddenly announces that he and Watson are on their way there, but since the securities are lost, he cannot hope to recover them; no other explanation is provided BLAC.

Norwood NORW, SIGN.

nose: Holmes's hawk-like SIGN, STUD; long-curved, like beak of eagle (Sylvius) MAZA; curved (Milverton's murderess CHAS,

Baldwin VALL); *see* **Bellinger, Lord; bird; Emsworth** (Colonel); **Holdernesse, Duke of; Milverton, Charles Augustus; Moran** (Colonel Sebastian); **Mortimer** (James); **Musgrave, Reginald; powder; Prendergast, Jack; Ras, Daulat; sheeny; Slaney, Abe; Stark, Colonel Lysander; Sterndale, Dr. Leon.**

nostrils: Holmes's quiver BRUC; for Turner's, *see* **lip.**

note: Holmes tells Watson to take it to Mrs. Ferguson SUSS.

nothing new under the sun: Holmes quotes the Bible (Ecclesiastes 1:9) STUD.

Notting Hill: hooligan, Gregson treats Mrs. Lucca like REDC; murderer (Selden) HOUN.

novel, yellow-backed: Hunter reads bits of one to Rucastle COPP; Watson nods over one CROO.

number: in titles: one SOLI, two SECO, three 3GAB 3GAR 3STU, four SIGN, five FIVE, six SIXN; 2704, of cab HOUN; 97613 inscribed in Drebber's watch STUD; seventeen, steps from ground floor to Holmes's apartment at 221B SCAN; nine to seven, seven to five: Avenging Angels' sign and countersign STUD; V. V. 341, Scowrers' Lodge VALL; seven of ten: papers (parts of the submarine plans) in Cadogan West's pocket BRUC; sixteen characteristics of typewriter type-face, Holmes identifies IDEN; forty-two prints of bicycle tyres, Holmes can identify PRIO; one hundred forty varieties of tobacco ash, Holmes can identify BOSC; seventy-five perfumes, Holmes can distinguish HOUN; one hundred sixty ciphers, Holmes analyzes DANC; thirty-one, Watson's old school number RETI; nine, days between Presbury's injections CREE; twenty-seven, a sweet age (Watson *re* M Morstan SIGN); X2473, identifying number for Mycroft's advertisement in the *Daily News* GREE; of Holmes's last fifty-four cases, the police have had all the credit in forty-nine; twenty-three, Holmes's years in practice, Watson cooperating for seventeen VEIL; telephone: *see* **XX.31;** *see also* **seven; treasure.**

nurse: nanny, Effie's daughter's; speaks in a northern accent (wantin', ye) YELL; medical, Phelps's, pours out some stimulating medicine for him NAVA.

nuts: can't sprint for (Moorhouse, rugby player; i.e., he cannot run fast) MISS; nutshells, old Trevor's face in GLOR.

Oakshott: Mr. and wife Maggie, poulterers BLUE; Sir Leslie, famous surgeon who attends Holmes ILLU.

Oberstein, Hugo: agent; one of the three capable of playing so bold a game as the theft of the letter from the foreign potentate SECO; gets fifteen years for spying, though he murdered Cadogan West; Holmes calls him a cunning dog BRUC.

observe: *see* **see.**

Odessa: *see* "**Dolsky in Odessa**"; "**Trepoff murder in Odessa.**"

*****Offenbach, Jacques** (1819–1880): French composer; *see* **Hoffmann Barcarolle** MAZA.

oil: Watson prescribes ILLU, LION; castor, two drops: Watson warns against any larger dosage SIGN.

Oldacre, Jonas: ferret-like (*cf.* **Lestrade, G.**), shifty, light gray eyes, white eyelashes; whines incessantly; alias Cornelius NORW.

old brick and timber gables: Riding Thorpe Manor DANC.

old: Holmes's disguises: lady, sporting man MAZA, man, opium addict TWIS, priest FINA, bookseller EMPT; old woman be damned! Holmes exclaims, re Hope's disguise STUD; "old Russian woman": records of this case are in Holmes's tin box MUSG; there are many old women, most of them daft, deaf, or dead – *see* **Dobney, Susan;** Kirwan, William (half-witted mother); **Mac-Namara, Widow; Merrilow, Mrs.; Spender, Rose; Westphail, Honoria.**

Oldmore, Mrs., and maid HOUN.

old sweet song, the: Holmes says Von Bork's *I shall get level with you!* was the favourite ditty of Moriarty, and Moran has also been known to warble it LAST.

Only one important thing has happened in the last three days, and that is that nothing has happened (Holmes) SECO; *see* **dog, non-barking; Holmesisms.**

opalescent London reek: fog ABBE.

Openshaw: Joseph; son John; brother Colonel Elias, aversion to negroes and to the Republican policy toward them FIVE; *see* **unbreakable.**

opium LION, SIGN, STUD, TWIS; Burnet drugged with WIST; Holmes knows that it is by no means tasteless; powdered, added to curried mutton SILV; does Holmes really smoke it? TWIS; *see* **cocaine; morphine.**

optical instruments: *see* **field-glass; glass** (magnifying); **glasses (spectacles); microscope; nightglasses; telescope.**

oranges: dish of, Holmes knocks over, to divert attention REIG (*see* **cigarettes; watering-pot**); Holmes tears one to pieces FIVE; redheads look like coster's barrow full of REDH.

orchid: among mare's tails, Beryl Stapleton asks for HOUN.

organisation: *see* **agency.**

Ormstein: *see* **Bohemia, King of.**

Orontes: troopship, brought Watson home from India STUD.

ostrich feather: smoke from burning house is like ENGR; Straker's mistress's dress is decorated with one SILV; *see* **dress;** *cf.* **flamingo.**

out (i.e., abroad in the United States and Canada): when he was out, Sir Henry had something to do with **dogs,** q.v. HOUN.

outhouse: you must go to the (Susan Cushing to Lestrade) CARD; Peter Carey had built himself a wooden one BLAC; in it you will find a considerable quantity of straw (Holmes to three policemen) NORW; by the kitchen door COPP; in corner of orchard HOUN; room accessible from top of WIST; Ferrier's servants sleep in STUD; several small ones BLAN; Gregory has searched every stable and SILV.

Out of Doors (1874): by J. G. Wood; Holmes's little chocolate and silver volume, in which he reads of Cyanea LION.

ouvrier: = French worker; Holmes's disguise LADY.

overcoat: Watson carries burglar-tools in his BRUC.

Overton, Cyril: captain of rugby team, Trinity College, Cambridge MISS.

ox: *see* **pole-axed.**

Oxford: *see* **Cambridge; Camford; Eton and Oxford.**

oysters: subjects of Holmes's feigned feverish ramblings; he cannot think why the ocean bed is not one solid mass of them DYIN; oysters and a brace of grouse, and something a little choice in white wines SIGN.

Pacific slope: includes Utah STUD; *see* **North America.**

packet: of incriminating papers, Anna withdraws from bosom (along with poison?) GOLD.

Paddington: northwestern borough of London; one of Watson's surgeries there ENGR; for Paddington railway station, *see* **trains.**

pads of cotton-wool soaked in salad oil: prescribed and applied by Holmes for Murdoch's lion's-mane wounds LION.

*Paganini, Niccolò (1782–1840): Italian violinist CARD.

page: missing from Watson's letter to Holmes HOUN; *see* **Billy; buttons.**

pail: of raw meat VEIL; of blood WIST.

painters: *see* ***Bouguereau, Adolphe William; *Corot, Jean Baptiste Camille; *Greuze, Jean Baptiste; *Kneller, Sir Godfrey; *Raphael; *Reynolds, Sir Joshua; *Rosa, Salvator; *Vernet, Émile Jean Horace.**

palimpsest: manuscript, Holmes deciphers; nothing more exciting than an abbey's accounts dating from the second half of the fifteenth century GOLD; *see* **manuscript.**

*Palladio, Andrea (1508–1580): Italian architect ABBE.

Palmer: bicycle tyre PRIO; *see* **Dunlop.**

Palmyra: ship on which the Douglases sail for South Africa VALL.

paper: of native Indian manufacture (Holmes deduces) SIGN; pink, not English SCAN; blue-tinted, KKK document FIVE; gray roll of, secret treaty between England and Italy NAVA; St. Clair uses the fly-leaf of a book to write to his wife TWIS; crackling ABBE; for papers thrown into fire but unburned, *see* **letters;** *and see* **blotting-paper; en-**

velope; fly-paper; foolscap; handwriting; litmus-paper; packet; sundial; watermark.

paperweight: Holmes uses his cigarette case as, to hold down his farewell note to Watson FINA; *see also* **collections.**

"Paradol Chamber": unexplained and inexplicable FIVE.

parcels: unwelcome, grotesque, or surprising, containing ears CARD, ape-serum CREE, ivory box DYIN, pearls SIGN.

paregoric: Holmes (not Watson) prescribes 3GAB.

parasol: *see* **umbrella.**

park (evidently Hyde Park): Sir Henry imprudently walks in, observing the folk HOUN; Holmes and Watson walk in YELL.

Parker: garrotter; Moran's sentinel, set to watch 221B; *see* **jew's harp** EMPT; Coxon's manager STOC; vicar DANC.

paroxysm: of terror HOUN; of energy (Holmes's) SECO.

Parr, Lucy: maid BERY.

Parthian shot: Holmes fires at Lestrade and Gregson STUD.

partridge: cold VEIL.

passenger enters vehicle: at end of journey, has disappeared IDEN, STUD; *see* **vehicles.**

passion(s): Sutherland's oath of fidelity a sign of IDEN; softer, Holmes sneers at SCAN.

pâté-de-foie-gras: pie; along with woodcock, pheasant, and ancient wines — the friendly supper Holmes offers to St. Simon, who refuses to partake NOBL.

Pathan: vile; pronounced pah-TAN; an Afghan tribesman SIGN.

pathology: Watson plunges into latest treatise on SIGN; for Holmes's research, *see* **scales.**

Patrick: *see* **Cubitt** DANC.

Patterson, Inspector: policeman FINA.

Pattins, Hugh: seaman; long, dried-up creature, lank hair, sallow cheeks; given a half-sovereign and sent on his way BLAC.

pavement (sidewalk): slimy SIGN; slippery BERY; Holmes beats REDH; *see* **affaire; asphalt.**

pawky humour: Holmes says that Watson is developing a certain unexpected vein of, against which he (Holmes) must learn to guard himself, after this exchange: Holmes: You have heard me speak of Professor Moriarty? Watson: A famous scientific criminal, as famous among crooks as − . Holmes: My blushes, Watson! Watson: I was about to say, as he is unknown to the public VALL; *see* **touch.**

P. C.: by coincidence, the initials of both Patrick Cairns and Peter Carey BLAC; *see* **F. H. M.**

*Peace, Charlie (1832–1879): criminal and violinist ILLU.

peacock: Tonga as proud as, when he kills Sholto SIGN.

pea-jacket: Lestrade's, wet NOBL; Holmes wears, part of disguise SIGN; Holmes wears again, not part of disguise REDH; McMurdo wears VALL.

pearl: pearl-box replaced in Morstan's bosom SIGN; *see* **Borgias; jewels; treasure.**

peasants: tell story of phantom hound HOUN; Holmes dispatches one (a peat-cutter) to Huxtable PRIO; *see* **clogs.**

pebbles: or gravel, Presbury CREE and Sterndale DEVI throw; *see* **jewels.**

peculiarities of style, Conan Doyle's: folding it carefully up DANC; my participation in some of his adventures was always a privilege which entailed discretion and reticence upon me DEVI; simious and ape-like appearance

STUD; apocrypha (esoterica?) of the agony column VALL; a coloured purple stole round his neck VALL; knife driven blade-deep (haft-deep?) REDC; ventilate the facts THOR; Sierra Blan*co* (mentioned several times) STUD; Signora Durando, Signor Rulli (since they are from a Spanish-speaking country, one would expect *Señor, Señora,* rather than the Italian forms) WIST; pacing up and down . . . with restless, picking fingers SIGN; one is liable . . . CREE, art in the blood is liable . . . GREE, simple things which are extremely liable to be overlooked SIGN (purists would prefer *likely*); Holmes sat up with a whistle BLUE; long, whirling (surely "whirring"), grinding noise EMPT; I shall have the others, but he first FIVE; we stood with bitter hearts HOUN.

peering: and benevolent curiosity, general look of, adopted by Holmes in disguise as simple-minded Nonconformist clergyman SCAN; general air of peering benevolence (Mortimer) HOUN.

P-E-N: from these letters (the rest sawed off) on fluting between shotgun barrels, Holmes identifies Pennsylvania Small Arms Company, well-known firm VALL; *see* **NN.**

pen: broad-pointed, probably a J, and very inferior ink CARD; another J GREE; sharp-pointed WIST; bad (and ink), found only in hotels HOUN; thick VALL; with heavy heart Watson takes his up FINA; *see* **handwriting; quill.**

Penang lawyer: walking stick HOUN, SILV.

pencil: indelible RETI; Holmes breaks his twice, intentionally 3STU; lodger prints in broad-pointed, violet-tinted REDC; St. Clair uses for his note his wife TWIS; Trevelyan uses for note to Holmes RESI.

perfume: white jessamine, Holmes identifies HOUN; *see* **number; smell.**

Perkins: driver HOUN; young Perkins, murdered by Steve Dixie outside the Holborn Bar; Holmes knows all about it 3GAB; groom HOUN.

"Persano, Isadora, well-known journalist and duellist": found stark staring mad with a match box in front of him which contained a remarkable worm said to be unknown to science; an unfinished case whose records are at Cox and Co. THOR; *see* **box; lunatic.**

Persian: slipper, in which Holmes keeps tobacco EMPT, ILLU, MUSG, NAVA; saying, by Hafiz, which Holmes quotes: There is danger for him who taketh the tiger cub, and danger also for whoso snatches [not *snatcheth*, which would be consistent with *taketh*] a delusion from a woman IDEN.

Peter: groom SOLI.

Peters, Henry ("Holy"): real name of Shlessinger LADY.

Peterson: commissionaire BLUE.

*Petrarch (Francesco Petrarca, 1304–1374): Italian poet BOSC.

pheasants: Gibson's estate has a preserve for THOR; *see* **paté.**

Phelps, Percy: "Tadpole"; fiancée Annie, sister of Harrison NAVA.

"Phillimore, James": stepped back into his house to retrieve his umbrella and was never more seen in this world; an unfinished case whose records are at Cox and Co. THOR.

philosophical instruments, fragile: what are they? We are not told; they probably include paraphernalia for chemical experiments; test-tubes could perhaps be considered fragile; anyway, Holmes manipulates them STUD; *see* **touch.**

philosophy: Watson says Holmes's knowledge of is nil STUD; but *see* **man.**

phlegmatic exterior: red-hot energy underlies Holmes's DEVI; an alert light of interest replaces Holmes's listless expression when he discerns that the case may be interesting after all ABBE.

phosphorus: Watson identifies, from hound's muzzle (how: sight? taste? it has no smell) HOUN.

photograph(s): incriminating (*see* **letters**): Adler's; Holmes asks king for SCAN; of circus performance VEIL; of regal lady CHAS; of wife, Amberley tears up RETI; of Lady Hilda, does not do her justice SECO; of three Cushing sisters, Holmes observes CARD; of women, Gruner collects ILLU; full-length, of Effie Munro, on mantel of stranger's house YELL; St. Clair TWIS, Blessington RESI, Lady Hilda SECO, and Beppo SIXN identified from theirs; enlarged, Holmes makes, of wounds LION; Holmes asks for one of Straker SILV; Sterndale carries one of Brenda DEVI; photography (hobby, ruse, smoke-screen) COPP, REDH.

piano, clatter of: Holmes and Watson overhear at children's party BRUC.

Pickwick, Mr.: Dickens character CHAS.

Pierrot: nom de plume of Oberstein BRUC.

pig: Holmes practices stabbing with harpoon (see cadaver) BLAC; pig's bristles, Holmes reads, and exclaims, We are undone, my good Watson VALL; *see* **fly-paper.**

Pike, Langdale: gossip; if ever, far down in the turbid depths of London life, there was some strange swirl or eddy, it was marked with automatic exactness by this human dial upon the surface 3GAB.

pike, lean-jawed: Watson's metaphor for Stapleton, used twice in two pages HOUN.

pillows: *see* **pipe, smoking, and tobacco.**

pince-nez FIVE, GOLD (of course), IDEN; golden glasses on a cord (St. Simon) NOBL.

Pinkerton: agency, agents REDC, VALL.

pinna: Holmes of course knows this term for part of the ear CARD; *see* **Holmes Bibliography.**

Pinner: Harry, Arthur: the so-called brothers are one man, the criminal Beddington; Arthur removes his beard and appears as Harry in Birmingham, where he is described as blond in English editions, dark in American STOC; Effie Munro has lived in Pinner, Middlesex YELL.

Pinto: Maria, *see* **Gibson** THOR; Jonas, McMurdo's alleged murder victim VALL.

pipe, smoking, and tobacco: A D P briar-root (brier in American editions) pipe SILV; mended pipe YELL; SILV; smoking concerts VALL; metal (opium) pipe TWIS; hookah, with Eastern tobacco (balsamic odour) SIGN; sealskin tobacco pouch BLAC, SILV; Holmes's pipes are brier SIGN, TWIS, cherrywood COPP, black clay BLUE, COPP, CREE, HOUN, IDEN, REDH, never meerschaum or calabash; a three-pipe problem, Holmes says REDH; Holmes solves case with an ounce of shag, sitting on five pillows TWIS; Holmes smokes one pound in half a day HOUN; Holmes refers to tobacco-poisoning, says fumes are not so poisonous a few paragraphs later DEVI; wreaths of acrid tobacco RETI; strongest black tobacco SILV; cavendish (tobacco); Watson smokes ship's STUD, Arcadia mixture CROO; Grant Munro smokes Grosvenor mixture at eightpence an ounce

YELL; honeydew tobacco box, filled with salt and two severed ears CARD; shag (tobacco) CREE, HOUN, SCAN, STUD, TWIS; Holmes's pipe filled with yesterday's plugs and dottles ENGR; Holmes's oily old (black) clay pipe is his counsellor HOUN, IDEN; he pulls on his meditative pipe SOLI; unsavoury VALL; filthy habit VEIL.

pips: to set the pips on = send seeds to – the Klan's bizarre death-threat FIVE.

pistol: Holmes practices indoors with MUSG; Holmes dunks Watson's in pond (ruining it?) THOR; Watson refuses to use his against an unarmed man (Selden) HOUN; Holmes orders Watson to pick up Williamson's SOLI; Holmes says his revolver is his search-warrant LADY; in most of the adventures, Watson is the one to carry and use a pistol or revolver; *see* **V.R.; weapons.**

pistol-shots: breath of passers-by blows out into smoke like so many BLUE.

***Pitt, William (1759–1806):** British prime minister (1783–1801, 1804–1806) HOUN.

plaster: sticking: covers Douglas's shaving-cut VALL; used to twist lip TWIS; Holmes covers prick (on his finger) with, since he dabbles with poisons STUD; Kratides' face criss-crossed with GREE; of Paris: Holmes uses to preserve footprint impressions SIGN; for busts SIXN.

***Plato (427?–347 B.C.):** Greek philosopher; *see* **best.**

platitudes: *see* **chain** (none stronger than weakest link); **game** (Watson says is hardly worth the candle); **iron** (strike while it is hot); **milk** (Small says he has learned not to cry over spilled); **queen** (Holmes remarks, All the –'s horses and all the –'s men cannot avail).

plethora: Holmes says he and Watson are suffering from a plethora of surmise SILV; plethoric, used to describe both **Jones** (Athelney) and **Milverton, Charles Augustus,** q.q.v.

plough: misspelled "plow," Watson says 3GAR.

plumber: Sutherland's father was one; business sold for £4700; *see* **Escott; Horner, John.**

plumber's smoke rocket: self-lighting; long, cigar-shaped roll SCAN.

Plymouth: Sterndale spends night at hotel there; Holmes wires to make sure DEVI; Holmes suggests that he met Mrs. Straker there SILV; decorators and furnishers of Baskerville Hall are from there HOUN.

pocket: Holmes's must bulge, since he carries **cards** (playing, visiting); **compass; handcuffs; jemmy; lantern; glass; nightglasses; notebook; pocketbook; sandwiches; slips; tape-measure,** qq.v.; cheques and money; often a pistol, and evidently a pocket-knife, since he whittles a peg MUSG, sharpens a pencil 3STU, and rips up Watson's trousers 3GAR; he also has a waistcoat pocket where he keeps at least one half-crown SILV, and a watch-pocket, with watch GREE; Stackhurst's pocket does bulge, from which Holmes deduces that he is going swimming LION.

pocketbook: not a wallet but a memorandum-book; Holmes carries DEVI, pretends that he has lost HOUN.

*Poe, Edgar Allan (1809–1849): American writer; creator of Dupin, q.v. CARD, STUD.

poetry: cut out the (Holmes, impatiently, to Watson, who is describing a wall) RETI.

points: railroad rails, tapered at one end, used in switches; Holmes deduces important matters from their occurrence or placement BRUC, NORW.

poison: alkaloid SIGN, STUD; unidentified, Anna apparently withdraws from bosom (or has she already swallowed it?) GOLD; unidentified white pellet – Holmes prevents Amberley from swallowing RETI; curare SUSS; both Holmes STUD and Jack[y] SUSS try out a poison on a dog; *see* **pipe, smoking, and tobacco; plaster.**

poker: fireplace implement, Watson uses to open treasure chest SIGN; *see* **Roylott, Dr. Grimesby; weapons;** card game, played by Scowrers VALL.

pole-axed: Staunton (metaphorically) MISS; Gorgiano must have gone down like a pole-axed ox REDC.

poles: circus employees drive away Sahara King with VEIL.

police: *see* **Algar; Anderson; Bardle, Inspector; Barrett; Baynes, Inspector; Bradstreet, Inspector; constable; Cook; Coventry, Sergeant; Downing; Dubuque; Dupin, C. Auguste; Edmunds; Forbes; Forrester; Gregory, Inspector; Gregson, Tobias; Hill, Inspector; Hopkins** (Stanley); **inspector; Jones; Le Brun; Lecoq; Lestrade, G.; Leverton; MacDonald, Alec; MacKinnon, Inspector; MacPherson; Martin, Inspector; Marvin, Captain Teddy; Merivale; Montgomery, Inspector; Morton** (Inspector); **Murcher, Harry; Patterson, Inspector; Pollock; Rance, John; sergeant; Tuson, Sergeant; von Waldbaum, Fritz; Walters; Warner; Wilson** (Sergeant); **Youghal;** there are, of course, no female officers, but at Scotland Yard a female searcher searches Mrs. Tangey for lost papers NAVA; St. Simon hires two policemen in private clothes for his wedding NOBL; *see* **Lestrade, G.,** for another example of police moonlighting; *see also* **evaluation; Norberton, Sir Robert.**

"politician, lighthouse, trained cormorant": alas, there are no details about this bizarre case VEIL.

Pollock: policeman STOC.

polo: Gruner plays ILLU.

Pompey: beagle and foxhound mix, or draghound; keen scent MISS; *cf.* **Toby.**

ponderousness, Conan Doyle's stylistic habit (three examples): truncated fowling piece (for sawed-off shotgun) VALL; suffering from a plethora of surmise SILV; any delay in arresting the assassin might give him time to perpetrate some fresh atrocity STUD.

pony: miserable moor − , swallowed by mire HOUN; dogs as large as a small pony or calf COPP, CREE, HOUN; *cf.* **lions.**

poop: Fairbairn knew more of, than the forecastle (= he was more than a common seaman) CARD.

*Pope, Alexander (1688–1744): English poet REIG, STUD.

"Pope, His Holiness the" BLAC, HOUN; *cf.* **"Tosca, Cardinal"; "Vatican cameos."**

Porlock, Fred: pseudonym of Moriarty's aide VALL.

port: wine GLOR, SIGN; above mediocrity, says Holmes; famous vintage, says Watson CREE.

porter: day MISS; railway STUD; porter, the heavy malt-and-barley drink, is not mentioned, though Holmes drinks **beer** and **half-and-half,** qq.v.

Porter, Mrs.: elderly Cornish housekeeper DEVI.

possess our souls in patience: Holmes says, paraphrasing the Bible 3GAR, VALL, WIST.

post (mail): innumerable references; the Royal Mail delivers three or four times each day; Watson goes to the Wigmore Street post-office SIGN; Holmes

Jack Prendergast.

asks Watson to ring for an express messenger SIXN; Wilder, Holdernesse's secretary, says, with some heat, His Grace is not in the habit of posting letters himself PRIO; *see* **letters; messenger.**

post-hypnotic influence: Gruner over Violet de Merville ILLU; Kemp has mesmeric influence over Melas (or almost has) GREE.

postmarks: from them Holmes and Watson deduce that sender is at sea CARD, FIVE.

Pott, Evans: super-boss of Vermissa; gray-haired rat VALL.

pounds: Holmes deduces that Watson has gained seven and a half from the benefits of wedlock;

Watson huffily admits to only seven SCAN; *see* **money; stone.**

powder: none on inscrutable woman's nose SECO; *see* **Margate; nose;** gun-powder marking, on Mrs. Cubitt's face, not on her hand; Holmes says this means nothing DANC.

practical: joking, Holmes's impish habit MAZA; *see* **documents; humour; jewels; surprise;** joke, newspaper calls the box of severed ears; Holmes and Lestrade agree that it is not CARD; police think that pips are practical jokes FIVE; Cubitt at first thinks that dancing men are DANC; Hope says that Holmes's joking is very ill-timed SECO.

prejudice (ethnic, class): Von Herling is aware of British prejudice, in all its queer manifestations LAST; *see* **black fellows; cockneys; country; dooties** (low-class pronunciation); **dress** (low-class garb); **food and drink** (beer, gin, and rum are low-class); **Germans; Gorot, Charles; gypsies; Italians; Irish; Jews; Melas, Paul; negro; peasants; pubs; social strata; voodoo; white man; Wiggins; Wilson** (Jabez); **women; workmen;** Holmes states, I make a point of never having any prejudices (using the word in the sense of premature judgments) REIG; *cf.* **Board schools.**

Prendergast, Jack: six-foot-six; clear, hairless face; long thin nose; rather nutcracker jaws; swears By God! GLOR; *see* **nose.**

"Prendergast, Major": wrongfully accused of cheating at cards FIVE.

Presbury: Professor, keen eyes, observant, and clever to the verge of cunning; under shaggy brows, large horn glasses; spits out an atrocious word at Bennett, to whom his daughter Edith is engaged; Holmes hypothesizes that he takes a strong drug every nine days; Edith, a bright, handsome girl of a conventional English type CREE.

Prescott, Rodger: alias Waldron; killed by Evans 3GAR.

press: bookcase REDH; presses ransacked REIG.

Price: Watson's pseudonym; he claims to be a clerk SHOS.

priest: venerable Italian; Holmes's disguise FINA.

Prime Minister MAZA; Premier (Herbert Asquith [1852–1928]?) LAST; Bellinger – twice Premier SECO; future Premier (Holdhurst) NAVA; upset BRUC; Moran earns six thousand (pounds) a year, more than the Prime Minister VALL.

***Prince of Wales (Albert Edward [1841–1910]; later King Edward VII [reigned 1901–1910]):** never identified by name or title, but is obviously intended; needs a huge loan BERY; has an indirect interest; motives are, to the last degree, honourable and chivalrous ILLU.

Prince, Shoscombe: horse SHOS.

Pringle, Mrs.: Lucas's elderly housekeeper SECO.

prisoners escape or are released, followed by murder or other mischief CROO, GOLD, GLOR, RESI, SIGN, SIXN, 3GAR.

prize: *see* **Bruce Pinkerton; Fortescue** (scholarship); **Jackson.**

problems caused by Conan Doyle's carelessness: (perhaps some were intentionally designed to tantalize the reader): notable are Holmes's travels during the **Great Hiatus,** q.v. – why so long? why Tibet? why chemical experiments in France? EMPT; Wisteria Lodge case is dated 1892, when Holmes should have been on the Great Hiatus WIST; Watson's travels – why was he in Australia (he claims to have visited Ballarat)? He has knowledge of women, he boasts, on three continents – which three? And how do we interpret "knowledge"? SIGN; most famous are Watson's name – we are told repeatedly (PREF, SIGN, STUD, THOR) that it is John, but his wife calls him James TWIS; and the location of his wound – at first it is in the subclavian artery of his left shoulder (STUD); in the next published tale it is in his leg, or, as we are explicitly told, the Achilles tendon (SIGN); still later it is, vaguely, in "one of my limbs" NOBL, and, even more vaguely, it is simply his "own old wound"; eventually the (leg-)wound ceases to bother him, and he boasts, I am reckoned fleet of foot HOUN; other problems: Scott Eccles has a watch – we are told that he consults it; how, then, can Garcia persuade him to go to bed early by jug-gling (Holmes's term) the clocks in the house? Surely he would again consult his watch to ascertain the time WIST; which pistol wounded Elsie Cubitt, her husband's or Slaney's? DANC; whatever happened to Mrs. Mortimer? HOUN; how can Holmes be certain that the vicarage lamp was full when lit? DEVI; and how can he be certain that the pearl has not been discovered among the shards of bust number three – and removed? SIXN; similarly, how can he be sure (or almost) that Alec Cunningham would thrust the incriminating scrap of paper into his dressing-gown pocket? REIG; the steps to Watson's front door are worn three inches deeper than those of his neighbor – a deep and dangerous cavity – why does Watson, a successful medico, not have them repaired? STOC; what is the card that Holmes insists Watson tie around his neck (perhaps a misprint for *cord,* which would be equally incomprehensible) SIGN; why do Holmes and Watson suddenly dash off for Norway? BLAC; they send their luggage to Paris to decoy Moriarty – what happened to it? (French *Holmesiens* have searched the Gare du Nord without success) EMPT; why does the crack shot Moran not shoot Holmes at the Reichenbach Falls instead of throwing rocks at him? And since Moran knows that Holmes did not perish in the falls along with Moriarty, what is the point of Holmes's pretending to be dead for the next three years?

EMPT; *see* **dates; sanitary facilities.**

professions: alternative, for Holmes: **actor, boxer, burglar,** qq.v.; women's: *see* **cook; governesses; housekeeper; landladies; maids; nurse; typewriting;** music teacher SOLI; singer (Adler) SCAN; violinist STUD; circus performer VEIL; *danseuse* NOBL; barmaid RETI; whore (Winter?) ILLU; Anna is a professional anarchist, but she commits suicide GOLD.

professors: Coram; Moriarty; Presbury, qq.v; all are scoundrels; their specialties are ecclesiastical history, mathematics, and physiology, respectively; Holmes speaks with the air of a clinical professor SIGN.

propose: Holmes makes advances to Watson FINA; *see also* **engaged; relations.**

Prosper, Francis: one-legged greengrocer BERY.

Providence: killed Barclay, Wood claims CROO; goodness of, Holmes deduces from a rose NAVA.

Priory, The: without exception, the best and most select preparatory school in England, its headmaster claims PRIO.

public (= American private) schools: *see* **Blackheath; Eton (and Oxford); Priory, The; Uppingham;** Stapleton (as Vandeleur) kept one in Yorkshire; it failed HOUN.

pubs (public houses): coarse glare and tawdry brilliancy SIGN; but Holmes tells Watson that a pub is the centre of country gossip – a far better source of information than the house-agent whom Watson consulted; but Holmes gets into a fist-fight there SOLI; Holmes tells Watson that he (Watson) could have whispered soft nothings with the young lady at the Blue Anchor and received hard somethings in exchange RETI; Henry Baker acquired his Christmas goose at the Alpha Inn, near the British Museum BLUE; *see* **Ivy Plant.**

pulse: feeble, Pinner's STOC; thready, Huxtable's PRIO; high, Mrs. Ferguson's SUSS – all three survive.

pumpkin, rotten: Brackenstall's head crushed like ABBE; *cf.* **eggs.**

Pycroft, Hall: cockney; fired, along with twenty-seven other clerks, when a Venezuelan investment turns sour; can quote any stock-value from memory STOC; *cf.* **Dodd, James M..**

queen: McMurdo calls Ettie a queen VALL; Watson calls Violet Smith queenly SOLI; Small accepts the queen's shilling (enlists in the army) SIGN; Holmes remarks, All the queen's horses and all the queen's men cannot avail in this matter BRUC; *see* **platitude.**

*Queen Anne (1665–1714): queen of Great Britain (1702–1714); Street, Watson's rooms there ILLU; architecture REIG, 3GAR.

*Queen Victoria (Victoria Alexandrina, 1819–1901): queen of

Great Britain (1837–1901); never named in stories; called a certain gracious lady, exalted person BRUC; *see* **emerald, V. R.**

queer: ideas (Holmes) STUD; Holmes fond of queer mysteries; would not be able to find a queerer one; the queer part of Cubitt's story, the appearance of dancing men DANC; queer, queerer, Browning says of Mary Cushing CARD; queer card with V. V. 341 on it; McGinty calls McMurdo a queer card; shove the queer: McMurdo's slang for pass the counterfeit money; queer throne for such a queen: McMurdo to Ettie; queer cipher: Morris's unnamed correspondent VALL; queerest thing, say both Holmes and Sir Henry, describing double boot theft HOUN; British prejudice, in all its queer manifestations LAST; queerest club (Mycroft's) GREE; one queer thing, two queer things, everything he does is queer (Mason, re Norberton) SHOS; Small says to Sholto that there is a queer thing about the ownership of the treasure SIGN; Ras looks at Holmes and Watson in a queer way 3STU; Lestrade says the case is queer madness SIXN; queer shade (cook's skin) WIST; *see* **fit(s); milk.**

Queer Street: Watson says Norberton is down it (= in debt) SHOS; Lestrade tells MacPherson that he would have been in it (in trouble) if anything had been stolen from the Lucas house SECO.

quick, Watson, the needle: part of the Holmes folklore, but it does not occur in the canon; *cf.* **deerstalker; Elementary; meerschaum.**

quill-pen: MISS, NOBL, REDH; *see* **handwriting; pen.**

quiver: *see* **Ames; bell; eyebrows; eyelids; finger; laughter; nerves; nostrils; wink;** *cf.* **Shiver;** *for quake and tremble, see* **hand; lip; rabbits.**

quotation marks, multiple: three sets, for quotations within quotations within quotations CROO, GLOR, MUSG, STOC.

rabbits: Oldacre darts out of his hiding place, like a rabbit out of its burrow; couple of rabbits would account for blood and charred ashes in wood-pile; Watson can make rabbits serve his turn if he ever writes an account of the case NORW; dead man rolls like a shot rabbit SIGN; Spaulding dives like a rabbit into a hole, ostensibly to develop photos REDH; Openshaw feels like a rabbit with a snake writhing towards it FIVE; Norberton and Stephens quake in bushes like two bunny-rabbits SHOS; rabbit-warren, house as full as, Jones complains SIGN; for rabbit-skin cap with hanging lappets, *see* **dress.**

Rache: German for "revenge," as Holmes superciliously points out; Lestrade thinks it is the start of the name Rachel STUD.

racing: Watson pays half his wound pension for SHOS; Holmes keeps Watson's cheque-book locked in a drawer to help him resist the temptation of wagering REDH; McCarthys fond of BOSC; the Wessex cup (or plate) is the main topic of conversation the length and breadth of England; Holmes himself bets on the following race SILV; Gilchrist's father ruined himself on the turf 3STU; *see* **games.**

radix pedis diaboli: devil's foot root; Watson translates the Latin DEVI.

Rae and Sturmash: coal-owners VALL.

railway: *see* **trains.**

Railway Arms: horrible country inn where Watson and Amberley are forced to spend the night RETI.

rain FIVE, GOLD, HOUN, NAVA, NOBL, SILV, STUD, WIST; lack of makes it hard to find clues NORW, PRIO; in BOSC Holmes reads footprint evidence with ease, even though the crime-scene is sodden with rain and the locals have wallowed all over it, like a herd of buffalo.

Ralph: butler; and wife (nurse) BLAN.

Rance, John: policeman; Holmes bribes STUD.

Randalls: father and three sons; burglars ABBE.

Rao, Lal: Sholto's butler; Holmes conjectures that he was Small's secret confederate; *cf.* **Chowdar, Lal** SIGN.

*Raphael (Raffaello Santi or Sanzio, 1483–1520): Italian painter 3GAB.

Ras, Daulat; silent, little (shorter than McLaren, who is five-foot-six); hook-nosed 3STU; *see* **nose.**

rashers (bacon) and eggs ENGR.

rat: "giant, of Sumatra, a story for which the world is not yet prepared": perhaps related to the Netherland-Sumatra case SUSS; Windibank glances about like a rat in a trap IDEN; Douglas calls his hiding-place a rat-trap VALL; rat could not hide himself NAVA; Pott is a gray-haired rat VALL; Holmes calls Oldacre a rat NORW; Ryder BLUE, Norlett SHOS, and Lestrade STUD are rat-faced; Irregulars scamper downstairs like so many rats; Gregson begins to smell a rat STUD; *see* **Ballarat.**

Ratcliff Highway: in Stepney; Sumner Shipping Agency located there BLAC; "Ratcliff Highway Murders" STUD.

rate: (i.e., speed) of train, fifty-three and a half miles per hour; Holmes says the calculation is a simple one; it is not SILV; *see* **height.**

rattle: (= death-rattle) I'm yours to the – (remarks Winter) ILLU.

raved in the air: Holmes FIVE.

razors, small case of: Lucas's gift to Mitton SECO.

*Reade, William Winwood (1839–1875): Holmes recommends his *Martyrdom of Man* (1874) to Watson, twice SIGN.

red-covered volume: probably *Burke's Peerage;* Holmes consults NOBL.

"Red-Headed Men" (=REDH) WIST.

red-Indian: Holmes's composure, which had made so many regard him as a machine rather than as a man (Holmes) CROO; *see* **native American.**

***Red King:** William II (William Rufus), king of England (1056?–1100; reigned 1087–1100) VALL.

"red leech, repulsive": unhappily, we have no more details about this case GOLD.

red tape: Holmes uses to tie up bundles of case records MUSG.

refuges: Holmes has at least five in London, where he can change his identity BLAC.

Regent Street: Stapleton in a cab on HOUN.

registration agent: one who compiles lists of eligible voters; Holmes's disguise CROO.

Reichenbach Falls: Holmes and Moriarty evidently fall to their deaths there FINA; Holmes reveals that he did not EMPT; WIST is dated 1892, but Holmes was thought to be dead at the bottom of the Falls in that year; *see* **Great Hiatus; problems caused by Conan Doyle's carelessness.**

reigning houses of Europe: three, Holmes has solved cases for NAVA – **Bohemia, King of; Holland; Scandinavia,** qq.v.

reincarnation: study of family portraits is enough to convert a man

to the doctrine, says Holmes HOUN.

relapse: Watson relapses into his chair SIGN; *see* **curled.**

relations: very intimate, between Holmes and Watson FINA, GREE, LADY, SPEC, YELL; intimate friend, Holmes re Watson SPEC; intimacy ENGR; Watson calls Holmes his master HOUN; Holmes calls Watson my boy, dear boy, my dear CHAS, MUSG, SIGN, STOC, 3STU; Holmes says Watson is his old friend EMPT, only friend FIVE; Holmes to Watson, Then it makes it all the easier for me to propose . . . that you should come away with me for a week to the Continent FINA; *see* **double; engaged; hand; lip; love; side.**

religion: Holmes has no belief in organized, but he acknowledges the existence of the powers of darkness; and the genius loci VALL; he mentions God's own wind LAST; remarks, God knows there was sin enough ILLU; exclaims, God help us! Why does fate play such tricks with poor, helpless worms? BOSC; says to Klein, original sin was yours 3GAB; *see* **Bible; chance; David, Uriah, Bathsheba; Providence; reincarnation; soul; supernatural.**

repeated passage: Holmes's mind-reading stunt CARD, RESI.

repetitions, Conan Doyle's stylistic habit: strangest and most unique things . . . the facts are unique (same paragraph) REDH; absolutely, very, quite, perfectly, almost unique BRUC, CHAS, MUSG, NAVA, NORW, SILV, WIST; dull eyes had regained their fire, and there, sitting by the fire TWIS; whole-souled admirer . . . whole-souled answer (same page) VALL; Douglas to Watson, I've heard of you; to Holmes, I've heard of you (same page) VALL; my last dollar . . . their last dollar (same page) VALL; I dislike the man (Morris) . . . I have a liking for Morris (within a couple of pages) VALL; sufficient for to-morrow is the evil thereof . . . Evil indeed is the man who has not one woman to mourn him (same page) HOUN; Watson exclaims The brute! the brute!; Holmes, a few pages later, The brute! HOUN; it is surely rather fanciful . . . No doubt you thought me fanciful (same page) EMPT; Holmes remarks, The plot thickens (twice within four pages) STUD; the danger . . . in danger . . . this danger (same page); threw up . . . threw open . . . throw down (same page) MAZA; and now you must on no account lose another instant . . . You must get home instantly and act FIVE; but you are joking . . . You are certainly joking, Holmes (same page) CARD; No, no, you are joking, Holmes! MAZA; I am not joking TWIS; My dear Holmes, you are joking. No, Watson, I am very serious THOR; I thought he was joking NAVA; *see also* **plethora; queer; yellow;** writers frequently try to find synonyms for *said* and *asked* in their representation of dialogue; in HOUN Conan Doyle

uses *cried* (seventeen times), *remarked* (twice), *broke in* (twice), *gasped* (twice), *stammered* (four times), *whispered* (four times); elsewhere we find *panted* COPP, *ejaculated* BOSC, COPP, GOLD, NAVA (three times, within a few paragraphs), *shrieked* COPP, *shouted* STOC, *groaned* STOC; in NAVA Holmes insists that Phelps accompany him on an hour's train journey, though the poor fellow can hardly walk; then Phelps spends a sleepless night in Holmes's spare bedroom – no wonder Phelps cries, ejaculates thrice, and, at last, gasps.

restaurants: *see* **Holborn; Goldini's; Marcini's; Simpson's.**

retriever: Holmes compared to DANC; *see* **foxhound.**

revenge: *see* **motives**

reverend abbess: like a, receiving leprous mendicants: Holmes, re V. de Merville ILLU; *cf.* bench of bishops, s.v. **butler.**

revolver: large, butt of, Milverton opens coat to reveal; little gleaming, withdrawn from bosom by Milverton's murderess CHAS; never out of his pocket (Douglas's), Smith and Wesson (McMurdo's) – the same weapon? VALL; Sylvius sits on his MAZA; *see* **pistol; weapons.**

***Reynolds, Sir Joshua (1723–1792):** English painter HOUN.

rhododendron bush: Holmes squats in NAVA.

ribston-pippin: (spelled with capital *R* and without hyphen in Doubleday edition) a kind of apple – used metaphorically to describe James Lancaster, a little ribston-pippin of a man, with ruddy cheeks and fluffy white side-whiskers BLAC.

Richards, Dr.: called to care for the Tregennis family DEVI.

*Richter, Jean Paul Friedrich (pseudonym: Jean Paul, 1763–1825): German writer SIGN.

"Ricoletti of the club foot and his abominable wife": records of this case are in Holmes's tin box MUSG.

rifles: Winchesters, pointed by police at McMurdo VALL.

ring: brilliant (= diamond), Holmes's, from reigning family of Holland IDEN; wedding, found STUD; wedding, lost VALL; wedding, new NOBL; signet TWIS; **Masonic,** q.v. STUD; *see* **emerald; jewels; snuff-box.**

roast beef sandwich: Holmes constructs BERY.

robber, highway: Turner became one in Australia BOSC.

*Roberts, Lord (Frederick Sleigh Roberts, first Earl Roberts, 1832–1914): British general; Boer War military leader BLAN.

*Robespierre, Maximilien de (1758–1794): French revolutionist VALL.

Robinson, John: James Ryder's alias; note that initials are identical in the real name and in the alias BLUE.

*La Rochefoucauld, Duc François de (1613–1680): French writer SIGN.

Rock of Gibraltar: ship on which Croker and Fraser meet ABBE.

rocks: Holmes, Watson, and Lestrade hide behind for their ambush HOUN; Moran throws at Holmes EMPT.

*Rodney, George Brydges (1719–1792): English admiral HOUN.

romanticism: *see* **Watson, John H.**

Ronder: porcine circus owner; human pig, human wild boar; cursed and slashed at everyone who came in his way; wife, Eugenia, cries out, Cruel beast! Monster! VEIL.

roof: Holmes crawls along SIGN; of railway carriage, body rested on BRUC; of outhouse, room accessible from WIST.

rope: Blessington's fire escape, used to hang him RESI; blood on SIGN.

rose: Holmes effuses, What a lovely thing a rose is . . . . [W]e have much to hope for from the flowers NAVA; Watson compares Lyons's complexion to the dainty pink which lurks at the heart of the sulphur-rose HOUN.

*Rosa, Salvatore (1615–1673): Italian painter and poet; painting by (?) in Sholto's collection SIGN.

Ross: Duncan, one of Archie's aliases REDH; Colonel, irascible, skeptical horse owner; cavalier manner toward Holmes; calls Straker villain! scoundrel!, though earlier he says he was an excellent servant SILV; and Mangles, dog dealers HOUN.

rotting vegetation: Nature throws before Baskerville's carriage HOUN.

Roundhay, Mr.: vicar; Watson glares at him with no very friendly eyes DEVI.

rowing LION; *see* **games.**

Roy: wolfhound CREE.

royal duke: Clay's grandfather REDH.

royalty, peers, knights: Conan Doyle and his readers were evidently much impressed by titles; Conan Doyle himself was, of course, knighted, but Holmes refused a knighthood 3GAR, though he did accept the French **Legion of Honour,** q.v.; Holmes characterizes the aristocracy as a caste who do not lightly show their emotions SECO; *see* **Adair,** Hon. Ronald; **Appledore, Sir Charles; Backwater, Lord; Balmoral; Baskerville; Bellinger, Lord; Belminster, Duke of; Blackwater, Earl of; Bohemia, King of; Brackenstall; Brackwell, Lady Eva; *Brinvilliers, Marchioness; Burnwell, Sir George; Cantlemere, Lord; Carfax, Lady Frances; Chandos, Sir Charles; *Clarendon, Lord; Clay, John; Colonna, Prince of; Dovercourt, Earl of; "Dowson, Baron"; Falder; Ffolliott, Sir George; Flowers, Lord; *Franz Josef; Green,** Hon. Philip; **"Greyminster, Duke of"; Gruner, Baron Adelbert; Hardy** (Sir John and Sir Charles); **Harringby, Lord; Holdernesse; Holland; Hope** (Right Honourable Trelawney and Lady Hilda Trelawney); **Klopman; *Kneller, Sir Godfrey; Leverstoke, Lord;** "Lewis, Sir George"; **Lomond, Duke of; "Maupertuis, Baron"; Maynooth; Meek, Sir Jasper; Merrow, Lord; Miles, Honourable Miss; Montalva, Marquess of; Morcar, Countess of; Morland, Sir John; Mount-James, Lord; Norberton, Sir Robert; Oakshott** (Sir Leslie); **Ormstein;** "Pope, his Holiness the"; **Prince of Wales; Queen Victoria; *Reynolds, Sir Joshua; Rufton, Earl of; St. Simon; Saltire, Lord; Saxe-Meningen, Clotilde Lothmann von; Scandinavia; Singleford, Lord; Soames** (Sir Cathcart); **Southerton, Lord; Sylvius, Count Negretto;** "Tosca, Cardinal"; "Turkey, Sultan of"; "Von Bischoff of Frankfort"; **Von Bork; Von Herder; Von Herling, Baron; Von Kramm, Count; Von und Zu Grafenstein, Count;** von Waldbaum, Fritz; **V.R.; Walter, Sir James; Whittington, Lady Alicia; *Zeppelin, Ferdinand, Count von.**

Roylott, Dr. Grimesby: though a medical man, he sends to the village for medical aid when his stepdaughter is dying; bends Holmes's poker with bare hands; Holmes bends it back SPEC.

rubber: Merryweather misses his; presumably of **whist,** q.v. REDH; *see* **games.**

Rucastle: Jephro and wife; son Edward, slipper-slapper and cockroach killer; daughter Alice;

Jephro threatens to throw Hunter to the mastiff COPP.

Rudge-Whitworth: bicycle VALL.

Rufton, Earl of: Lady Frances's forebear LADY.

rugby: Watson played at Blackheath; Ferguson played for Richmond SUSS; Cambridge 'varsity MISS; *see* **games.**

Rulli: *see* **Lopez** WIST.

rum: in Carey's hut; chosen instead of whisky or brandy; ergo, drinkers were seamen (Holmes) BLAC; for a peculiar choice of drinks, *see* **champagne; sherry.**

rupee: thought to bè a bad florin CROO; *see* **money.**

Ruritania: actual Cunard ship; Gruner is on the passenger list ILLU.

***Russell, (William) Clark (1844–1911):** American novelist; Watson reads his sea stories FIVE.

Russian: *see* **old.**

Ryder: James, rat-faced; sister, Maggie, calls him "Jem" BLUE; *see* **Oakshott.**

safe: Holmes tells Watson to put gem in his (Holmes's) BLUE; tall, green (Milverton's), Holmes burgles CHAS; large, brass-bound (Von Bork's); its combination is *August 1914* LAST; elaborate, containing submarine plans BRUC; large iron, in Roylott's chamber, with a saucer of milk nearby; serves as snake kennel SPEC; Mawson's, Beddington rifles RESI; bankers' have been forced,

says Holder, so he takes the coronet home and locks it in his bureau BERY; Oldacre's, left open, with papers on table NORW; Amberley's is really a strong room, like a bank's, with iron door and shutter RETI; most of these safes have keyholes, not dial combination locks.

Sahara King: lion VEIL.

sailors BLAC, BRUC, CARD, FIVE, GLOR, NAVA, SIGN, STUD; German and Finnish on *Lone Star* FIVE; Chinese, Holmes has been working among DYIN; *see* **hands,** for Holmes's study of sailors'.

St. Clair: Neville, respectable suburbanite with a secret source of income (begging); wife TWIS.

St. George's, St. Monica's, St. Saviour's: churches; *see* **weddings.**

"St. Pancras case": involves a dead policeman; Holmes catches the culprit, a picture-framer, by identifying trace evidence, including hairs, threads, and glue, by using his microscope SHOS.

St. Paul's: last rays of the sun were gilding the cross upon its summit SIGN; the artificial knee-cap manufactory is near REDH.

St. Simon: Lord Robert, stooped, walks with bent knees; Lord Eustace; Lady Clara NOBL; *see* **Tudor.**

salad-oil: medicine; *see* **pads.**

"Samson of New Orleans": perhaps escaped justice because of the lack of a reliable test for blood stains STUD.

sandwich: and cup of coffee, Holmes and Watson dine on REDH; sandwiches, paper of, Holmes pockets NAVA.

sanitary facilities: the genteel Miss Harrison nurses Phelps for weeks, never leaving his side, at least in the daytime; would she have used Phelps's chamber-pot in his presence, even though he is comatose? NAVA; in GOLD, NORW, RETI, and VALL people are confined in cramped quarters for long periods of time; how did they manage? At the end of RETI two people finally die in their sealed room; but first, one writes on the wall "We we"; it is interpreted as the beginning of the phrase "*We we*re murdered,*" but surely it was a final, desperate cry for bladder relief.

salt, rough: severed-ear preservative CARD.

Saltire, Lord PRIO; *see* **Holdernesse.**

***Sand, George (pseudonym of Amandine Aurore Lucie Dupin, Baronne Dudevant, 1804–1876):** French writer REDH.

Sandeford, Mr., of Reading: bust owner; Holmes pays him ten pounds for a fifteen-shilling statue, makes him sign a release SIXN.

Sanders, Ikey: diamond cutter; Merton says, he has split on us, without intending a pun MAZA; *see* **Van Seddar;** *also see* **hands,** for Holmes's study of diamond-cutters'.

***Sanger, "Lord John" (1816–1889):** English showman VEIL.

***Sarasate y Navascués, Pablo Martín Melitón (1844–1908):** Spanish violinist and composer REDH.

sarcasm: Holmes's, *see* **coruscation; courteous; cunning; flying; impossible; intellect; mind; scintillating;** Barker speaks with acrid irony VALL.

saturnine figure: Holmes MAZA.

Saunders: housemaid DANC; Mrs., housekeeper 3GAR; Sir James (Dr.), dermatologist BLAN.

savages: Tonga SIGN; mulatto cook WIST.

Savage, Victor: Smith's nephew, murdered DYIN.

Sawyer, Mrs.: name invented by Hope or his accomplice; bleared eyes, wrinkles STUD; *see* **Dennis.**

Saxe-Meningen, Clotilde Lothmann von: second daughter of King of Scandinavia; betrothed to King of Bohemia SCAN.

scales: epithelial, Holmes identifies with microscope; the epithelium is membraneous tissue, which suggests that Holmes is doing pathological research; the word is from Greek *epi* + *thele,* the second element of which means "nipple," which may give us some clue SHOS; *see* **glue.**

"Scandal in Bohemia" (= SCAN) IDEN.

Scandinavia: King of NOBL; royal family of FINA.

Scanlan, Mike: vicious Scowrer VALL.

scent (used figuratively): Holmes, we must cast round for another scent HOUN; Holmes like a foxhound running on a breast-high scent BRUC; Holmes taciturn when on a scent NAVA; numerous subtle signs that Holmes is on a hot scent WIST; Holmes and Watson, like two old hounds, will get a sniff of the scent PRIO; for literal scents, *see* **smell.**

schemer falls into the pit which he digs for another, the: Holmes paraphrases Ecclesiastes 1:2; the biblical passage ends, A serpent shall bite him SPEC.

schoolmaster: Stapleton ill-advisedly admits that he has been one; no one easier to trace, says Holmes HOUN; Brunton has been one MUSG; Huxtable and Soames are educators (headmaster and tutor, respectively) PRIO; Moriarty (EMPT, FINA, VALL) and Murdoch and Stackhurst (LION) have been coaches (private tutors); Aveling and Heidegger are Masters (mathematics and German, respectively) PRIO; the schools of both Huxtable and Stapleton are in Yorkshire; *see* **education; public schools; universities.**

scientific: Holmes is a little too, for Stamford's tastes; it approaches to cold-bloodedness STUD; *see* **automaton; cadaver; pig.**

scintillating: Holmes's ironic term for Watson MISS; Holmes re Watson, you scintillate ILLU; *see* **impossible; intellect.**

scissors, nail: used to cut notepaper WIST, newspaper HOUN.

Scotch bonnet (= tam o'shanter): Baker wears, though it is unbecoming BLUE.

Scowrers: local nickname for the Eminent Order of Freemen, a secret society, almost all members of which have Irish names VALL.

scrambled eggs (cold) BLAC.

scratch, off you go at: Holmes tells Wilson, using race-track lingo REDH.

scratches: made by shoes on a table, from which Holmes deduces the direction the fleeing culprit took 3STU; *cf.* **key,** for the scratches it makes.

screams: horrible, Moriarty's EMPT, murdered manager's wife's VALL; muffled, Brunton's MUSG; wild, hoarse, Smith's GOLD; hoarse, Amberley's RETI; piercing, Nancy Barclay's, CROO; woman's, bursts from laurel bushes SOLI; Boone (St. Clair) breaks into a scream TWIS; Phelps screams when Holmes surprises him NAVA; Lady Mary screams when Brackenstall strikes her ABBE; Roylott screams at Holmes; later emits one dreadful shriek SPEC; Holmes screams Help! Help! Murder! REIG; Watson tries to scream but only emits a hoarse croak DEVI; *see* **child, cries.**

Scylla and Charybdis: Watson's term for contrasting tales (GLOR, STUD) RESI.

Sea Unicorn: Carey's ship BLAC.

"Second Stain" (= SECO) NAVA, YELL.

secret codes: *see* **codes.**

secret panels: *see* **hiding places.**

secret societies: Vehmgericht, Carbonari, Italian, Avenging Angels STUD; Ku Klux Klan FIVE; Circolo Rosso (Red Circle), allied to the old Carbonari REDC; Mafia SIXN; Ancient Order of Freemen (Scowrers) VALL; Irish LAST; Brotherhood or Order (Russian Nihilists) GOLD; the Joint (American gangsters) DANC; Freemasons NORW, REDH, RETI, STUD.

securities: stocks BLAC, DANC, IDEN, NAVA, RETI.

see: but you do not observe, Holmes to Watson SCAN; details not invisible but unnoticed by Watson IDEN; see everything, but are too timid about drawing inferences TWIS; see everything but fail to reason from what you see BLUE; I see no more than you, but I have trained myself to notice what I see BLAN; Watson has seen all that Holmes has but Holmes has deduced a little more SPEC.

Selden: Mrs. Barrymore's brother; Notting Hill murderer; evil yellow face, terrible animal face, seamed and scored with vile passions; screams out a curse; dressed in Baskerville's cast-offs, he is killed in a fall while being chased by the hound HOUN.

Senegambia: Holmes recalls details of a case from SIGN.

senses: Holmes's keener than Watson's EMPT; for his ability to see in the dark, *see* **eye(s).**

sere and yellow: Holmes quotes Shakespeare, *Macbeth* STUD.

sergeant: police LADY; the one in VALL is anonymous until Chapter 4, where we are told that his name is Wilson.

Sergius: *see* **Coram, Professor.**

serpents: unlike other snakes, the swamp adder is gifted with a sense of hearing: it responds to Roylott's whistle SPEC; Milverton CHAS and Moriarty FINA are reptilian; Hope writhes along the ground like one STUD; wisdom of, Watson develops HOUN.

serum: of anthropoid, or black-faced langur; injected to cure impotence CREE.

servant(s): Barrymore has the subdued manner of a well-trained servant; he and his wife are the only ones at Baskerville Hall HOUN; Brackenstalls have eight ABBE; Musgraves have eight maids, cook, butler, two footmen, and a boy; the garden and the stables, of course, have a separate staff, including gamekeepers (Janet Tregellis is daughter of head gamekeeper) MUSG; Douglases have butler, housekeeper, and six other servants VALL; Cubitts have at least six farm lads, a groom, a cook, and a stable-boy DANC; Turners have a man and a girl; McCarthys have lodgekeeper, gamekeeper, and plenty of indoor help BOSC; Holder has three maids, a groom, and a page

BERY; Hopes have butler, valet, housemaid, personal maid SECO; Barclays have maids, cook, coachman CROO; doctor thinks it remarkable that people of the Shlessingers' class have no servant LADY; university students have dips 3STU; Blessington and Trevelyan have maid, cook, page RESI; Straker, a horse trainer, has one maidservant SILV; Ferrier, an independent Utah farmer, has several who sleep in the outhouse STUD; the Watsons have a couple CROO, ENGR; Holmes and Watson have a maid (BRUC, FIVE); they are also attended by **Hudson, Mrs.,** and **Billy,** qq.v.; *also see* **butlers; cook; footmen; housekeeper; maids; man-servant; stable-boy; valet.**

settings of tales: English: most in London, but frequently in the Home Counties and some a little farther from the great city: Sussex BLAC, LION, MUSG, SUSS, VALL; Surrey NAVA, REIG, SOLI, SPEC, WIST; Kent ABBE, FINA, TWIS, VALL; Norfolk DANC, GLOR; Hampshire COPP, THOR; Berkshire ENGR, SHOS, VEIL; Herefordshire BOSC; Devonshire HOUN, SILV; Bedfordshire BLAN; Cornwall DEVI; Holmes never leaves 221B in DYIN, IDEN, MAZA; European: for a paragraph or two in REIG, the setting is France (Lyons); the case of Huret, the Boulevard assassin, apparently took Holmes to France GOLD; FINA and LADY are set, in part, on the Continent; for non-European settings, *see* **America; Australia; India** – all

of which are violent, lawless places.

seven (Holmes has): explanations COPP; schemes MISS; clues NAVA.

sex: there is some confusion of sex in a couple of names – Norman Neruda (female) STUD, Isadora Persano (male) THOR; and Irene Adler admits to being a cross-dresser SCAN.

shadows: long, trail down the walls and hang like a black canopy above Sir Henry; long, black, trailing down corridor; spring up and down from shaking candle HOUN; long, black, streaming backward down the corridor SIGN; black, Holmes and Watson hide in, near Laburnum Villa; Beppo glares from the shadow of his matted hair SIXN; Howells is a black-eyed shadow of her former self; Holmes uses the shadows of an oak and a fishing-rod in his trigonometric computations MUSG; dark shadows round Holmes's bright eyes NORW; shadow passes over the gaunt face of Sterndale DEVI, the expressive face of Holdhurst NAVA, the mobile face of Jack SUSS; shadow of a woman's head REDC; Norberton's career has outlived its shadows SHOS; *see* **smile; surmise.**

Shafter: Jacob, McMurdo's landlord; daughter Ettie, slight German accent; for her father's accent, *see* **leetle;** their nationality is changed to Swedish in English editions, but the representation of dialect remains the same VALL.

shake-down: not extortion, but accommodations for the night; Stark offers Hatherley ENGR.

*Shakespeare, William (1564–1616): English playwright and poet LADY, 3GAB; *see also* **age; airy; conscience; course; game; green peas; grinned; journeys; method; sere; sucking; thrice.**

shark: Sylvius a shark, Merton a gudgeon MAZA.

sheeny: offensive term for Jew; Arthur Pinner (Beddington) had a touch of the – , about the nose, Pycroft says STOC; *see* **nose; prejudice.**

sheep: singular epidemic among SILV; scabby, no room for, says McGinty VALL; in a pen, Openshaw will not be cooped up like FIVE; Hope shoots a big-horn STUD; *see* **bleat.**

Sherman: old bird-stuffer, Toby's owner SIGN.

sherry, brown: mutineers' odd choice in drink; mixed with blood on the table GLOR; *see* **money.**

shingle (beach): of Southsea, Watson yearns for CARD, RESI.

ships: *see "Alicia"*; *Aurora; Bass Rock; Conqueror; Esmeralda; "Friesland"; "Gloria Scott"; Hotspur; Lone Star; "Matilda Briggs"; May Day; Norah Creina; Orontes; Palmyra; Rock of Gibraltar; Sea Unicorn; "Sophy Anderson"* (s.v. **Anderson**); sailing and steam, speeds of FIVE.

shiver: of assent, passes through drooping tail SUSS; convulsive, after administration of poison STUD; *see* **dogs;** Sir Henry's eyelids HOUN; Pinner's eyelids STOC; Baldwin's every limb VALL; Von Bork's car LAST; *cf.* **quiver.**

Shlessinger: Dr. and wife, missionaries; exercise apostolic duties; he has a bitten left ear LADY; *see* **Fraser; Peters, Henry ("Holy").**

shoes: rubber-soled tennis, Watson wears for burgling CHAS; ribbed tennis, Sterndale wears DEVI; varnished, Damery's ILLU; canvas, unlaced, McPherson's LION; Amberley's left wrinkled, right smooth RETI; satin NOBL; patent-leather, Watson's slippers; scorched STOC; jumping, clay-clotted 3STU; size twelve WIST; Heidegger wears shoes, no socks PRIO; Holmes buys a pair of Sir George's for six shillings BERY; *see* **boot(s).**

Sholto: Major, drunkard, gambler, thief; sons Bartholomew, Thaddeus SIGN; "Sholto murder" (= SIGN) REDH.

shooting: sport THOR; wild-duck; Hudson treats himself to shooting trips, with Trevor's best gun GLOR; Holmes says, I could not shoot him [Moran] at sight, or I should myself be in the dock EMPT; Moran EMPT and Sylvius MAZA are big-game shots, Sterndale is a lion hunter DEVI.

shorthand: Gregson takes; later Lestrade takes STUD.

shout: loud, of triumph, Holmes's, on discovering black pearl SIXN.

shriek: of delight, Holmes's, when he succeeds in poisoning the terrier STUD.

shrimp: Holmes calls Ryder one BLUE.

shrubbery: mulatto cook breaks through; Holmes crawls in, while Baynes watches from a tree WIST; *see* **laurel.**

shuffling, lying: *see* **gypsies.**

shutters: iron BRUC, RETI; ordinary wooden? – Holmes flings them together and bolts them for protection against air-guns FINA; old-fashioned with broad iron bars SPEC.

side by side: Holmes and Watson lie together on grass plot DEVI; couches, for Holmes and Watson ILLU; *see* **double bed; relations.**

Sigerson: Holmes's pseudonym during the Great Hiatus EMPT.

"Sign of the Four, The" ("The Sign of Four" in Doubleday edition; = SIGN): CARD, FIVE, IDEN, REDH, STOC.

Silver Blaze: in disguise, wins Wessex Cup by six lengths SILV.

silver nitrate: on Watson's forefinger SCAN; *see* **iodoform.**

simple: Holmes says that simple crimes are, paradoxically, more difficult to solve BOSC, IDEN; case was simple and direct though it appeared to be complex HOUN; *see* **absurdly simple; height; rate.**

Simpson: Baldy, one of Emsworth's fellow soldiers in South Africa BLAN; Fitzroy, his red and black silk cravat in Straker's hand SILV; street Arab, Baker Street Irregular; Holmes orders him to mount

guard over Wood, pats him on the head CROO.

*Simpson's: (full name, Simpson's Dining Rooms) restaurant in the Strand DYIN, ILLU.

Sinclair, Admiral: Sir James Walter a guest at his house in Barclay Square (error for Berkeley? *London Street Guide and Index* lists no Barclay Square; *Berkeley* and *Barclay* are pronounced the same by the English) BRUC.

Singleford, Lord: his horse entered in race SILV.

single-stick: Holmes expert at ILLU, STUD.

sister: none of Holmes's should ever have accepted such a situation COPP.

six-shooters VALL.

skeleton: of Mortimer's spaniel, hound-gnawed HOUN.

skirts: dwindling frou-frou of SECO; whisk of LADY.

skull: Holmes's is dolichocephalic HOUN; Moriarty remarks on Holmes's frontal development FINA; MacDonald has a great cranium VALL; Baker's BLUE and Smith's DYIN have enormous capacity; Garrideb collects plaster ones 3GAR; Mrs. Ronder's heart leaps with joy when she hears the crash of her husband's smashed skull VEIL.

skunk: Fairbairn CARD, Morris VALL.

Slaney, Abe: American gangster; great, aggressive, hooked nose; blazing, black eyes; Cubitt calls him a skulking rascal DANC.

slang: used primarily in dialogue of low-class or American characters, but Holmes and Watson are sometimes guilty: *see* **barney; boob; bumper; chevy; chokey; copper; cove; croaker; crib; cross; darbies; dibbs; dig(s, - gings); Gar!, by; growler; guy; heeled; jack-in-office; jarveys; jay; junk; let in; mate; money** (for **bob; tanner; quid**); **nark; nuts; queer; rattle; scratch; shake-down; sheeny; slop-shop; snibbed; split; stiff, old; sucker; yarn;** for correct, though unfamiliar, terms, *see* **gasogene; spud; tantalus; vesta.**

Slater: stonemason BLAC.

slavey: (servant) London, boot-slitting SCAN.

Sleepy Hollows: Holmes's term for country villages; refers to *The Legend of Sleepy Hollow* (1820), by ***Irving, Washington,** q.v., though not naming him MISS.

sleeves, thumb-nails, boot-laces: Holmes draws conclusions from; Sutherland's plush sleeve bears a mark which suggests that she is a typist or a seamstress; the position of the mark causes him to opt for the former IDEN; *cf.* **fingertips.**

slippers: bedroom, Brunton MUSG and Barker VALL wear; Holmes holds his slippered feet to the fire ABBE; *see* **shoes; Persian; Turkish.**

slips: Holmes takes from his pocket the various slips of the dancing men DANC.

*Sloane, Hans (1660–1753): physician, collector, founder of British museum 3GAR.

slop-shop: slang for small store selling clothing to sailors (from Middle English *sloppe,* a kind of garment; *slop* [mud, viscous matter] is from an identical Middle English word); *see* **Upper Swandam Lane.**

slow-witted: Holmes confesses that he has been ABBE.

slow-worm: one of Sherman's pets; a legless lizard; keeps down the beetles; *cf.* **badger; stoat** SIGN.

Small, Jonathan: one-legged ex-convict; Holmes describes him as small, active; later Watson writes that he is good-sized, powerful; clubs a man to death with his wooden leg; curses his pursuers; drops his mask of stoicism SIGN.

smell: Roy knows by smell that Presbury is simian CREE; Holmes tells Dixie, I don't like the smell of you 3GAB; Watson smells of iodoform SCAN; Holmes sniffs Drebber's lips and identifies poison STUD; Holmes identifies jessamine; Watson sniffs (possibly) and identifies **phosphorus,** q.v.; Watson identifies fetid, stale tobacco smoke GOLD; Watson and Holmes sniff bottle and identify the pleasant almondy odour of prussic acid VEIL; Holmes sniffs string CARD, gloves BLAN, and identifies tar; Watson sniffs cigar CHAS, creosote SIGN; Holmes sniffs cigar and identifies it as a Havana RESI; Stoner smelled Roylott's cigar (Holmes deduces presence of ventilator); Holmes and Watson smell burning oil and heated metal SPEC; Phelps did not check for scent of tobacco NAVA; smell of gunpowder, servants sniff DANC; dogs follow aniseed MISS, creosote SIGN; Holmes retires to thyme-scented Sussex downs LION; fresh paint hides the smell of rotting bodies RETI; *also see* **scent (used figuratively)**.

smile: Holmes's, enigmatical NORW; tolerant RETI; sardonic, bodes little good EMPT; whimsical CREE, ILLU; curious DANC; languid 3GAB; rises with one SECO; Hudson's, loose-lipped GLOR; faintest shadow of, flickers over Mrs. Douglas's face at mention of wedding ring VALL; Smith's, malicious and abominable; but shortly thereafter he smiles pleasantly DYIN; Milverton's, broad, insufferable, and complacent CHAS; Pinner's, ghastly STOC; Rucastle's hardens into a grin of rage COPP; Barclay's, struck from his mouth CROO; Hope's, placid, on his dead face STUD; Sholto's, ghastly, inscrutable SIGN; police listen to Openshaw's story with a FIVE; *see* **Hippocratic;** *and see* **laugh.**

Smith: James, orchestra conductor; Ralph, his illiterate dead brother; Violet, daughter of James, teaches music SOLI; Culverton, tries to kill Holmes; great, yellow face, coarse-grained and greasy; sullen, menacing, gray eyes DYIN; Mordecai, rents boats; wife, son Jack; son Jim SIGN; *Joseph (1805–1844), American founder of Church of Jesus Christ of Latter-Day Saints (Mormons) STUD; "Smith-Mortimer succession case": Holmes solves GOLD.

snarl: Holmes, in disguise, snarls contempt at Watson; Moran snarls with rage EMPT; Holmes snarls at vampires SUSS; Holmes withdraws empty hand with a bitter snarl of anger SECO; Hudson snarls at Victor GLOR; Moriarty snarls at Holmes FINA; three of Boone's teeth exposed in a perpetual snarl TWIS; fierce, Hope's, when he takes wedding ring from Lucy's dead hand STUD; *see* **snort.**

snatches: of song, Tregennises sing DEVI; *see* **violin.**

sneer: distinct, in Cantlemere's words to Holmes MAZA; bitter, on Windibank's face IDEN; Ross's lips curl in a SILV; Barker sneers with acrid irony VALL; *see* **passions.**

snibbed: Holmes's word for bolted, fastened (Sholto's window) SIGN.

snort: Holmes snorts contempt BRUC; Mason says (at least three times) that the case is a snorter VALL.

snow BERY.

snuff GREE, IDEN, REDH.

snuff-box: gold, with amethyst, Holmes's IDEN; tortoise-shell, Mycroft's GREE.

Soames: Sir Cathcart, son at the school PRIO; Hilton, tutor and lecturer 3STU.

social: questions, Watson tries to interest Phelps in NAVA; strata,

Douglas's offhand manners reveal that he has lived on some far lower horizon than that of the country society of Sussex VALL; *cf.* **poop;** summonses, unwelcome, call upon a man either to be bored or to lie (Holmes says) NOBL.

socks: Heidegger goes out without PRIO; Garrideb jokes about the cut of his 3GAR; for Holmes's, *see* **boots.**

soldiers, retired: Holmes (along with Mycroft in GREE) identifies them, their ranks, and their regiments at a glance BLAN, GREE, STUD; they are likely to become commissionaires or watchmen, but Dodd is a stockbroker BLAN.

*Solomon (tenth century B.C.): king of Israel; McGinty makes an unlikely allusion to VALL.

son: Alexander Holder's carried himself in the matter as Holmes should be proud to have his own do, should he ever chance to have one BERY.

Sotheby's: auctioneers and art dealers; actual firm 3GAR.

sots: Holmes's term for opium addicts TWIS.

soul: Holmes says he may be saving Ryder's when he lets him go BLUE; Kemp to Melas: if you speak to a human soul about this – one human soul, mind – well, may God have mercy upon your soul! GREE; Amberley's is distorted RETI.

South Africa: securities (gold shares) of, Watson decides not to buy DANC, Sir Charles made his money from HOUN, Carruthers is deeply interested in SOLI; Green has spent time there LADY; two people are from there; another dies there SOLI; background (Boer War) BLAN; gold king from there built Smith's house, an architectural nightmare; *see* **architecture** ILLU; Gilchrist leaves university, avoiding scandal, to accept commission in Rhodesian Police 3STU.

South America: Shlessingers are missionaries from LADY; exotic brides from (South or Central), Gibson THOR, Ferguson SUSS, Stapleton HOUN; arrangements made to send the murderer Selden there, but he dies HOUN.

Southerton, Lord: owns lands round the estate COPP.

spaniels HOUN, SHOS, SIGN, SUSS; the one in SHOS howls outside well-house, snaps at black skirt; *see* **skeleton; Toby.**

sparking plugs: code words for naval signals LAST.

spasm: of merriment, seizes Holmes NORW; *see* **laughter; smile.**

spats: from his spats to his gold-rimmed spectacles, he [Scott Eccles] was a Conservative, a churchman, a good citizen, orthodox and conventional WIST; *see* **dress; lavender.**

Spaulding, Vincent: Clay's alias; Holmes calls him the fourth smartest man in London – perhaps the third REDH; *cf.* **Milver-**

ton, Charles Augustus; Moran, Colonel Sebastian.

"Speckled Band": (= SPEC) NAVA.

Spencer John gang: crooks, Holmes has knowledge of 3GAB.

Spender, Rose: Mrs. Peters's old nurse; imbecile; dead of senile decay LADY.

*Spenser, Edmund (1552–1599): English poet; called *Chaucer, Geoffrey, q.v., a well of English undefiled; Holmes uses the phrase but does not identify either the author or the subject LAST.

spider, foul: Moriarty compared to NORW.

spies: see agents.

spirit: Holmes goes to Devonshire in HOUN.

spirits: half-bottle in Holmes's hut on the moor HOUN; see flask; spirits of wine used to wash horse's face SILV; Holmes offers Watson the spirit-case SCAN.

split: slang for inform on, McMurdo uses VALL; see Sanders, Ikey.

sport: see games.

spring: Holmes springs sown with an ejaculation of satisfaction ABBE; like a tiger, springs on Moran's back EMPT; Amberly springs to his feet, and like a tiger Holmes springs at his throat RETI; McMurdo makes a tiger-spring at his fiancée VALL.

spud: spadelike tool WIST.

squealing: coolies used to do some, says Smith DYIN.

squirrel: Croker as active as ABBE.

stable-boy: half-clad, waits with Holmes's and Watson's trap TWIS; throws light on the matter by telling Holmes about Elrige's DANC.

Stackhurst, Harold: coach, Holmes's neighbor in Sussex; tells Holmes there is a curse on the place LION.

stage: what the law had gained the stage had lost (Dowson, re Holmes) MAZA; see actor.

staghounds: Holmes's characterization of Gregson and Lestrade; later they, along with Holmes, spring on Hope like staghounds STUD; see dogs; spring.

stairs: badly carpeted, at Mrs. Merrilow's VEIL; well-carpeted, Trevelyan's RESI; Watson's steps worn three inches deeper than neighbor's, from which Holmes deduces that Watson's medical practice is better STOC; worn hollow at the centre by the ceaseless tread of drunken feet TWIS; worn stone 3STU; stair-rods, bright SIGN; Holmes rushes to the top of the stairs to draw in the fresh air GREE; top steps swilled down (to remove blood), others dry SIXN; for steps at 221B, see number.

Stamford: map-seller; error for Stan-? HOUN; Archie, forger; apprehended by Holmes and Watson near Farnham, also the locale of SOLI; young, introduces Holmes and Watson STUD.

Stamford's: map-seller; error for Stanford's Geological Establishment, actual firm HOUN.

Stanger, James: editor of *Vermissa Herald*, beaten almost to death VALL.

Stangerson, Joseph: murderous Mormon, acts as Drebber's secretary; stabbed, in self-defense, by Hope STUD.

Staples: Culverton Smith's apologetic butler DYIN.

Stapleton: Jack, pseudonym of Rodger Baskerville; gray eyes, flaxen hair, lean jaws; also uses pseudonym Vandeleur; wife Beryl, née Garcia (spelled Garçia in Baring-Gould edition); though she is a Costa Rican beauty, at Dartmoor he passes her off as his sister; dark, eager eyes; she calls her husband This villain! HOUN.

staring brick: Deep Dene House NORW.

Stark, Colonel Lysander: called Fritz; long, sharp nose; something of a German accent; **Elise,** q.v., also speaks broken English and has some unexplained relationship – wife? sister? Stark, Ferguson, and Elise disappear at end of tale ENGR.

Starr, Dr. Lysander: mayor of Topeka, Kansas; Holmes invents (recalling **Stark, Colonel Lysander,** q.v.?) 3GAR.

starve: Holmes occasionally goes without food for days, ingesting only tobacco smoke DYIN, FIVE, MAZA, MISS, VALL; he explains, the faculties become refined when you starve them MAZA;

but normally he is a hearty trencherman – *see* **drink; food.**

Staunton: Godfrey, athlete; Blackheath, Cambridge; *see* **landlady's daughter;** "Arthur H., rising young forger"; "Henry," whom Holmes helped to hang MISS.

Steiler, Peter: Swiss hotelier FINA.

Steiner: traitor LAST.

stepfathers, stepmothers: COPP, IDEN, SPEC, SUSS, YELL.

Stephens: butler SHOS.

Stepney: London district, location of Gelder & Co.; riverside city of a hundred thousand souls, where the tenement houses swelter and reek with the outcasts of Europe SIXN.

steps: *see* **stairs.**

Sterndale, Dr. Leon: lion-hunter and explorer; passed out (and closed window); fierce eyes and hawk-like nose DEVI.

"Stevens, Bert": terrible murderer; mild-mannered, Sunday-school young man NORW.

Stevenson: one of Staunton's rugby teammates MISS.

Stewart: Jane, housemaid CROO; "Mrs., of Lauder," Moran probably responsible for her death EMPT.

stiff, old: = chap, fellow, coot; Evans's American slang term for Garrideb 3GAR.

Stimson & Co.: undertakers; proprietors, Mr. and Mrs. Stimson LADY.

stoat: one of Sherman's pets; *cf.* **badger; slow-worm;** for the stoat's red eyes, *cf.* **Teddy.**

Stockdale: Barney; wife Susan 3GAB.

stocks: Stock Exchange debt, Walter owes BRUC; *see* **securities.**

stone: unit of weight = 14 pounds; Overton weighs 16 (= 224 pounds) MISS; stones on the moor look like the fangs of some monstrous beast HOUN; Holmes hunts among heather and ferns for a considerable stone THOR; for gemstones, *see* **jewels;** *and see* **weapons.**

Stone, Rev. Joshua: Garcia's neighbor WIST.

Stoner: Helen, engaged to Armitage; Julia, engaged to a half-pay major of marines but dies before the wedding SPEC.

stormy petrel of crime: Holmes says Watson is NAVA; *see* **fixed point.**

Stradivarius: violin, Holmes's CARD Holmes an expert on SIGN, STUD; *see* **Amati; Cremona.**

strait-jacket: Sir Henry wonders whether he or Stapleton should be in one; a little later he says he is sure Stapleton is a crazy man HOUN.

Straker: John, alias Darbyshire; and wife; his overcoat found flapping from a furze-bush; Ross says that he has always been an excellent servant, but he is an adulterous horse-maimer; buys his dashing mistress (never named) expensive dresses SILV.

Strand: major London thoroughfare; Watson stays at hotel in, before meeting Holmes; American Exchange there STUD; location of **Simpson's,** q.v.; Sir Henry bought boots at shop there HOUN; Holmes asks Clay for directions to, from Saxe-Coburg Square REDH; Holmes and Watson stroll there RESI; telegram postmarked there; Staunton ran in direction of MISS; Watson takes hansom to Strand end of Lowther Arcade FINA.

Straubenzee: air-gun maker MAZA.

straw: Holmes directs Watson to light a couple of bundles NORW; *see* **outhouse.**

string: Holmes ties knots in one at every yard MUSG.

strychnine: Watson, flustered by Morstan's presence, recommends large doses as a sedative; identifies poison as strychnine-like substance SIGN.

"Study in Scarlet, A": (= STUD) original title, "A Tangled Skein"; alluded to BOSC, IDEN, RESI.

*Stuart: Charles I (1600–1649; reigned 1625–1649) MUSG and II (1630–1685; reigned 1660–1685) VALL, kings of Great Britain; *see also* **kings.**

students, fellow: Holmes's, at university, provided him with cases in the early years MUSG; these include Trevor GLOR and Musgrave MUSG.

style, Conan Doyle's: like Holmes, the author had a remarkable gift of observation, and he provides the reader with precise details, as entries for **eyes, hands, dress, fingers,** and **food** will demonstrate; but *see* **absurdities; alliteration; formulas; peculiarities; ponderousness; repetitions.**

sucker: they are playing him for a, says Sir Henry, lapsing into broad Western dialect HOUN; *see* **jay; slang.**

sucking dove: Von Bork says any pan-German Junker is one, compared with Altamont; he is possibly quoting Shakespeare, *A Midsummer Night's Dream.*

Sudbury: *see* **Blount.**

sugar: lump of, Lady Beatrice gives Shoscombe Prince; SHOS; Watson befriends Toby with SIGN; though Holmes and Watson drink lots of coffee and tea, we are never told how many lumps each one takes.

suicides (real, apparent): hanging RESI; shooting THOR; poison GOLD, RETI, STUD; drowning in two feet of water FIVE; Howells thought to have drowned herself in eight feet of water, but she probably escaped MUSG; Holmes wonders if Sir James Walter was a suicide BRUC; attempted, DANC, RETI, STOC.

Sumatra: country that produces the giant **rat,** q.v., and the mysterious coolie disease from which Holmes claims he is suffering DYIN.

Sumner: shipping agent BLAC.

sundial: code appears on DANC; Openshaw is instructed to leave the (Klan) papers on FIVE.

superficial (very, remarkably): Holmes's term for his ratiocination CARD, CROO, REIG, RESI; *see* **absurdly.**

supernatural: Holmes disbelieves in DEVI, HOUN, SUSS; but *see* **Bible; David; devil; religion; rose.**

supper, cold: Mrs. St. Clair lays for Holmes and Watson TWIS.

supposititious: case, Holmes proposes VALL.

surgeon, local: old white-haired (gray-haired in the next paragraph), attends Elsie DANC.

surgery: Watson deep in recent treatise on GOLD; for the locations of his surgeries, *see* **Watson, John H.**

surmise: and conjecture – that's all we have, says Holmes; not a shadow of a case HOUN; *see* **plethora.**

surprise: Holmes throws Watson into a **faint,** q.v., EMPT; surprises Watson in moor hut; loves to dominate and surprise HOUN; surprises others with dramatic revelations NAVA, NORW, SILV, SIXN; Watson surprises Holmes with news of Lucas's death SECO; *see* **practical.**

Susan: maid, like some huge awkward chicken; Stockdale's wife 3GAB.

Sussex: location of poisonous jellyfish (Cyanea) LION, vampires SUSS, Holmes's bees LION, SECO.

Sutherland: Mary, vacuous face; Ned, her New Zealand uncle who left her money; her father was a successful plumber IDEN; *see* **dress;** "Mary Sutherland" (= IDEN) COPP, REDH.

Sutro: Maberley's lawyer 3GAB.

Sutton: Blessington's real name; bank robber and informer; murdered by fellow gang members Biddle, Hayward, and Moffat, who hang him RESI.

William Gillette (1853-1937), American actor and playwright, famous for his stage performances as Holmes

swan: solitary, swims in frozen pond ABBE.

Swan and Edison: brand of electric lights; actual firm – Sir Henry will install 1,000 candle power at Baskerville Hall HOUN.

Swedes: *see* **Germans.**

swimmer: Holmes, in retirement, is one; so are McPherson and Murdoch LION; Small admits that he foolishly took a swim in the Ganges SIGN.

Swindon, Archie: escapes Scowrers; he would rather be a free crossing-sweeper in New York than a large mine owner VALL.

Sylvius, Count Negretto: cruel, thin-lipped mouth; curved nose like the beak of an eagle MAZA.

syringe: Watson is horrified to see it in Holmes's hand, but it is filled with aniseed, not cocaine MISS; Presbury uses one for his ape-serum injections CREE; *see* **drugs.**

system: *see* **method.**

tailing (shadowing, following): Holmes bungles it HOUN, STUD; Holmes: I followed you. Sterndale: I saw no one. Holmes: That is what you may expect to see when I follow you DEVI.

tall, thin man: *see* **detective.**

Tangey, Mr.: commissionaire; wife and daughter; calls his wife My old woman NAVA.

"Tankerville Club" FIVE; Colonel Moran is a member EMPT.

tantalus: frame or holder for decanters of spirits BLAC.

"Tarleton murders": records of the case are in Holmes's tin box MUSG.

Tarlton, Susan: Coram's maid GOLD.

tattoos: anchor STUD; fish REDH; initials J. A. GLOR; triangle inside a circle – not a tattoo but a brand VALL; *see* **Holmes Bibliography.**

Tavernier: maker of wax bust of Holmes MAZA.

tea: ABBE, RESI, CREE, CROO, LION, NAVA, SIGN, SUSS, 3STU, VALL; flown to, as an agitated woman will CROO; pretext for liaison between Mary Cushing and Fairbairn CARD; high, Watson orders for Holmes VALL.

tears: spasm of pain blurs Watson's eyes with; Mrs. Barrymore weeps bitterly in her apron HOUN.

Teddy: mongoose, ichneumon, snake-catcher; leaves footprints, which Watson mistakes for those of a dog or monkey, on curtain; finest red eyes CROO; Sherman's stoat also has red eyes SIGN.

teeth: a too visible line of yellow and irregular teeth (Sholto's) SIGN; chattering, Drebber's, Holmes's, Watson's, MacDonald's, Mason's STUD, VALL; Holmes cries between his SIGN; Boone's, *see* **snarl;** for false teeth, *see* **"Dundas separation case"; fake, false, feigned, phony (not including disguises, impersonations, or aliases).**

telegram, -graph, -phone: from the first (STUD – sends a long telegram) Holmes uses frequently; he has never been known to write where a telegram would serve DEVI; but, instead of a wire, Holmes sends Gregson a rather long letter, delivered by hand SIGN; cipher telegram SECO; weird one (Overton to Holmes) MISS; Holmes's hotel room ankle-deep in congratulatory telegrams REIG; Holmes asks Watson if he has telegraph forms and then dictates two wires BLAC; from Charing Cross office, sends one to Croker ABBE; sends one to determine if Baskerville is actually at the Hall HOUN; similarly for Sterndale at the Plymouth hotel; throws answer into grate; Roundhay also wires Sterndale DEVI; sends one to Watson, asking about Shlessinger's left ear LADY; sends several at telegraph office GREE; scribbles off several and hands them to the page-boy NAVA; sends a cable to the Savannah police FIVE; has an agent send Amberley a wire with an innocent clergyman's (Elman's) name forged RETI; Holmes summons Lestrade to Croydon; jumps out of cab to send another wire CARD; Lestrade sends one to Holmes: Come instantly SIXN; in Stangerson's pocket, a wire from Cleveland: J. H. is in Europe STUD; long telegram from Paris appears in London newspaper SECO; police trace Eccles through telegram he sent to Holmes WIST; Cubitt wires Holmes that he is coming; they exchange wires; then Cubitt sends a letter, while Holmes sends a cablegram to America DANC; exchange between Staunton, Overton, and Mount-James MISS; Mycroft wires Holmes that he is coming at once; Holmes later wires Mycroft some news of the case; the latter responds by note, delivered by a government messenger BRUC; the telephone comes into use only late in Holmes's career – ILLU, RETI, 3GAR; *see* **bitter curse; come at once if convenient – if incon-**

venient come all the same. –S. H.; letter.

telescope: Frankland uses to spy on the countryside; Holmes identifies it by the light flashing on its lens; Sir Henry's rear-admiral forebear is painted with one HOUN.

tempestuous, melancholy (weather) HOUN.

tennis: does Watson play? *see* **shoes;** he does play **billiards,** the **horses,** and **rugby,** qq.v.

terrier: Holmes asks Watson to fetch; he poisons it STUD; *see* **dogs.**

terror: paroxysm of, Selden experiences when confronted by hound HOUN; Lady Hilda exhibits – not beauty SECO; on M. Tregennis's face DEVI; some men strike terror into others: But, my word! I had rather not be the man that crossed him!, Ames re Douglas VALL; A hard, fierce man, I should think, and one whom I should be sorry to offend, landlord of the Englischer Hof re Green LADY; *see* **Abrahams; handwriting** (Porlock's terror); *cf.* **horror.**

test: the Sherlock Holmes's, for blood stains STUD.

Texas: Watson knows that it is the Lone Star state, Holmes does not FIVE.

Thames: scene of boat chase in SIGN; *see* **body; key; money; treasure.**

theatre: tickets BRUC, RETI, SECO; Imperial, James Smith conducted

orchestra SOLI; Woolwich BRUC; Haymarket RETI; Lyceum SIGN.

thieves: (their thefts are usually thwarted or the stolen object returned): *see* **Beppo; Brunton, Richard; Burnwell, Sir George; Carey, Peter; Clay, John; Gilchrist; Harrison** (Joseph); **Hope** (Lady Hilda Trelawney); **Pinner, Harry, Arthur; Ryder, James; Shlessinger, Dr. and Mrs.; Sholto** (Major); **Small, Jonathan; Stapleton** (Jack); **Sylvius** (Count Negretto); **Walter** (Colonel Valentine); Holmes himself steals things (BRUC, CHAS, ILLU, LAST, RETI) but always in the interests of justice, of course; he snorts his contempt for petty theft BRUC; *cf.* **blackmail; murderers.**

theorist: Athelney Jones addresses Holmes as Mr. Holmes, the theorist; later as Mr. Theorist SIGN.

theory: Watson asks Holmes if he has one; Holmes responds, At least I have got a grip on the essential **facts** (q.v.) SILV; Lestrade to Holmes: You are too many for me when you begin to get on with your theories; Holmes: I much fear that British juries have not yet attained that pitch of intelligence when they will give the preference to my theories over Lestrade's facts NORW; Holmes says, It is a capital mistake to theorize before you have all the evidence STUD; Insensibly one begins to twist facts to suit theories, instead of theories to suit facts SCAN; Still, it is an error to argue in front of your data. You find yourself insensibly twisting them round to fit your theories WIST; It is a capital mistake to theorize in advance of the facts SECO.

thermometer: at (of) ninety no hardship for Watson CARD, RESI; in the first of these tales it is a blazing hot day in August; in the second it is a close, rainy day in October; *see* **Afghanistan.**

thick fog BRUC, COPP, HOUN.

think: I am inclined to (Watson begins); I should do so (Holmes continues, cuttingly) VALL; *see* **intellect; scintillating.**

*Thoreau, Henry David (1817–1872): American writer; Holmes quotes his example of very convincing circumstantial evidence: finding a trout in the milk (some readers are puzzled by Thoreau's witticism: fish live in water; ergo, the milk has been watered) NOBL; see **circumstantial evidence.**

thorn: from Tonga's blow-pipe; Holmes asks, Is that an English thorn? Watson responds, No, it certainly is not SIGN.

thought: Watson is afraid to break into Holmes's TWIS; *see* **deaf.**

threads: Holmes's frequent metaphor for lines of investigation, e.g., HOUN; *see* **net;** for literal threads, *see* **St. Pancras.**

threats, by Holmes and against him: *see* **box** (coffin); **break; crush; Dangling Prussian; dogs; entrances; fist; hunting-crop; laughter** (Holmes's response to threats); **Tut!;** Stark to Hatherley, Not a word to a soul. You will not tell a human being ENGR; Latimer to Melas, If you try any tricks, God help you! But say no more than you are told to say, or – you had better never have been born. If you speak to a human soul about this – one human soul, mind – well, may God have mercy upon your soul! GREE.

threw up: Holmes says Browner did CARD; St. Clair threw up reporting TWIS; Sylvius threw up his eyes MAZA; *see* **window.**

thrice is he armed that hath his quarrel just: Holmes quotes Shakespeare, *2 Henry VI* LADY.

thrill: vague, runs through Watson when Holmes says that severed ears are not a joke CARD.

throat: Holmes's acrid tobacco-fumes assault Watson's; hound worries Sir Henry's HOUN; villainous stuff (fumes) linger about Holmes's; Sterndale clutches his own, beneath his brindled beard DEVI; chin hangs in folds over Rucastle's; later, dog's muzzle buried in it COPP; dog's fangs buried deep in Presbury's CREE; Morstan's hand goes to, choking sobs SIGN; Von Bork clutches his own in despair LAST; white haft of a knife emerges from Gorgiano's REDC; great gash in Venucci's SIXN; weak, Angel's IDEN; Holmes springs at Amberley's RETI.

*Thucydides (471?–?400 B.C): Greek historian; passage from, for examination; instead of copying it, why did Gilchrist not simply obtain the printed text, after identifying it, by borrowing the book or making use of the library? 3STU; *see* **Fortescue.**

thumb: print, mark NORW, REDC, SIGN, TWIS; compositor's COPP; Downing's nearly chewed off by suspect WIST; for thumb-nails, *see* **sleeve.**

Thurston: Watson plays billiards with DANC.

ticket, railroad: nonexistent BRUC; half SPEC; *see* **theatre.**

tide-waiter: (= customs-officer) one of Holmes's correspondents NOBL.

tie-pin: *see* **emerald.**

tiger: Holmes springs like EMPT, RETI; bounds like SIXN; -skins, thrown on Sholto's thick carpet; - cub, Watson tells Morstan about one in his tent in Afghanistan SIGN; Green springs at Watson like a tiger LADY; McGinty springs at Baldwin like one; McMurdo makes a tiger spring at Ettie; Cormac nicknamed Tiger; older Scowrers have tigerish lawless souls VALL; thief or murderer could pounce like one, in the fog BRUC; Moran's bag of tigers remains unrivalled EMPT; *see* **hearth-rug.**

time: *see* **Big Ben; clock; cuff; dates; dinner; lamp; luncheon; noon; watch.**

tin mine: Stapleton's refuge and hound-kennel HOUN.

tiptoe: Mortimer says Sir Charles's footprints indicate that he walked on; no, says Holmes, he was running – for his life HOUN; similarly for McCarthy's BOSC and Barclay's CROO assailants, and for Arthur BERY.

"Tired Captain" NAVA; some believe that this case = MISS, since Overton was skipper of the rugby team and was haggard with anxiety.

tissue-change: increased, by Holmes's drug habit, Watson warns SIGN.

toast: Holmes munches silently (quite a feat!) STUD; sits with mouth full of VALL; and coffee, Holmes and Watson engaged in SCAN.

tobacco: chewing, used by man who sealed gummed flap of envelope, Holmes speculates TWIS; smoking kills the appetite, says Holmes GOLD; *see* **cigarettes; cigars; number; pipe, smoking, and tobacco; snuff.**

Toby: dog; half spaniel, half lurcher; keen sense of smell SIGN; *cf.* **Pompey.**

toilet: Eccles has given no thought to his WIST; Holmes comes into Watson's room just as he has finished his 3STU; at intervals of his, Holmes drinks claret and eats biscuits DYIN.

Tokay: wine; Sholto apologizes – he keeps only Chianti and Tokay SIGN; heavily sealed dust-covered bottle, Altamont has taken a fancy to LAST.

Toller: sottish groom, and wife COPP.

Tonga: Andaman Island savage; unhallowed dwarf; small eyes, thick lips; shot, drowned in Thames SIGN; *see* **mace; meat.**

tooth: badly stuffed with gold STOC; weaver's COPP; viper's, spring in ivory box is as sharp as DYIN; *see also* **"Dundas separation case"; fake, false, feigned, phony (not including disguises, impersonations, or aliases); teeth.**

"Tosca, Cardinal": Holmes investigates his death at the request of the Pope BLAC.

Tottenham Court Road: location of the Jew broker CARD; plumbing business, Sutherland's father's IDEN; Morton and Waylight's REDC; and Goodge Street, site of altercation between Baker and a little knot of roughs BLUE.

touch: a distinct, says Holmes, re Watson's pawky humour VALL; undeniable, says Holmes, re Stapleton calling himself Holmes HOUN; Holmes's delicacy of, when manipulating his fragile philosophical instruments STUD; *see* **artist; sheeny.**

touts: one of those damned, stable-boy calls Simpson SILV; Norberton is jealous of them SHOS.

towel: Holmes uses to bind Hope's ankles STUD; *see* **cord.**

tradesmen: distinct from professional men and servants; Holmes's practice brings him into contact with many, including artificial knee-cap manufacturer REDH; bric-a-brac merchant and manufacturer SIXN; builder NORW; electrician SOLI; engineer (not considered professional?) ENGR; innkeeper PRIO; paint manufacturer RETI; paperhanger STUD; pawnbroker REDH; plumber BLUE; undertaker LADY; wine merchant IDEN.

trains: Holmes and Watson ride in almost every case, sometimes using the wrong stations (e.g., King's Cross for Liverpool Street MISS); Holmes pulls Watson from one ABBE; Moriarty engages a special to pursue Holmes and Watson FINA; one of Holmes's clients is a railway porter in his velveteen uniform STUD; stationmaster greets Holmes and Watson DANC; stationmaster laughs heartily at Hatherley ENGR; railroad guard brings Watson a patient ENGR; Holmes and Watson take a Pullman car from Winchester to London SILV; they always take first-class carriages (FINA, HOUN, SILV, STOC); Cadogan West and Amberley travel third-class; Watson views the latter as infra dig BRUC, RETI; railway official (very helpful) walks Holmes along the Underground tracks BRUC; robbery in the train deluxe to the Riviera MAZA; Holmes says that he is not like a time-table and that criminals' movements are not scheduled like railway trains VALL; Holmes returns to London by train, leaving the scene of the crime (or pretending to), to the puzzlement of others HOUN, NAVA, SILV; Holmes and Watson use King's Cross, Euston, Liverpool Street, Waterloo, Paddington, Charing

Cross, Victoria stations; *see* **Bradshaw; milk; points; Underground.**

tra-la-la-lira-lira-lay: *see* ***Chopin, Frédéric François.**

tramp: Holmes hypothesizes the existence of one to explain murder NORW.

trap: door in top of cab, through which passenger can communicate with driver HOUN.

treasure, Agra: one hundred and forty-three diamonds, including the Great Mogul; ninety-seven very fine emeralds, one hundred and seventy rubies, forty carbuncles, two hundred and ten sapphires, sixty-one agates, three hundred pearls, plus beryls, onyxes, cats'-eyes, turquoises, and other stones – all dumped into the Thames; Watson unblushingly effuses, Whoever had lost a treasure, I knew that night that I had gained one (Morstan, his bride-to-be) SIGN; "Agra Treasure" (= SIGN) REDH; *see* **jewels.**

trees: Holmes knows that some grow to a certain height and then develop some unsightly eccentricity (metaphor for Moran's life) EMPT; an oak and an elm are important in MUSG; *see* **flora.**

Tregellis, Janet: head gamekeeper's daughter MUSG.

Tregennis: Mortimer, Owen, George, Brenda; Cornish family, members of which are dead, mad, or murderous; Mortimer's eyes are averted; Brenda is (or was) beautiful DEVI.

"Trepoff murder in Odessa": Holmes was involved, but we are given no details SCAN.

Trevelyan, Percy: doctor; author of monograph on obscure nervous lesions, which Watson has read RESI; *see* **nitrite.**

Trevor: old – pugilist, mutineer, gold-digger; last words, written in a shaky hand, Sweet Lord, have mercy on our souls; son Victor, Holmes's only university friend, calls his father "the dad"; leaves England for a tea-plantation in India GLOR; *see* **Armitage.**

trifles: nothing so important as, says Holmes TWIS; he has a strangely retentive memory for LION; *see* **data; facts.**

trigonometry: Holmes uses MUSG.

Trincomalee: town in Ceylon; *see* **Atkinson.**

trout: *see* **fisherman; *Thoreau, Henry David.**

Tudor: chimneys SOLI, SUSS; half Tudor, half Georgian THOR; Tudor and Plantagenet blood, St. Simon has NOBL.

"Turkey, Sultan of": Holmes has a commission from him that calls for immediate action, thus delaying his visit to Tuxbury Old Hall BLAN.

Turkish: bath, Watson takes LADY; Holmes and Watson take ILLU; slippers, Roylott wears SPEC.

Turner, Mrs.: Holmes's housekeeper? cook? SCAN; John and daughter Alice; she is one of the most lovely young women Watson has ever seen in his life; in love with James McCarthy BOSC.

Tuson, Sergeant: policeman STOC.

***Tussaud, Madame Marie Grosholtz (?–1850):** Swiss founder of London wax museum MAZA.

Tut!: Sylvius twice remarks MAZA; Tut! tut!, cries Holmes to Openshaw, You must act, man, or you are lost FIVE; Tut, tut, we have solved some worse problems, says Holmes to Watson PRIO; Tut-tut!, says Holmes, when he learns from Hopkins that the road was trodden into mire GOLD; tut, tut, this sounds serious, says Smith DYIN; tut, tut!, Moriarty exclaims as he threatens Holmes FINA.

twaddle: ineffable, says Watson re Holmes's *Book of Life* STUD; *cf.* **bleat.**

twine: tarred, and brown paper smelling of coffee CARD.

twitch: various body parts do so, including eyebrows VALL, faces 3STU, features PRIO, fingers and hands DYIN, lips CHAS, various parts of Sholto's body twitch SIGN; Whitney is twitching and shattered TWIS; Bates twitches THOR; *cf.* **quiver; shiver.**

typefaces: Holmes identifies *Times* leaded bourgeois, but confesses that when very young he confused the *Leeds Mercury* with the *Western Morning News* HOUN; identifies agony column of *Daily Telegraph* by print and paper BRUC.

typewriting: Holmes almost mistakes for piano playing SOLI; Lyons's fingers play nervously over the stops of her Remington typewriter HOUN; Sutherland is a professional typist; Holmes identifies peculiarities of typewriter (slurred *e*, tailless *r*, plus fourteen other characteristics) used by Angel (Windibank) IDEN; Lady Hilda pretends to be enquiring about typewriting when she dupes MacPherson at Lucas's house SECO; *see* **Holmes Bibliography.**

tyre: *see* **Dunlop; number; Palmer; unbreakable tyre;** spelled *tire* in Doubleday edition.

Uffa: *see* **"Grice Patersons in the Island of Uffa."**

ulster: worn by both Watson and Adler; Watson hides the rocket under his; Adler's is part of her cross-dresser's costume SCAN; worn by Holmes and Watson, with cravats BLUE.

ululation: *see* **women.**

umbrella: ivory head, Bellinger's SECO; Watson's, Holmes borrows VALL; "Phillimore" returns home for his, disappears THOR; streaming, Openshaw's FIVE; baggy parasol, part of Holmes's disguise; Sylvius hands it to him in the Minories MAZA; Holmes carries harpoon around London like an umbrella BLAC.

unbreakable tyre: bicycle, invented by Openshaw's father FIVE.

Uncle Sam: Holmes, in disguise as Altamont, looks like LAST.

Underground: London's underground railway system BERY, BRUC, REDH, STUD; Watson says, I should like to see him [the author of *The Book of Life* – i.e., Holmes, though Watson is unaware of the fact] clapped down in a third-class carriage on the Underground, and asked to give the trades of all his fellow-travellers STUD.

undertaker's: mute, Mount-James resembles MISS; man, Holmes offers money, addressing him as "my man" LADY; *see* **dress; Stimson and Co.**

Underwood, John, and Sons: hatters; Drebber's hat obtained from them STUD.

universities: Cambridge, London, Oxford; Holmes attended one (unspecified) but evidently did not take a degree GLOR, MUSG; does research on early English charters at one (again unspecified) 3STU.

unpredictability: Holmes uses a couple of railway metaphors VALL; *see* **trains.**

Upper Swandam Lane: north side of the Thames, east of London Bridge; vile alley between slopshop and gin-shop, location of the Bar of Gold TWIS.

Uppingham: Smith's public school GOLD.

"Upwood, Colonel, atrocious conduct of in connection with the famous card scandal at the Nonpareil Club": one of the cases that Holmes solves after the conclusion of HOUN.

urchin: small (actually, Cartwright) crosses moor HOUN.

vacation: Holmes on, nonetheless becomes involved in a criminal case DEVI, FINA, REIG.

valet: Trelawney Hope's; Mitton, Lucas's SECO; treacherous valets and maids CHAS.

"Vamberry, the wine merchant": one of the pretty little cases whose records are in Holmes's tin box MUSG.

Vandeleur: Stapleton's alias HOUN.

"Vanderbilt and the Yeggman": records in Holmes's index SUSS.

"van Jansen in Utrecht": Holmes cites as a parallel case STUD.

Van Seddar: diamond cutter MAZA; *see* **Sanders.**

vaseline DYIN; *see* **make-up.**

"Vatican cameos": no details, but perhaps related to **"Pope, his Holiness the"** or **"Tosca, Cardinal,"** qq.v. HOUN.

V.C.: Victoria Cross, British Army medal for conspicuous valor; *see* **Emsworth,** Colonel.

vehicles: barouches, broughams, buses, cabs, carts, dog-carts, drags, four-in-hands, four-wheelers, gigs, growlers, hansoms, landaus, traps, waggons, wagonettes, vans – too numerous to enumerate – rattle throughout the canon; *see also* **Benz; bicycle; Ford; train; trap; Under-**

ground; wherry; *and see* **passenger.**

Vehmgericht STUD; *see* **secret societies.**

veils NOBL, SPEC, TWIS, VEIL.

veins: (knotted, passionate) start (stand) out on Rucastle's COPP, Sterndale's DEVI, Sylvius's MAZA foreheads.

velvet smoking cap: Culverton Smith's falls off DYIN.

ventilator: Holmes knows that he will find one before he visits Stoke Moran SPEC; *see* **bullet; vesta.**

verbs: the German is uncourteous to his (putting them at end of sentences) SCAN.

Venner & Matheson: well-known firm of engineers ENGR.

Venucci: Pietro, Mafioso, one of the greatest cut-throats in London; pocket contains apple, string, shilling map of London, photograph; sister Lucretia, the Countess of Morcar's maid SIXN.

Verner, Dr.: buys Watson's practice; distant relation of Holmes, who actually put up the money NORW.

*Vernet, Émile Jean Horace (1789–1863): French artist; Holmes's forebear GREE; *see* **art.**

vesta: match; Holmes finds because he was looking for it SILV; *see* **bullet; ventilator;** Boone pretends to sell wax vestas TWIS.

Vibart, Jules: lover of Devine LADY.

vices: Watson says that Holmes has none, save for occasional use of cocaine YELL; elsewhere, Watson admits that one of Holmes's most obvious weaknesses is impatience with less alert intelligences than his own BRUC; *see* **admiration; cigarettes; cigars; drugs; food and drink; pipe, smoking, and tobacco.**

Victorian: portico, Tuxbury Old Hall BLAN; *see* **Elizabethan; Jacobean.**

"Victor Lynch, the forger": oddly, alphabetized in Holmes's index by his first name SUSS.

view-halloa: fox-hunting cry; Holmes is like an old hound that hears DEVI; one of Milverton's servants raises when Holmes and Watson emerge from the veranda; *see* **foxhound** and **hound;** note that Von Bork hunts with the English LAST.

vigils: Holmes, often with Watson, spends interminable hours, usually at night, to trap a suspect BLAC, BRUC, EMPT, HOUN, LAST, NAVA, REDC, REDH, SIGN, SIXN, 3GAR, VALL; the shortest is only a minute, but it fills Watson with anxiety DANC; *see* **whining.**

"Vigor, the Hammersmith wonder": no mention of his wondrous feats; the case is recorded in Holmes's index SUSS.

villain!: *see* **Holder; Ross** (Colonel); **Stapleton** (Beryl).

Villard, François le: French detective, consulted Holmes SIGN.

vinegar and water: Wright bathes Lady Brackenstall's plum-coloured swelling with ABBE.

violence: plenty of it; most notable: Roylott beats his native butler to death, hurls blacksmith over parapet SPEC; Carey flogs wife and daughter, attacks old vicar BLAC; Norberton horsewhips Sam Brewer in Newmarket Common SHOS; Browner clubs, mutilates wife and lover CARD; Prendergast shoots, cuts throats, throws men overboard, all amidst a muck of brown sherry and blood on the table GLOR; Holmes attacked by van, bricks FINA; by two men with sticks ILLU; *see also* **cat; dogs.**

Violet: first name of de Merville, Hunter, Smith, Westbury.

violin: Holmes scratches on plays Watson's favourite airs on STUD; orders Watson to hand to him FIVE, HOUN, NOBL; drones away on NORW; plays snatches on SECO; plays chords (triple-stops?) on STUD; Holmes in violin-land REDH; improvises air on SIGN; plays recording of on gramophone MAZA; plays while his client is being murdered FIVE; to Holmes Watson had become an institution, like the violin, the shag tobacco, the old black pipe, the index books, and others perhaps less excusable CREE; *see* **Amati violins; Cremona; Hoffmann Barcarolle; *Norman-Néruda, Wilhelmine; *Paganini, Niccolò; *Peace, Charlie; *Sarasate y Navascués, Pablo Martín; Stradivarius.**

"Vipers": an entry in Holmes's index SUSS; *see* **tooth.**

visitors: *see* **friends.**

vitriol: sulfuric acid; *see* **acid, weapons.**

"Vittoria, the circus belle": an entry in Holmes's index; evidently not connected with the Ronder case SUSS.

voice: Holmes's, high, quick CARD; high, somewhat strident STOC; sinks when speaking of Klan FIVE; soothing 3GAR, WIST; feeble; high, thin DYIN; unsteady DEVI; Mortimer's, high, cracking, but it sinks almost to a whisper when he tells of his sighting of hound pawprints; Stapleton could not silence hound's voice HOUN; Sholto's, thin, high, piping; Small's, thick and foggy, later high, cracked SIGN; Smith's, high, screaming, petulant, penetrating DYIN; Presbury's, high screaming CREE; Mrs. Ronder's, well-modulated and pleasing VEIL; Dunbar's, low, agitated THOR; Damery's, pleasant, mellow; de Merville's, like wind from an iceberg ILLU; Holdernesse's, like a dinner-gong PRIO; female in barouche has a harsh one – a man's voice SHOS; Merton's, deep and raucous MAZA; Ferguson's, still deep and hearty SUSS; Mrs. Barclay's, shaking CROO; Melas's, wailing GREE; Milverton's, fear vibrates in CHAS; leper utters wild-beast cries BLAN; seven of these voices are high, two are deep; *see* **Latimer, Harold.**

von, Von: for some names with this prefix, *see* second part of name.

"Von Bischoff of Frankfort": Holmes cites as a parallel STUD.

Von Bork: German spy, like some wandering eagle; has cousin Heinrich; gives a guttural expression of disappointment; curse you, you double traitor, he says to Holmes, glaring murder from furious eyes LAST; *see* **cigars.**

Von Herder: blind German mechanic, constructs air-gun SCAN.

Von Herling, Baron: Secretary of German Legation LAST.

Von Kramm, Count: King of Bohemia's pseudonym SCAN.

von Waldbaum, Fritz: Dantzig specialist (detective) NAVA.

voodoo: figurine; black and leathery; Watson mistakes it for a mummified negro baby or for a very twisted and ancient monkey; Holmes consults Eckermann's *Voodooism and the Negroid Religions* WIST; *see* **cock.**

voyage: under *V* in his index, Holmes has a record of the Voyage of the *Gloria Scott* (a bad business) SUSS.

V.R. (Victoria Regina): Holmes inscribes this patriotic monogram by firing bullets into the wall at 221B MUSG.

***Wagner, Richard (1813–1883):** German operatic composer and one of the most influential cultural forces of the nineteenth century REDC.

waggon-tracks: *see* **wheels.**

Wainwright: artist; famous criminal; Holmes recalls ILLU.

waiter: agitated German; he evidently does not serve in the dining room but is in charge of guests' boots HOUN.

Waldron: Prescott's pseudonym 3GAR.

walk: Holmes and Watson go from Baker Street to the Alpha Inn in fifteen minutes (via Wimpole, Harley, Wigmore, and Oxford Streets, a curiously roundabout route); it is about four miles – they are fast walkers! BLUE.

***Wallenstein, Albrecht Eusebius Wenzel von (1583–1634):** Austrian general SCAN.

Walter: Sir James, dead scientist, famous Government expert; his brother, Colonel Valentine, wild eyes; cravat falls from lips BRUC.

Walters: policeman; terrified by cook's face at window WIST.

war: then, sir, prepare for (Holmes to Bellinger) SECO; a cleaner, brighter, stronger land will lie in the sunshine after the storm (i.e., World War I) has cleared (Holmes to Watson) LAST; *see* **German.**

"Warburton, Colonel, madness of": one of the two or three cases which Watson brought to Holmes ENGR.

Wardlaw, Colonel: his horse is entered in race SILV.

Warner: Holmes's agent; discharged gardener; excited rustic WIST.

warrant: Holmes, Watson, and Gregson ignore their lack of one- and enter houses CROO, LADY, REDC; Oberstein has no need to fear; Holmes says there is not enough evidence to obtain one BRUC; Holmes cannot enter Henderson's house because he does not have enough evidence to apply for one WIST.

Warren: Mrs., landlady — that is her profession! — and Mr., time-keeper at Morton and Way-

to visit Coram GOLD; Holmes pulls his out and invites Watson for a stroll GREE; Holmes consults to determine whether he can make a train THOR; Holmes looks impatiently at — a client is overdue SHOS; Lestrade looks at his and gives McFarlane half an hour NORW; Norton looks earnestly at his gold one SCAN; gold, by Barraud of London, No. 97613, among Drebber's effects STUD; *see* **Camberwell;**

light's; Watson calls her the expectant landlady REDC.

Warrender, Miss Minnie: Holmes has collected her history in a fat notebook; evidently she was ruined or murdered, or both, by Sylvius MAZA.

warships of the future: Holmes discourses on SIGN.

wash-hand stand: in Blessington's bedroom; apparently = American washstand RESI.

washing, face: Boone's TWIS; Silver Blaze's SILV.

watch: winding-up of, from which Holmes deduces the dead man's bedtime FIVE; Lestrade and Mycroft look twice a minute at theirs BRUC; Holmes suddenly looks at his and says he is expecting developments ABBE; Holmes glances at his — it is two o'clock, time

Watson, John H.: elder brother.

watch-chain: keys on CREE, LAST, SECO; Hope fidgets with seals on SECO; *see* **Albert.**

watching: Holmes describes the scoundrel's or suspect's movements so precisely that he is convinced that Holmes has been watching him DEVI (Sterndale), SILV (Brown), STUD (Rance).

watchman: at Woolwich Arsenal, an old soldier BRUC.

water (pond, moat), items hidden or thrown into: silver ABBE, pistol THOR, wedding dress NOBL, clothing and dumb-bell VALL; Neligan Sr. BLAC, Moriarty FINA, Openshaw FIVE, Douglas VALL, Stapleton HOUN, Howells MUSG, Biddle RESI, Hayward RESI, Moffatt RESI, and Leonardo VEIL are lost or drowned in bodies of water – ocean, water-fall, pond, river, lake, mere, mire; Watson pours a carafe over the face of an attempted suicide STOC; pours a Venetian carafe for Morstan – and later pours more, when she almost faints SIGN; pours carafes for the hysterical Hatherley ENGR and the injured Gruner ILLU, but we are not told whether they drink it or if it is put to some other use; maid pours carafe over Smith's forehead GOLD; *see* **hot water.**

watering-pot: Holmes upsets, to divert attention DEVI; *see* **oranges.**

Waterloo: Bridge, Openshaw drowned near FIVE; Holmes says that the Brackenstall case is not his – ABBE; railway station CROO, FIVE, HOUN, NAVA, SOLI, SPEC; *see* **trains.**

watermark: Holmes deciphers, identifies SCAN; none on paper used for St. Clair's TWIS or Garcia's WIST notes; *see* **handwriting.**

water-pipe: Holmes climbs down, as Small and Tonga had climbed up SIGN; Presbury uses for a foothold in climbing the wall of his house CREE.

Watson: I have always done you an injustice. There are others (Holmes re Watson's stupidity) 3STU; not luminous, but a conductor of light (says Holmes) HOUN; Oh, if you (Watson) find your own cases more interesting than mine . . . . (Holmes, with some asperity) NAVA; Holmes: my trusted comrade and biographer; I knew you would not

shrink at the last BRUC; my (astute) friend (and partner) CHAS, RETI; best of messengers DYIN; the same blithe boy as ever LAST; compound of the Busy Bee and Excelsior CREE; ideal helpmate BLAN; severely practical, as usual REDC; dangerous ruffian (Holmes's tongue is, of course, in his cheek) LADY; Holmes commends his zeal and intelligence HOUN; Holmes remarks, When you had formed your inevitable and totally erroneous conclusions EMPT; Brilliant, Watson! Only one flaw in your diamond VEIL; Watson knows an English **thorn** (q.v.) when he sees one SIGN; and he knows women – *see* **fair sex;** police-report (he is suspected of murder) describes him as middle-sized, strongly built, square jaw, thick neck, moustache CHAS; Watson admits his own stupidity BLUE, REDH; says, I am out of my depths . . . I miss the point STOC; describes his own personality as insignificant VALL; he is sometimes a bore – see **Afghanistan; social;** people forget his **name,** q.v.; Holmes forgets about him (he is hiding behind Holmes's bedstead) and offers him a thousand apologies DYIN; another thousand apologies for frightening Watson into a faint EMPT; Holmes says Watson has made a pretty hash of the investigation upon which Holmes has sent him; he has omitted no blunders LADY; he is similarly caustic in SOLI; Holmes hides information from him, much to Watson's discomfiture

DYIN, EMPT, HOUN; Watson lights Gregson's lantern REDC; Holmes tells Watson to touch the bell BLUE, start up the Ford LAST, set fire to straw NORW; Watson holds, carries, or fetches things for Holmes – see **boots; coat; field glass; match; messenger; note; pistol; telegraph forms; terrier; violin;** Holmes says Watson tells stories wrong end foremost WIST; his accounts are stories rather than scientific exercises ABBE; he embellishes COPP; they are fairy-tales, tinged with romanticism EMPT, SIGN; see **intellect; meretricious; write;** for Watson's reading, see **British Medical Journal;** for his platitudinous remarks, see **chain; game;** for his wagering, see **racing. As a doctor:** a case of great gravity occupies him – he is at the sufferer's bedside all day IDEN; cures a railway official of a long and lingering illness ENGR; Holmes says (but does not really believe) that Watson has limited experience, mediocre qualifications DYIN; Holmes says, Not one of your cases, Watson – mental, not physical 3STU; as medicaments, Watson uses **brandy** (and ammonia), **castor oil, cotton, strychnine, water,** qq.v.; he diagnoses **tissue-change;** see also **pads; paregoric; vinegar and water.**

elder brother: from a watch, Holmes deduces that he died from drink SIGN.

surgeries (professional offices): in Paddington ENGR, STOC; Kensington EMPT, NORW, REDH; the location of the surgery in FINA is a problem, since it seems to be somewhere near the old Baker Street lodgings.

wife (wives): see **Morstan** (Mary), after whose death there are a couple of mysterious references to a Mrs. Watson; is the author nodding or was there a second – or even a third – marriage? As a wooer, Watson is embarrassing: see **dreamland; hands; number; treasure, Agra.**

wax: thumb-mark on NORW; imprint of cuff-link on WIST; Mrs. Lexington is as close as NORW; figures of Holmes EMPT, MAZA; see **Meunier, Oscar; Tavernier.**

weapons: air-gun EMPT, MAZA; arsenal THOR; axe, blow-gun (-pipe) SIGN; battle-axe MUSG; bludgeon FINA, GREE; brick FINA; boulder LION, STUD; chair CHAS; charcoal fumes GREE; cleaver ENGR; club CROO, VEIL; cudgel ABBE, LADY, SIGN, STUD; dagger REDC, SECO; decanter ABBE; devil's-foot fumes DEVI; dog-whip WIST; dynamite REDC, VALL; elephant-gun BLAN; firelock (thrown, not fired) SIGN; garrot EMPT; gas RETI; gun (=shotgun) BOSC, GLOR; hammer (possible weapon) VALL; harpoon BLAC; hatpin ABBE; hunting-crop (loaded) HOUN, IDEN, REDH, SIXN, SPEC; knife (clasp) SIXN; knife (blunt, for otectomy) CARD; knife (sealing-wax) GOLD; knife (long, deadly, sheathed) VALL; knife (Carey tries to murder Cairns with) BLAC; knife with white haft, in Gorgiano's throat REDC; knife at Drebber's throat STUD; knife,

large, in McPherson's pocket
LION; life-preserver (blackjack)
BERY, BRUC, GREE; mace SIGN;
pistol (revolver) BERY, BLAC,
CHAS, COPP, DANC, DEVI,
EMPT, FINA, FIVE, GLOR, GREE,
HOUN, LADY, MAZA, MUSG,
REDH, REIG, RESI, SIGN, SIXN,
SOLI, SPEC, STUD, THOR, 3GAR,
VALL, WIST; poison darts SIGN;
poison pills GOLD, RETI, STUD;
poisoned arrow (and bird-bow)
SUSS; poker ABBE, SIXN, SPEC,
STOC, 3GAB; rifle (Winchester)
VALL; rock FINA, HOUN; sand-
bag WIST; sawn [sawed]-off shot-
gun; six-shooters; spanner VALL;
stick (walking) ABBE, BLUE,
CARD, HOUN, ILLU, LADY,
MAZA, NORW, PRIO, SIGN,
SHOS, SILV, SPEC, STUD, SUSS;
stone BOSC, EMPT, HOUN; vitriol
BLUE, ILLU; wooden leg SIGN.

weather: *see* **bitterly cold; blazing;
bleak; blizzard; bright; close;
cloud; cold; dull; elemental;
equinoctial gales; fine rain; fog;
gale (hurricane); gloomy; mud-
coloured; opalescent; rain;
snow; tempestuous; thick; wild.**

web: Moriarty is like a spider at the
centre of a foul one NORW; Cubitt is entangled in a dangerous
one DANC; *see* **net.**

**weddings (actual, aborted, or
forced), locations of:** St.
George's church (Doran's)
NOBL; St. Monica's (Adler's)
SCAN; St. Saviour's (Suther-
land's); outdoor bowling-alley
(Smith's) SOLI; Utah (Lucy Fer-
rier's) STUD; *see* **marriage.**

*Weiss & Co., London: knife-
makers, a real firm; they manu-
factured the cataract knife SILV.

Westbury,   Violet: Cadogan
West's fiancée BRUC.

Westhouse & Marbank: great
claret importers IDEN.

Westphail, Honoria: Stoner's aunt
SPEC.

Westville Arms: inn; Holmes and
Watson stay there VALL.

wheels: from depth of their tracks,
Holmes   draws   conclusions
ENGR, GREE, PRIO.

wherry: light rowboat; Holmes and
Watson cross river in one SIGN.

**whining of hinges and lapping of
agitated water, followed by
rasping of bolts:** vigil is over
VALL.

whispers: Bennett CREE; Mortimer
HOUN; Watson SPEC.

whisky: MacDonald accepts a wee
nip, evidently neat VALL; and
soda NOBL, REDH, SIGN; and
water SIGN, STUD; whisky-pegs
SIGN.

whist: Tregennises and Adair play
DEVI, EMPT; Holmes says,
When the other fellow has all the
trumps, it saves time to throw
down your hand MAZA; *see*
rubber.

whistle: Holmes sat up with a
BLUE; he whistles RESI, SILV,
3GAB, groans or sings and whistles at his work DANC, STUD;
gives a whistle of surprise BRUC;
whistles   in   astonishment   at
crowd gathered at murder site
SIXN; whistles, The drama has

come to a crisis 3GAB; whistles for a hansom after scaling Watson's wall FINA; whistles for police EMPT; Watson whistles for cab DYIN; coachman gives a shrill whistle for a street Arab, who brings a four-wheeler SIGN; Hayter whistles and exclaims By Jove!; inspector blows his whistle to summon constables REIG; Drebber whistles a popular hymn STUD; *see* **fingers; Jove; serpents.**

Whitaker's Almanack: used by Porlock as the key to his code; Holmes's edition is too up-to-date VALL.

White, Abel: indigo-planter, hires Small SIGN.

Whitehall: London district containing government offices NAVA.

white man: Croker compliments Holmes with this epithet ABBE.

Whitney: Isa, opium addict; wife Kate (*see* **dress**); brother Elias, D.D. TWIS.

Whittington, Lady Alicia: at St. Simon wedding NOBL.

Whyte, William: seventeenth-century owner of Holmes's copy of *De Jure inter Gentes;* he writes his given name in Latin (genitive case): Gulielmi (misprinted in Doubleday edition as Guliolmi) STUD.

wide-awake: hat; so-called because it has no "nap" (OED); worn by Munro, who has written his name in the lining YELL.

Wiggins: spokesman for the Baker Street Irregulars SIGN, STUD;

Watson refers to him as insignificant and unsavoury SIGN, STUD.

Wigmore Street Post Office SIGN; *see* **post.**

wild: morning THOR; wild, tempestuous night CHAS, GOLD; wild, bleak STUD.

*Wild, Jonathan (1683–1725): English criminal; sold his brains to crooks on a fifteen percent commission VALL.

Wilder, James: secretary, and bastard son, to Holdernesse; furtive eyes and twitching features; seeks fortune in Australia PRIO.

Williams: driver, boxer SIGN; James Baker, Garcia's neighbor WIST.

Williamson, Reverend (?): he was in Holy Orders but his career has been a dark one; now defrocked; white-bearded (later gray-bearded); utters a string of foul oaths SOLI.

Willows, Dr.: attends Turner BOSC.

Wilson: Jabez, commonplace British tradesman, obese, pompous, slow; small, fat-encircled eyes; Holmes laughs at him and then shoves him back into a chair REDH; *see* **clever;** Sergeant, policeman; slow, bucolic common sense; also, a Scowrer (presumably no relation) VALL; manager of messenger service HOUN; *Brig. Gen. Sir Archdale (1803–1874), British army officer SIGN; "Wilson, notorious canary-trainer": his arrest removes a plague-spot from the East End of London BLAC; sham chaplain (no Christian name); musket-fire brings him down, with eight others, wriggling on the floor GLOR.

Windibank, James: Sutherland's stepfather; **disguises** (q.v.) himself as Angel IDEN.

Windigate: landlord of Alpha Inn BLUE.

Windle, J. W.: Scowrer official; in his letter, appends the initials D. M. A. O. F. = Division Master, Ancient Order of Freemen VALL.

window: -fasteners, preposterous English (says Holmes) SCAN; -sill with newly severed human thumb on it ENGR; three dirty windows, a fourth shuttered up COPP; dirty, vacant, melancholy, at 3, Lauriston Gardens; Hope hurls himself through one at Baker Street STUD; Murdoch hurls dog through LION; Holmes throws up GREE; bedroom, Watson's – Holmes deduces that it is on right-hand side, from Watson's slovenly shaving BOSC; Porter throws open; servant throws up DEVI; Harrison uses long-bladed knife on NAVA; *see* **blood.**

Windsor: Holmes spends a day there, having been received by the Queen BRUC.

wines: *see* **Beaune; chianti; claret; Montrachet; port; sherry, brown; Tokay;** ancient, cobwebby bottles NOBL; Stamford and Watson drink STUD; Watson and Frankland drink a decanter, celebrating the latter's latest legal triumph; Stapleton and Sir Henry drink HOUN; Holmes and Watson invite Barnes to share a glass of his own wine SHOS; *see* **comet vintage.**

wink: MacDonald's eyelid quivers VALL; a wink quivers in Baynes's tiny eyes WIST; Hope gives Holmes a jocose wink STUD.

Winter: James; Evans's real name; alias Morecroft 3GAR; Kitty, flame-like, worn with sin and sorrow; her arm shoots out among the leaves, throws vitriol ILLU; *see* **cripes; rattle.**

witchcraft: MacDonald accuses Holmes of VALL.

wizard: Hopkins calls Holmes ABBE.

wolf: Beppo snaps at Watson's hand like a hungry wolf SIXN; hungry wolf after caribou (Douglas's metaphor for his enemies) VALL; wolf : Klein :: lamb : Maberley 3GAB.

Wolfe, Nero: Rex Stout's detective character; it has been conjectured that during the **Great Hiatus,** q.v., Holmes had a liaison with **Adler, Irene,** q.v., in New Jersey, U. S. A., the result of which was Wolfe; Mycroft Holmes has also been suggested as Wolfe's father.

wolf-hound: one of Presbury's dangerous pets CREE.

woman: young, in telegraph office MISS; shrill, broken whimpering of a frightened SIGN; sob of a HOUN; that little – Holmes calls Smith SOLI; nervous – Stoner's fiancé thinks her fears are the fancies of a SPEC; none safe from Sir Robert SHOS.

*Wombwell, George (1778–1850): owner of travelling menagerie; Ronder's is in competition VEIL.

women: Holmes's aversion to GREE; Holmes's remarks about: woman's heart and mind insoluble puzzles to male ILLU; women are never to be entirely trusted – not the best of them SIGN; naturally secretive SCAN; inscrutable; extraordinary conduct caused by hairpin or curling-tongs SECO; have seldom been an attraction for me LION; I am not a whole-souled admirer of womankind; absence of usual feminine ululation VALL; Watson says Holmes disliked and distrusted the sex but was always a chivalrous opponent DYIN; when he likes, Holmes can have a peculiarly ingratiating way with women GOLD; Holmes says, The most winning woman I have ever known was hanged for poisoning three little children for their insurance money SIGN; a more sensitive organism than man DEVI; landlady (Warren) has the pertinacity and also the cunning of her sex REDC; broken whimpering of a frightened woman (Bernstone) SIGN; Lucas's relationships with women were promiscuous but superficial SECO; Adler has beautiful woman's face but the mind of the most resolute of men (King of Bohemia avers) SCAN; *see* **Adler, Irene; Bellamy** (Maude); **daintiest thing under a bonnet on this planet; fair sex; frou-frou;** Hunter (Violet); **marriage; professions; tea;** *cf.* **analytic.**

women, exultant over death, dancing, singing, clapping hands, springing in air: Beryl Stapleton, when she knows that her husband is lost in the Great Grimpen Mire HOUN; Emilia Lucca, when she sees the ghastly bloody corpse of Gorgiano REDC; note that both are foreign born; English ladies are more controlled.

Wood: Dr., brisk and capable general practitioner VALL; Henry (Harry), bent back, sometimes speaks strange tongue (Hindi?); yellow-shot, bilious eyes CROO; *J. G., Reverend (1827–1889), English writer and lecturer LION.

Woodcock: Holmes and Watson dine on BLUE; St. Simon refuses it NOBL; *see* **paté.**

wooden leg: Small uses his as a lethal weapon SIGN; *see* **limb; weapons.**

Woodhouse: wants Holmes's life BRUC.

Woodley: Jack; red moustached; slogging ruffian (hits Holmes), drunken brute, foul-mouthed blackguard; utters a string of abuse SOLI; Elizabeth, engaged to Adair EMPT.

"Woodman's Lee, tragedy of": whatever it was, Holmes solved it BLAC.

work: Huxtable knows that Holmes will work for the work's sake PRIO; Holmes protests that the work is its own reward NORW; *see* **game; money** (for Holmes's fees).

workman: British – a token of evil, says Holmes CROO; Holmes's disguise, with a goatee and swaggering air CHAS; *see* **tradesmen.**

worm: remarkable, said to be unknown to science; *see* **"Persano, Isadora, well-known journalist and duellist";** *cf.* **religion,** for another reference to worms.

"Worst Man in London": original title of CHAS, referring to Milverton.

worst stories: even avid enthusiasts must admit that there are some bad ones. My own nominees are CREE (insanely implausible) and MAZA (repetitive and derivative). The plots of the novellas SIGN, STUD, VALL begin to limp when the author's point of view shifts from England to America or India, about both of which Conan Doyle had some odd preconceptions. These tedious inserted romances move creakily, but the first parts are among the best Holmes tales; *see* **best stories, Conan Doyle's own list, in order.**

wound, Watson's: by Jezail bullet: in shoulder STUD; in leg SIGN; in one of his limbs NOBL; Watson's hand steals toward CARD; subclavian artery grazed, but Holmes says it is a damaged *tendo Achillis* SIGN; Watson wounded (much later) by Evans's pistol 3GAR.

Wright, Theresa: maid ABBE.

wrinkles: Mrs. Sawyer (Hope's accomplice in disguise) has STUD; thousand on Roylott's face SPEC;

appear on Holmes's face when he is disguised TWIS.

write them yourself: says Watson to Holmes, about accounts of Holmes's cases; I will, says Holmes ABBE; he does: BLAN, LION; *see* **Watson, John H.**

writing: on wall RETI, STUD.

X2473: number of Mycroft's advertisement GREE.

XX. 31: Damery's private telephone number ILLU.

yachting: Von Bork yachts against the English LAST; Neligan Sr. sails North Sea in a yacht BLAC.

yarn, slinging you a: Cairns's slang for telling a [false] story BLAC.

yellow: face, fever, bar of light YELL; squares, bar, line, (flickering) tunnel(s), blaze, glare, little fan, circle, of light BRUC, ENGR, REDC, REDH, SIGN, SILV, 3STU, TWIS; golden square of light; tiny pin-point (speck) of light (mentioned three times); steady light HOUN; bright light VALL; light twinkles SPEC; screen (window at 221B) EMPT; the color turns up frequently – as in yellow-back novel COPP, CROO; features and skin WIST; Carter's parchment skin VALL; Whitney's pasty face TWIS; Smith's face DYIN; Selden's face; leaves; flame HOUN; fever CARD, COPP, CROO, NAVA; gloves (and overcoat, s.v. **dress**); hair VEIL; tresses (of Cyanea) LION; eyebrows VALL; bilious eyes CROO;

fog BRUC, COPP, SIGN; brick-(work) CARD, REDC; cardboard box CARD; diamond MAZA; khitmutgar's clothing; Sholto's teeth SIGN; barouche SHOS.

yeoman's daughter: imprisoned in a room by Hugo Baskerville; she escapes by climbing down the ivy; Hugo and his dissolute companions pursue her and she dies HOUN; *see* **ivy;** for Hugo's fate *see* **Baskerville.**

yew: trees HOUN, VALL; hedge SOLI.

Yorkshire: the schools of both Stapleton HOUN and Huxtable PRIO are there.

Youghal: of the C. I. D., policeman MAZA.

*Young, Brigham (1801–1877): American Mormon leader STUD.

youth: dispatched with note for Slaney DANC; Swiss, probably in the pay of Moriarty; a few paragraphs later Watson is more certain: the youth was one of the numerous agents whom Moriarty kept in his employ FINA.

Zamba, Signor; an invalid, partner in the fruit-importing business REDC; *see* **Castalotte.**

*Zeppelin, Count Ferdinand von (1838–1917): German general and flier, inventor of dirigible; Von Bork implies that zeppelins (airships) will soon make English skies less tranquil LAST.